The Preschooler Problem Solver

Tackling Tough and Tricky Transitions with Your Two- to Five-Year-Old

Carol Baicker-McKee, Ph.D.

PEACHTREE
ATLANTA

For my husband Steve—
who makes
cinnamon buns for Sunday breakfast,
things I need like garden gates and treehouses,
ten out of ten free throws every time,
the printer work again,
and me happy

Published by
PEACHTREE PUBLISHERS
1700 Chattahoochee Avenue
Atlanta, Georgia 30318-2112
www.peachtree-online.com

Text © 2009 by Carol Baicker-McKee

Cover Design by Maureen Withee
Interior Design by Melanie McMahon Ives and Regina Dalton-Fischel

Printed in the United States of America
10 9 8 7 6 5 4 3 2 1
First Edition

Library of Congress Cataloging-in-Publication Data

Baicker-McKee, Carol, 1958-
  The preschooler problem solver : tackling tough and tricky transitions with your two- to-five-year-old / written by Carol Baicker-McKee.
    p. cm.
  ISBN 978-1-56145-445-7 / 1-56145-445-1
  1. Preschool children. 2. Parenting. 3. Child rearing. I. Title.
HQ774.5.B353 2009
649'.123--dc22   *167720 6*
                    2009011165

Table of Contents

Chapter Four

Chapter Five

Chapter Six

Conclusion

INTRODUCTION

There are already tons of parenting books on the market, many of them packed with good advice on how to raise normal, well-adjusted children, so you might justifiably wonder why the world needs another one. Well, the world needs another one because none of those other books have an adequate solution to the following nerve-wracking parenting dilemma:

Q. Suppose you never should have signed your four-year-old daughter up for ballet lessons because you have all the poise and grace of a psychotic robot (only without its fine sense of rhythm) and your daughter has unfortunately inherited your bad-dancing genes, but you let yourself get talked into it anyhow and now it is time for the end-of-year recital. And you are perched on a seat in the middle of a row in a hot auditorium packed with a gazillion people, most of them darling little girls in absolutely adorable pastel tutus, tiaras, butterfly wings, etc., except for your daughter and her classmates, who have ended up in the only number where the dancers are attired in what appear to be enormous hot pink loofahs with *slightly* smaller hot pink loofahs fastened atop their heads, and to make matters worse your kid is glommed on to you like some sort of giant mutant barnacle with bad fashion sense. And she is refusing to go backstage to wait with her best friend, cousin, and other classmates for her turn, much less tippytoe onto the stage and perform that classic ballet piece "Daddy's Little Girl," even though a mere hour ago she was so excited and eager to be in the show that she made you leave the house a half hour early. And the relatives are coming to watch, and the teacher has stressed how essential it is for everyone to be there as the number will not work properly without all the performers, plus her name is already in the program and all the other moms are staring at you and looking rather smug and superior. What the heck do you do?

A. According to one parenting book I'd just read at the time this happened to me and my daughter, I should gather my young daughter up gently and take her home, since rushing children into new experiences they don't feel ready for only harms their psyches and sets them on a path of seeking out experiences that exceed their maturity, like juvenile alcohol use, premature sex, and maybe even talking to people on the phone the way pathetic grown-ups do instead of texting them like normal, wholesome teens should.

Of course, a couple weeks before that, I'd read another book by a different noted child development expert that said pretty much the opposite: that you should always take a firm tough-love stance and order your child in no uncertain terms to follow through when she starts something, whether it was joining a soccer team or doing an art project at home, because to do otherwise would set her on a path of shirking responsibility, avoiding challenges, and not paying at least the minimum balance on her credit-card bill, thereby triggering a global credit crisis.

Consequently, I was sitting there nearly as paralyzed as my daughter. But thanks to the combined body heat of the gazillion people around me and the loofah girl pressed tightly to my chest, I was sweating so much that I could feel little rivers of perspiration running down my legs into my shoes. And that reminded me that I really, really, really needed to pee, which finally unfroze my leg muscles enough that I could head to the ladies' room. With my daughter still plastered against me, I squeezed past the twenty-seven grandmothers sitting next to us, a process akin to going through a gauntlet of turnstiles while nine months pregnant with quintuplets, and made my way out of the auditorium into the relative cool and calm of the lobby, where both Sara and I instantly relaxed. I was able to peel her off of me, only losing a little skin in the process, and head to the bathroom.

We both peed and washed our faces, and I dabbed at the pools of sweat under my blouse and at the streams still coursing down my thighs until my brain began to function again. Then I reached a decision about what would *probably* be best for my daughter and devised my strategy.

I offered Sara a sip from my water bottle, and commiserated. "Pretty overwhelming, isn't it?" I said. "No wonder you got cold feet."

Sara looked down at her little pink ballet slippers. "My feet aren't cold! They're hot!"

I tried again. "I mean, I understand why you don't feel like being in the show anymore."

"Yeah," said Sara, "let's just go home."

"I guess we should," I agreed. "Though it's too bad after you practiced so hard and got so good at your plié. And at that cute little part where you bend at the waist and poke your fingers in the dimples you don't have."

"Yeah," said Sara, heading for the exit. "It's too bad."

"And it's a shame lots of people will be disappointed," I said. "Like Daddy, your brothers, your aunts, and the other girls who are counting on you to start the curtsy at the end of the dance."

"Yeah," said Sara, tugging on the heavy door. "It's a shame."

"And I'm really sorry about the sundaes," I said. "I was going to let you get hot fudge *and* caramel sauce. You know, to celebrate."

"Yeah…wait!" said Sara. "I can get hot fudge *and* caramel?"

"Well, you could have," I said, "if you'd done the recital. But since we're just going home, we can hardly go out for a celebration." I stepped out the door.

"Just a minute," said Sara. "I changed my mind. I feel like dancing now!"

"Are you sure?" I asked. "Because I wouldn't want to damage your psyche or anything."

"I'm sure," said Sara, grabbing my hand. "And can I have two cherries on top? And extra whipped cream?"

"We'll see," I said. And we skipped to where her class was waiting and got her settled in with her best buddy.

In the end, Sara performed pretty well, just a half beat or so behind the other dancers as usual, but with a practically elegant arabesque and curtsy at the end. And I managed to snap one of my favorite photos of her on the stage after the performance. In the snapshot her friend Rachel has her toes turned out in first position, her arms extended back gracefully, and she's laughing. Sara's cousin Erin stands tall in fourth position, arms curved delicately overhead and a slight smile on her lips. Sara, on the other hand, looks like a street tough with her legs spread and arms crossed, glaring suspiciously at the camera out of the corner of her eye. I think she's just figured out she might have been sort of tricked. But the sundaes were really good, and Sara, who back then had the appetite of a ladybug with a stomach virus, actually ate all of hers. Which meant I didn't get to finish it. But it was worth it.

If you're the kind of parent who frowns at ever using a little guilt or trickery or invoking the persuasive powers of sweets, this may not be the right parenting book for you. In fact, if the account above has left your lips pressed tightly together and your eyes narrowed, you should probably stop reading this right now and see if you can exchange it for one of those other high-minded, here's-the-right-answer books. I do have a Ph.D. in clinical child psychology from the University of Virginia; years of experience working with young kids as a volunteer, teacher, and therapist; and the wisdom that comes from being the parent of three creative, lively, and strong-willed children—but I'm not above using guilt induction, deceit, and bribery occasionally, in the right situation, with the right parent and kid, along with other non-traditional methods like extreme silliness, peer pressure, and hoping the problem will just go away on its own.

If there's one thing I've learned from all my years with preschoolers, it's that not only is there more than one way to skin a knee, there's more than one way for Mommy or Daddy—and eventually even the kid himself—to make it better. What works best with a particular child at a given point in time depends on a complex array of variables, including the child's temperament and past experiences; his current stage of development; whether he's tired, hungry, thirsty, uncomfortable, sick, or in pain; whether there's some big stressful change going on his life; your family's values and your parenting style; the lunar stage; if it's a month with an "r" in it; and of course, whether he's wearing his lucky underpants.

All of which is a long way of saying that the main way this book differs from others on raising your preschooler is that it rarely prescribes just one approach to solving a problem, but instead offers options, usually lots of them—the behavioral techniques that experts have found to be most effective as well as the traditional methods that generations of parents have fallen back on, plus the occasional bizarre approach I've stumbled upon. You're free to choose the one that seems to fit best for your kid and circumstances. And if that doesn't work, you can try a different one.

By the way, this is not to say I don't believe that there are some fundamental principles that work for pretty much any set of parents and kids that you should probably consider as basic necessities for your parenting arsenal. If you read this book cover to cover, you'll probably figure them out, because I repeat them over and over. And if you need more details about these basics, consult any good puppy-training guide, as the principles are much the same. People will look at you a little strangely, though, if you opt for the clicker method, so you should probably skip that, at least in public. I'm only sort of kidding, by the way.

Another way this parenting book differs from others is that it's nuanced, which is a fancy way of saying that I try to take real-life variables into consideration. For example, there is lots of good information in books, magazines, and on the Internet to help you answer your preschooler's questions about sex and reproduction. But I have yet to find another source that addresses how you might handle things differently when your child asks these questions in a piercing voice in a forum like a crowded subway car at rush hour or a public restroom along the turnpike.

Obviously, this book differs from others on preschoolers in its content and goals. This book focuses on the turning points of early childhood and helping your child through the challenges, new experiences, and life changes of this period of development. Some of these are situations faced by nearly all children, such as moving from a crib to a big bed, throwing or attending birthday parties, and nose picking. Others are common but by-no-means-universal experiences, like welcoming a new sibling, attending school for the first time, or wondering whether God has boogers. And still others are relatively rare things I hope your family doesn't have to face, like divorce, natural disasters, and a debilitating fear of ladies' lingerie.

There are also many potential problems not covered in this book. Luckily for you, many of them are discussed in my other books. For example, if you need help with daily routines, like getting your jellyfish child dressed in the morning, figuring out how to talk on the phone without constant interruptions or preventing homicide during the evening Arsenic

Hour (the period just before dinner), you should consult *FussBusters at Home.* Or if you struggle to get your kids through outings like trips to the grocery store, attending plays, or accompanying you to the gynecologist after the sitter cancels, or if you're trying to figure out how to make your next family vacation more fun and less hassle, you can read *FussBusters on the Go.* You can also ask me questions by emailing me at baickermckee@gmail.com or submitting them to my blog, www.doodlesandnoodles.blogspot.com. Or check out my website: www.carolbaickermckee.com.

There are some problems of the preschool years not covered in any of my books, though. For example, you won't find anything in my books on coping with lice, scabies, ticks, or pinworms. Partly this is because although I'm *Dr.* Baicker-McKee, I'm not a medical doctor and thus not qualified to offer professional advice on that stuff. But mostly it's because even thinking about those gross guys makes me start itching so much I have to stop whatever I'm doing to scratch for the next fifteen minutes. Um, I'll be back to finish this up in a little bit.

My first goal is to help you and your kid get through the challenges of the preschool years with a minimum of whining, pinching, peeing one's pants, or vegging in front of the telly excessively. The next goal is to help you support your kid in such a way that she acquires her own coping skills, a sense of optimism, and an ability to bounce back after difficulties. And my final goal is to give you the skills and attitudes to create a family culture that's inviting, comfortable, and invigorating–one that encourages every member to welcome friends, tackle creative projects or meaningful work, and contribute to the running of the household, and one that's elastic and roomy enough to allow for growth as you add new members and everyone gets older and bigger and has different needs and desires. I'm sure I fall short in places in this book, just as I have with my own family, but I've really tried.

By the way, some of you may be wondering whether I in fact scarred my daughter for life by manipulating her into participating in her recital when she obviously didn't want to. It's been many years now, and I can state with absolute confidence that I don't think so. Sara whined and clung to me more than usual the next couple days, but that's typical for many preschoolers after any stressful event, and she soon resumed her usual daily activities of being a dog, playing with miniatures under the coffee table, and pottering about in the mud by the slide. And the next fall when Rachel asked Sara if she wanted to sign up for ballet again, I was prepared to say, "No way unless you threaten me with a Barney and Friends marathon," but Sara said, "Sure, and let's take tap-dancing class too." And she performed in those recitals with only her normal last-minute reluctance rather than full-blown panic attacks; I didn't even have to mention hot-fudge sauce. Although Sara gave up dance after that year (probably wisely), since then she's performed in many plays, programs, and band recitals, and she's not fazed a bit by public speaking. Over the years, it's gotten easier and easier for my slow-to-warm up daughter to try other new experiences, even all by herself. And not only has she not been arrested for underage drinking or surprised us with a teen pregnancy, she's amazingly responsible and undertakes all kinds of challenges without prompting or nagging. Most importantly, though, she would never dream of talking on the phone when a text would suffice. *Phew.*

CHAPTER ONE

It's a "Big" Deal!

* * *

Saying Ta-Ta to Cribs, Diapers, Bottles, and Other "Little Guy" Stuff

Your baby is growing up! Giving up the crib and pacifiers, learning to use the potty, sometimes managing to ask for a snack in something other than a whiny voice! Maybe even learning to put on a sock by herself or to break only three knickknacks when she "helps" you dust!

So, do you want champagne? Or Kleenex?

Me, I usually needed both. For as proud as I was to see my tyke reach a milestone like giving up diapers, I felt wistful too, watching her shed her snuggly, innocent baby persona along with the Pampers. And replacing it with a do-it-myself, swaggering, big-kid one that liked to say things like, "You're an old poopy butt! Ha, ha, ha, HA!" (Plus, for a while there, changing diapers seemed a heck of a lot more appealing than mopping up pee puddles from the living room rug. Also, the stiff back I got from all that bending over made me notice that I was getting older too…)

All this is by way of saying that change, even when welcome, is hard. For you, for your kid, for the carpet. And that's why this chapter not only has lots of practical ideas for nudging your kid toward more mature behaviors, but also has oodles of suggestions for dealing with the immature reactions that inevitably accompany the shift. And tips for things like cleaning the urine out of the carpet so the dog doesn't think, "Hey! I guess we're doing our business indoors now!"

Because I'm a trained Ph.D. psychologist, I know all the proper ways to potty train a toddler or help him substitute more mature comforting behaviors for his Nuk addiction. Luckily for you, though, my three kids have also taught me totally incorrect (but really effective) ways to accomplish these same tasks. You can pick whichever approach you prefer. And then you can try one of the ones that really works and know you at least tried to do it right.

Now that I've got you all freaked out about this growing-up business, I'm going to advise you to relax and enjoy it. Because really, life with kids just gets better and better (except for when they're thirteen). Babies are sweet and toddlers adorable—but preschoolers are so competent! Sort of! And funny as the dickens. And even though at times their growing maturity won't seem worth the trade-offs (like the loss of a certain baby cuteness or the rise of back talk), on the whole your kids will only get more interesting and capable as they grow. As the poet Robert Browning once said, "The best is yet to be."

Out of the Crib and into the . . .

✳ ✳ ✳

Strategies for a Smooth Move to a Big Bed

Usually kids move to a big bed sometime between the ages of one and a half to three and a half; two is most common. The standard expert advice is "Don't switch your toddler from a crib to The Big Bed during any other significant changes or stresses in his life." If you follow this advice, though, your kid will be crammed into a crib until he is seven or eight years old, because the odds of finding a window of calm with a toddler or preschooler range from slim to none. So ignore that, and try some of these tips that might make the shift easier, even during a less-than-ideal period.

That said, there are definite times *not* to move your child. Make sure that there aren't other *major* changes in the works: avoid making this shift when you're weaning, potty training, moving, or throwing away all his pacifiers in a sleep-deprived fit. You should also be sure to make the big move at least eight weeks before or after the birth of a new baby, so your child doesn't resent the baby for booting him out of his crib—but don't worry, he'll find plenty of other things to resent the baby for.

Of course, in real life, timing is often governed by practical issues, like the person you borrowed the crib from is having another baby and is starting to drop pointed hints about the due date. Or Houdini Jr. is risking a fractured skull nightly despite your having lowered the mattress as far as it goes and removed every item thicker than a sheet. The bottom line is that you'll just have to pick a relatively good time, take the plunge, and be prepared for some rough nights.

Sell the Idea

With some kids, you won't have to push at all—they can't wait to be grown up. Others need a little coaxing—or a good sales pitch. Peer pressure is always effective—a month or so before you switch, visit cool big kids and get them to show off their prized beds.

Offer some enticements and let your kid be involved. Go look at sheets together. Though most kids have zero interest in shopping for mattresses and headboards, linens are another matter. This is the time to be completely tacky—check out the options with licensed cartoon characters. Once your little guy has made his selection, make a big show of putting the new linens away "until he's big enough for a bed." When the time comes to make the switch, have your child help with the assembly and disassembly process. Getting to use real tools is enough incentive for many kids to tolerate *any* change! If your child is reluctant to "get big" and you need him to move, try linking the switch to some other big-person privilege (like staying up later) or big-person possession (like, say, your broken calculator or the ratty pocketbook he covets).

Don't forget to sell the idea to *yourself.* For me, the shift to a big bed, more than changes like walking or even weaning, marked the transition from baby to big kid. And losing your baby is bound to be bittersweet. Maybe you need a little consolation prize too! I recommend chocolate, which cures just about anything.

Ease into the Change

A gradual change is easier for many kids than an abrupt switch. There are a few different strategies you can employ to make the change at a pace that will be easier for your child.

At first, have him just sleep on his crib mattress on the floor. It will feel and smell familiar, and your little guy won't get hurt if he rolls off.

When he's ready to move to a big-boy bed, consider buying a small-size toddler bed, which uses a crib mattress, has low sides, and feels crib-cozy. Put the bed in the same spot as the crib, and continue to use the same quilt, stuffed animals, and other accessories in the new bed for a while. Wait to do major redecorating until after your child is used to the switch.

Alternately, you can set up the bed and leave the crib up too. Use the bed for naps, and the crib for night. Or do the bedtime routine—stories, kisses, water, etc.—in the big bed and transfer your child to the crib for sleeping. If you're going to adjust your bedtime routine, do it well before you take the crib down.

Now the only problem you have to worry about is that your kid can get *out* of his bed whenever he wants to...

Wander-Unlusting and Fall-Proofing

✷ ✷ ✷

Tips for Helping Your Preschooler Stay in Bed— Without Ropes or Magic

When my daughter Sara was two, I woke every night about 3:00 AM with a creepy feeling of being watched. Which I was—by Sara. She'd stand inches away, breathing heavily and staring at my face. A few weeks into this routine, Sara decided she had two mommies: the nice Day Mommy and the mean Night Mommy (though as more sleepless nights passed, the mean Night Mommy started to displace the nice Day one too).

Fortunately, the Good Sleep Chart described below turned out to be the cure for both our night terrors. It might work for your wanderer, too, but in case she has other tastes or issues, I'm offering a variety of stay-put tactics.

Bed Glue

Childproof your sleeper's room, and the rest of the house, in case she wanders at night. Gate off stairways, attach bookcases to the wall, and put up night-lights for the path to the bathroom. Also, close the door after your child falls asleep (if she objects while she's awake), as a fire-safety precaution. Then you can use one or more of these strategies to keep your child in her bed.

✳ *Teach the new rules.* It may seem obvious, but some kids get up simply because now they can—and they don't realize they aren't supposed to.

✳ *Make a sign.* Have your kid help you make a *big* sign that says something like "Stay in bed until morning" and hang it where she can see it from bed. (You might want to add the phrase "unless you have to go potty or barf.") Older toddlers are strong respecters of official signs even though they can't read them.

✳ *Create a good-sleep chart.* Charts and stickers work great with many toddler problems. Vary the incentive to fit your child, and be careful to keep rewards *small* and fairly easy to earn at first.

✳ *Lock her in—for pretend.* Sprinkle "fairy dust" across her threshold, telling her that it will keep her safe and happy *in her room* until morning, or "lock" a pretend gate across her corral. Or conjure up whatever barrier fits her current imagination passion. Some kids will prefer to pretend lock you *out!* (Boost this strategy by giving your child a real key.)

✳ *Lock her in—for real.* With a baby gate. If your child is constantly getting up, let her know the consequence will be a gate across her door (two-high if necessary). Just make sure you can hear her if she needs you during the night.

✳ *Provide a restroom pass.* Give your child a "ticket" she can use to go to the bathroom or if she feels sick. If she gets up, wordlessly collect her ticket and take her to the potty and then back to bed. (With or without a bathroom pass, the silent return method is *very* effective—just keep doing it, calmly.) If she gets up for another reason, give her another "ticket"—with a fine of no TV or something the next day.

✱ *Let her get up!* Just make the rule that she must stay *in* her (childproofed) room and be quiet. If she falls asleep on the floor, so be it.

Fall-Proofing

LITERATURE LINKS

Aside from the kind of books featuring licensed characters like Barbie or Elmo, there are surprisingly few books about giving up cribs. Try MY OWN BIG BED by Anna Grossnickle Hines for a choice that has literary merit. And kids who are Berenstain Bear fans will like MY NEW BED by Stan and Jan Berenstain.

If your kid is more the *fall*-out–of-bed than the *climb*-out-of-bed type, you'll need some special safety precautions. Although using portable bed rails is a popular approach, I think that option has a number of drawbacks. First, the rails have to be installed correctly and then checked *every night* (and naptime) to make sure they haven't loosened enough to pose an entrapment or strangulation hazard (and you should also monitor safety recalls religiously). Second, using them just delays your child's learning how to stay in bed; eventually, you'll have to go through that step anyhow. My preference is a simple and free approach: just put the new mattress on the floor at first (she won't get hurt if she does roll off), and add the frame and box springs later once she's become a champion in-bed sleeper.

When she's ready to sleep in her big bed, position it with the headboard against the wall, well away from windows and other hazards. Place pillows, cushions, or the old crib mattress on the floor next to the bed to soften her landing in case she does fall. You can also stuff a rolled-up towel or blanket under the fitted sheet to create a hard-to-roll-over hill along the edge of the bed. Alternately try a long "body pillow" or a million stuffed animals lined up along the open edge. Or, if she doesn't object, tuck her in nice and *tightly*.

Daytime training can also help minimize night falling. While your child's awake, get her well acquainted with the size and boundaries of her bed. Have her roll around the whole bed, noticing how it feels whenever she gets near the edge. (Make it a fun game by chanting the "There were three in the bed and the little one said, *Roll over, roll over!*" rhyme, and having all the stuffed animals fall out until just your child remains.) We also played this game whenever we traveled and slept in new beds.

Some people find a bigger bed does the trick; you can always get your child a full or queen-size bed. There are some drawbacks to this approach: it can be expensive; it still may not work; and you can't usually get cute kid bedding. On the plus side, it gives you a little more space when you're cuddling at night or reading stories (and if, say, you do doze off in the process, you're less likely to fall out yourself!)

Ready or Not, Here I Go!

✳ ✳ ✳

A Readiness Checklist for Potty Training

You can toilet train with *much* less fussing by everyone if you start it when your child is ready. Which brings us to the tricky question: how can you tell if the kid is ready? Let me count the ways! But first, a few notes on the whole process.

The Big Picture

Parents today mostly train their kids between the ages of two and three and a half. A few start as early as eighteen months or as late as four years old. Keep in mind (and this was recently confirmed in a large study) that *the earlier you start, the longer training takes.* On the other hand, if you wait too late (toward four), your kid may encounter teasing or develop a rebellious attitude about the whole process. In general, girls are ready sooner than boys, and most kids are trained during the day long before they achieve night control. One more note: age of training is *not* related to intelligence—and they don't ask about it on college applications, not even for Yale.

The Readiness List

Here are all the types of readiness you'll want to consider in deciding when to start. Almost no child will ready in all these ways at once, but the more ways everyone's ready, the easier training will be.

✳ *Physical readiness.* Is your child staying dry for several hours? Does he *notice* the sensation of a full bladder or the need to poop? (You'll be able to tell by signs like doing the pee dance, or making a funny face before he poops.) Also, can he *hold* his pee or poop, at least for a minute or so, after he feels the urge to go?

✳ *Language ability.* Can your child tell you in words or gestures that he needs to go? Does he understand related words, like toilet, underwear, flush, before (as in "Tell me *before* you have to go"), and, for boys, the all-important "aim"? Also, can he understand and follow simple directions? After training dozens of kids as a parent and day-care teacher, I'm convinced that language development *strongly* influences how easy it is to potty train.

✳ *Emotional readiness.* Is your kid out of the "Terrible Twos" and able to be cooperative? (Despite the name "Terrible Twos," most kids have stopped being reflexively oppositional by age two and a half, making it a good age to start.) Can he handle making mistakes or having his play interrupted? Also is your kid eager to be "big" like you or Superman or other cool potty-trained role models? Finally, if your kid is not preoccupied with other stresses in his life, it will be easier for him to devote the necessary energy and concentration to succeed.

✳ *Self-help skills.* Can your child can pull his own pants down and up, wash his hands without help, and get on and off a potty or the big toilet alone?

✳ *Equipment readiness.* Do you have a little potty? (I recommend a sturdy basic one that your child can empty himself—and skip the little guard things for boys; they're *dangerous* if you get what I mean.) Another option is a portable seat that fits on the big toilet, but most little guys feel less secure with this arrangement. You'll also need a stool for hand washing, stuff for cleaning up accidents (try the pet accident cleaners for carpets and upholstery), a rubber sheet for the mattress, and incentives of some sort (see suggestions on page 15).

✳ *Wardrobe preparedness.* I think nothing is cuter than a two-year-old in overalls—but they are a *big* mistake during training. So are one-piece ballerina outfits—one of my friends had a serious potty-training setback after her mother-in-law gave her daughter an all-in-one tutu thing that the kid insisted on wearing 24-7. Aim for easy-on, easy-off clothes with elastic waists. I'll also warn you that skirts end up in the stream pretty regularly. The main requirement of course is *LOADS* of underpants (at least ten pair). (See other underpants tips on pages 19–21.)

✳ *Family readiness.* Can an adult at home spend a *lot* of time over the next two or three weeks focusing on the process? And does that adult have reserves of energy, patience, and laundry-doing ability? Again, you'll want to avoid periods when the family is distracted by other big issues, like new babies, moving, or marital strife. Finally, try to complete potty training *before* your expensive new carpeting is installed.

Tinklers Anonymous

✳ ✳ ✳

A Twelve-Step Program for Becoming Clean and Dry

There is no one foolproof approach to training your child. This version borrows bits and pieces from methods recommended by a range of experts. If it doesn't work, or just doesn't seem right for your kid, check out the "innovative" methods that follow.

Step 1: Show . . .

When your child shows some signs of readiness, start inviting her into the bathroom with you. Let her watch what you're doing and ask you embarrassing questions (which you should answer). Or, better yet, find a slightly older sibling or peer to model the process.

Step 2: …and Tell!

Talk about what you are doing, from noticing you need to go and holding your pee to pulling your pants back up and washing your hands. Make sure you introduce all necessary vocabulary.

Step 3: Introduce Mr. Potty

After a couple of weeks, get the potty out and set it up in the bathroom. (Some parents put it in other rooms, but I think that just confuses the issue at this point.) Let your child sit on it, fully clothed, if she wants to. Talk about what it's for.

Step 4: Read All about It!

Casually add books about potties, poop, making mistakes, growing up, and so on to your child's pile of bedtime and snuggletime books. Good ones to try: EVERYONE POOPS by Taro Gomi (a kid favorite), ONCE UPON A POTTY by Alona Frankel (different versions for boys and girls), and WHAT DO YOU DO WITH A POTTY? by Marianne Borgardt (a cool pop-up book).

Step 5: Call Attention to Your Child's Plumbing and Products

While you're changing her, start commenting on the fact that she has peed or pooped, and note that soon she'll be big enough to make her pee or poop go in the potty instead of her diaper. Talk about how, where, and why these products come out of her. If you notice her doing the pee dance or showing other signs of needing to go, comment on these too, and praise her for getting big and noticing when she's about to go.

Step 6: Have Teddy Demonstrate

This step can be powerful, especially if you don't have access to other kid models. Have one of your kid's favorite stuffed animals or dolls sit on the potty. Then "pretend" together to have him pee or poop. (You might have your child pour water colored yellow with food coloring or dump some brown clay into the potty.) Then make a *moderate* fuss over Teddy. "Good job Teddy! You peed in the pot! Here's a sticker."

Step 7: Get Lucky!

If your child tends to go poop about the same time every day, invite her to sit on the potty at that time to "see if her poop comes out." Otherwise, offer her a chance to try to pee when she wakes up dry from a nap or has gone a couple of hours with a dry diaper. Give your child some time to be successful, but don't force her to sit on the potty. Some kids like to look at books or blow bubbles while they wait. Praise your kid for trying, even if nothing happens. If she does succeed, show her how proud you are—but don't go overboard. And let her help dump the pee or poop into the toilet (though she may make a bit of a mess). Wait to flush if the noise frightens her.

Step 8: Be Suggestive

Make a few tinkle sounds (e.g., *pssss, pssss, pssss*) when your child is sitting on the potty, or run the faucet on a low stream. You might laugh or feel silly—but a recent study shows this old grandma trick not only starts the flow, but it's also linked to lower incidence of urinary tract infections!

Step 9: Have a Go at the Real Thing

After your child has experienced a potty success or two, ask her if she'd like to try wearing underpants and using the potty. If she balks, back off, and ask again in a few days or so. But if she is interested, help her into those new pants!

Step 10: Remind—But Don't Nag

This is a fine line. I suggest the technique used in many childcare settings—a frequent schedule. Every hour or hour and a half, everyone (that means you too) treks to the bathroom to try. If nothing happens, so be it. Also stay alert for obvious signs, like the pee dance, holding herself, being restless, etc.—and whisk her off to try. Remind her she can return to making booger pies (or whatever she's doing) in a minute.

Step 11: Be Cool about Accidents

And hot about success! Remember that full training can take six months or more. It's very common for kids to start having accidents again after several weeks of seeming to have the hang of it. Just remind your child that learning new things takes time, and reassure her (and yourself) that she'll have the hang of it again soon.

Step 12: Night Train

If your child is normally dry in the morning, this step will be easy—but I'd still wait *at least* a month or two after day training to start, because the effort of staying dry all day is enough to make many kids *start* wetting the bed. When you're ready to try, put a protective sheet on the mattress and adjust your child's routine to increase success: reduce fluid intake in the evening, take her to go potty just before bed, and put her to sleep in thin underpants (or nothing at all). You might also start with the potty in her room next to the bed. If she does wake up needing to go, it's right there. Be matter-of-fact about accidents, and let her sleep on a sleeping bag if she does have one. Pile the wet linens in a laundry basket and deal with them in the morning.

Potty Games

* * *

Activities to Encourage Readiness and Cooperation

These games, which may *seem* to have nothing to do with peeing or pooping, can nonetheless help your child get ready—or ease issues that have cropped up in the process.

Monkey See, Monkey Do

Imitation games help kids develop the habit of watching models and copying what they do, including peeing in the toilet. Say, "Hey little monkey, can you do this?" and perform a simple action like hooting or jumping

up and down. Once your child can copy simple actions, increase the difficulty by stringing together a chain of several actions or having him copy
complex actions like putting together a puzzle. If your child prefers kitty
cats to monkeys, play Copy Cats instead. Other good games are Follow the
Leader and Simon Says, Jr. (Usual game but you just say Simon Says every
time—no tricking).

Wait, Wait, Go!

This game introduces both necessary vocabulary and your child's ability to postpone an urge. You can play it many ways. Start a race by saying,
"Wait... wait... wait... GO!" A similar game is "Hold It... Let Go!" Sit on the
floor while you and your child tug on opposite ends of a thick rope or hula
hoop. When you say "Let go!" she drops her end—and you fall over. Very
funny.

Before, After

Teach this important vocabulary in a playful way. Give your child silly
commands, emphasizing the key word, e.g., "*Before* you stick out your
tongue, clap your hands," or "Flap like a chicken *after* you give me a kiss."
Let your child give you silly commands too.

Oops! That's Okay!

Oops games are great for kids who are easily frustrated or get upset
when they make mistakes. Have your child do something like build a block
tower or make a Play-Doh sculpture, then say, "Oops!" and have him knock
it down or squash it *himself*. Follow up with, "That's okay! Try, try again!"
(Make sure that your child knows he should only wreck or squash his own
constructions.)

What a Mess!

Definitely, definitely increase opportunities for messy play and water
play when you are training your child. (I guess Freud had to be right about
something.) Try finger-painting on a cookie sheet with pudding or shaving

cream; "cooking" in the sandbox; making mud pies from "clean" potting soil; pouring soapy, bubbly water from container to container in the sink or tub; and "messing about" with small smooth objects like buttons, coins, or dried beans. (Watch to make sure they don't go in mouths or ears or up noses.) Some kids like to smash graham crackers to make a crumb piecrust (Let them use a toy truck to run over crackers sealed in a heavy-duty zipper bag—that's fun.). Some like to squish dough (Play-Doh or the real thing). Anything that involves dumping and filling is good too.

Yes Sir, That's My Baby!

A little extra babying is soothing during this difficult transition and gives your child a chance to express his ambivalence about growing up. Pretend to change his diapers, feed him from a bottle, hold him and rock him, and generally give him a little TLC. Your child might also like a turn to treat you like a baby and showcase how grown up he is now.

Control Freaks

Games that let your child control you may release any tension that builds up between you during the training process. My kids liked playing Mom Robot, where they "pushed my buttons" (e.g., nose, belly button, elbow) to make me do silly things like stick out my tongue, cross my eyes, or quack like a robo-duck. Try also Simon Says, Mother May I?, and similar commanding games.

Peeing for Fun and Profit

✳ ✳ ✳

Effective Potty-Training Incentives

Think about it. What's in potty training for the kid? Not much—most toddlers and preschoolers are content to keep doing their business in their diapers and let you take care of the mess. Fortunately, little kids like to please their parents and be big like them—and those things will be their main incentive. But sometimes, a more concrete reward acts as a reminder or cements a child's resolve and keeps her trying in the face of frustration, just as a reward or chart can help you acquire a new habit. Here is a menu of some popular incentives—pick one that suits your values and your kid's preferences.

Token Rewards

Small things can have a big impact when you choose them well and use them wisely; big rewards wind up feeling like a bribe or too much pressure, and so are likely to backfire in a power struggle. Increase your child's sense of involvement and control by letting her choose between two acceptable options, and letting her be in charge of obtaining/using the reward—such as reaching in a jar to pull out a coupon or pasting the sticker where she chooses on her clothes or a chart.

✳ *Stickers.* They're cheap, readily available, and come in an infinite variety, so you're bound to find some that please your child.

✳ *Money in the bank.* Most kids enjoy making a deposit in a piggy bank after they've made one in the potty. Our favorite bank for this purpose was one that looked like a toilet—and made flushing sounds as the penny swirled down the drain. (You can find these at stores like Spencer's Gifts or on eBay.)

✳ *Nibbles.* I know nutritionists are always warning parents not to use food as rewards, but, well, treats *work*. Just keep the reward small and unavailable at other times. And brush teeth a lot. My kids loved M&Ms, but other tiny candies or snacks work too.

✳ *Coupons.* She can use them for things like one extra story or ten more minutes at the playground.

✳ *Tokens toward a (slightly) bigger prize.* When your kid reaches the goal, celebrate with a moderate treat, like a new book, a small toy, or lunch at a fast-food restaurant.

Symbols of Pride

When your child has a success, she may want to make sure everyone knows about it. She can try one of these ways to communicate the big news.

✳ *Brag button.* Make—or get a copy store to make—a button that says, "I peed in the potty today!" and let your child choose to wear it after a successful pit stop.

✳ *A ribbon—or a trophy.* It can be a powerful incentive, especially for a child with older siblings who garner sports awards.

✳ *Announcements.* No, not fancy engraved ones. But let your child call Mommy or Daddy at work, Grandma, Aunt Sal, and her best friend who's already trained—if she's eager to do so.

✳ *Have a pee party!* Just an informal get-together with a couple of trained buddies or a cake and balloons with the family. Cap off the party with a reading of THE DUMB BUNNIES by Sue Denim (Goldilocks gets flushed down the merry toilet—very funny). Don't forget a potty break to prevent accidents while the cake is being cut.

Big-Kid Privileges

Growing up is a package deal, with both increasing demands and emerging opportunities. Underscoring the link between the big-kid *responsibility* of using the toilet with some big-kid *privilege* may help with a kid who wants the advantages of being a big guy without actually doing any of the work. This approach works best if you make sure the privilege is something your child really wants.

✳ *Wearing a cape.* Supergirl is potty-trained after all. Or maybe your kid prefers a tiara or a briefcase—just choose something off-limits to *little* kids. Purchase the desired item, and let your child know she can have it once she's trained like her role model.

✳ *A big-people-only outing.* Take her on a trip alone with one parent to a movie, a sporting event, a meal at a restaurant with waiters and tablecloths (during an off-peak time, please), a fishing expedition, or something else exciting that only potty-trained guys can do.

Peer Pressure

✳ ✳ ✳
Other "Different" Approaches to Training

These are methods you're unlikely to find in traditional childcare manuals. Some of them would even earn me a frowny face from various child-development experts. But all are tried-and-true and if other ideas haven't worked for your child, you *probably* won't scar him for life with these.

Peer Pressure

This was the method that trained my first child—though as a trained psychologist I don't exactly *endorse* it because I hate it when people give me those frowny faces. But I must say it worked! My first child was potty-trained at two, *just weeks after the birth of his little brother.* How? Well, his visiting four-year-old cousin Scott announced scornfully that only *babies* wore diapers. That afternoon, Kyle asked for big-boy pants. I told him he'd have to pee and poop in the potty if he had big-boy pants. He gave me a withering look and said, "I *know.*" And that was that. Since then I've heard numerous similar stories. It's not a method you can orchestrate, but if it happens, great!

Peer Tutoring

This is similar, but not *quite* so coercive. Most toddlers worship big kids and may well cooperate better with them than with you. You may be able to enlist an older sibling or friend to help by demonstrating and encouraging.

My second child had zero interest in even sitting on the potty, despite being offered every shade of M&M ever made. Then one day while I was trying to coax him to give it the old college try, his older brother said, "*I* want an M&M!"

"Okay," I answered, "you can have an M&M if you can get Eric to sit on the pot." Well, Kyle not only convinced Eric to sit on the potty, he got him to pee! We were all thrilled—and Kyle took over potty training, for which he charged us the better part of a bag of M&Ms. (And in a rare burst of generosity, he shared some with his little brother!) With my third child, I just offered candy to the older two as soon as I thought she was ready—and she was trained within days.

The IKEA Method

This was the other key component to training my daughter. When my kids were little, IKEA, the Swedish home furnishings place, was one of the first places to offer a playroom for kids while their parents shopped. The kicker was that only potty-trained kids could stay there. My daughter was so anxious to hang out with her brothers in the ball area instead of being dragged to look at bookcases with us that she announced she was ready to be potty-trained just before her second birthday. Be careful—this method only works when the push (so to speak) comes from the kid, not from you, and when he is in fact ready to be trained.

Group Training Sessions

If your child is in daycare or one of those tolerant preschools that accepts untrained kids, you may not have to do any actual teaching yourself—the group may take care of it. When I taught toddler daycare, we'd invite the kids who were untrained but ready to come along when the trained kids went potty, and soon they'd be trained too. We simply switched them from diapers after they'd used the potty successfully for several days.

Summer Training Camp

Lots of parents swear by this method, which is easier on the carpets—and often on stores of patience as well. Introduce the potty—outside. Then let your kid wander around *au naturel*. When he pees, as he surely will, suggest that he try doing it on the potty next time. For some reason, being naked seems to make it easier for kids to be aware of their urges, and it eliminates the hassles associated with getting pants pulled down in time.

Just Add Water—The One-Day Method

This technique was popular in the 1970s, following the publication of TOILET TRAINING IN LESS THAN A DAY by Nathan Azrin. (It's still in print and apparently still selling well.) The basic idea is that you spend one day trapped in the kitchen forcing liquids on the kid and trying out the potty until he "gets it." It uses many of the steps I recommend (using a doll to demonstrate, getting "lucky," and guiding the child through all the extra steps of the process, like pulling up pants), just in a compressed time frame. I know people who have used this method when they were desperate (e.g., had their kid enrolled in a preschool that only took trained kids—and it was starting in two days and their kid had zero interest in the whole matter). It worked well for them. I also know some parents who tried it and hated it. It feels strict and coercive to me, and, despite the title, it may actually involve more than one really intense day.

Sweetie, There's a Reason It's Called "UNDERwear"

* * *

Panty Problems and Solutions

One of my friends had what I thought was an unusual potty-training problem with her son: he insisted on wearing his underwear back-to-front— and *over* his pants. She finally figured out the issue was twofold: 1) he wanted to see the picture on his underpants, and 2) he wanted all his buddies to know that he'd taken the big step out of diapers. Since then, I've discovered this issue is hardly rare. And there are all those other panty problems too— like what kind to use, etc. So here are some common problems and possible solutions.

The Picture Problem

Boys' underpants often have the bigger, more interesting cartoon picture on the back, a fact that many boys find distressing. Since almost no two-year-olds can work the fly anyway, I say go ahead and let the boys wear their pants backward. For kids who need to see the picture outside their clothes, why not let them wear a boring plain pair *under* their clothes, and the fancy ones on top? Their friends will only occasionally tease them about it when they are teenagers—my twenty-year-old rarely brings up the under-wear-on-the-outside thing to his friend anymore.

Disposables Versus Training Pants Versus Underpants

What should your kid wear during the training process? Forget training pants. They're expensive, tricky to operate, and not absorbent enough to be worth the bother. As for expensive disposables, save them for times when you won't be able to get to a potty quickly. Regular underpants have many advantages: 1) they're cheaper, 2) they're easier to pull up and down, 3) kids can choose from a zillion designs, 4) they don't contribute to land-fill problems, 5) starting out in them eliminates another transition you'll have to make eventually, and most importantly, 6) *they're horribly uncomfortable when they get wet.* Why, you might ask, is this an advantage? Because feeling uncomfortable is one of the best motivators for a kid to use the potty! In my experience, kids who wear disposables take *much* longer to finish training.

Unsuitable Choices

One of my kids preferred to wear a ratty pair of Teenage Mutant Ninja Turtles underwear that had accidentally been included in a box of hand-me-down clothes. I confess I gave up and let him wear them almost daily (as often as they were reasonably clean) until they finally fell apart altogether. And that's the advice I'll give for most of the weird choices kids make. There are enough control battles inherent in toilet training that you don't have to go looking for more fights. Most kids will come around to reasonable choices before long.

The Part-Time Panty Guy

Some kids prefer to put diapers (or disposables) back on for certain activities (including pooping). As long as it's the kid's choice to wear a diaper, I see no harm in it. (You might even gently suggest the option of wearing a diaper during certain activities, such as when you're out shopping, if your child routinely has accidents then—just don't force him). Most kids choose to wear underpants full-time as they get more comfortable with the whole process.

Nightwear

If your child is not yet trained at night, feel free to keep her in a diaper or disposables until she's ready to try. Explain that it's hard for her to notice that she needs to go when she's asleep, and that her body will be able to hold her pee longer as she gets older. That's all the reassurance most kids need. If you're trying to night-train, though, I recommend either regular underpants or nothing at all (see page 12).

Remedial Potty Class

✳ ✳ ✳

Coping with Refusal, Regression, and Other Problems

Don't panic if your three-and-a-half-year-old covers her ears when you even mention the "P" words. Or if your previously trained child is suddenly having accidents every time you leave the house. Problems like these are common—and surmountable.

Refusal

Some kids are more than ready physically, but flat out refuse to try. Most of the time, backing off and waiting a bit before broaching the topic again is the best approach. But if you feel it's absolutely time—you can't bear to change one more diaper or, as happened to one of my patients, you've run out of diapers and money but not time until your next paycheck try one or all of these approaches:

✳ *Make wearing diapers a nuisance.* Many kids don't like the hassles and interruptions that going potty entails. The solution? Make wearing diapers at least as inconvenient! Interrupt your child's play to change his diaper, change him every hour and a half whether he's dry or not, and make him go in the bathroom to wash his hands after you change him—all the things that would happen if he were getting trained. Store the diapers in a distant spot, and make him fetch them—in short, anything you can think of to make going potty seem at least as easy as wearing diapers.

✱ *Preserve the advantages of diaper changes.* Some kids don't want to give up the warm interactions that are part of getting changed. Make sure you continue to play tickle games, give hugs and kisses, or incorporate whatever rituals are part of your child's diapering routines during toilet time.

✱ *Make using the potty worth his while.* This approach is only for those emergency situations—like you just can't afford diapers anymore—because it involves enough pressure to endanger the real goal of toilet training, which is having your child decide to control his own body. Choose a powerful incentive. You might have to go out on a limb here—my patient used gum, which her older son didn't get until he was four. Place the incentive where your kid can see but not reach it. When he asks for it, remind him he can have it once he starts using the potty.

✱ *Set a date.* Some kids like the structure of a timetable. Count down the days until it's time for underpants and the potty. Just be willing to be flexible if the big day arrives and he's clearly not ready after all.

✱ *Find a training partner.* Everything is more fun with a friend! If a neighbor's child is ready to train, let the kids spend a few days together focused on potty activities. Start with a day of training their teddies, reading books, watching videos, etc. Then take turns hosting the trainees.

Regression

Many kids regress. Sometimes they're just tired of the hassle, but often there's another cause. Has anything else changed in your child's life? Visitors? Holidays? Has he been sick or had his scheduled disrupted? Time plus a little TLC will usually take care of the problem. Other options:

✱ *Reassure him.* Some kids get so stressed out by the training itself that it starts to interfere with their skills. Normalize the accidents ("Everyone has them!"), tell stories about when you or other important people in your child's life had accidents (make up stories if necessary), and calmly predict that he'll be back on track soon.

✳ *Increase structure.* Offer a new incentive, resume a reminding schedule, make sure your child visits the potty to "try," have him clean up after an accident (in case he's just avoiding the hassle aspect), and play some of the potty games on pages 12–14.

Miscellaneous Problems

Your child may experience one or more of these common problems.

✳ *Fear of flushing.* If the noise or scariness of stuff disappearing down the drain bothers your child, allow him to leave the room before you flush.

✳ *Situational accidents.* Does your child always have accidents in certain situations, such as at a friend's house or while watching TV? Some kids feel uncomfortable using unfamiliar potties or are shy about asking where the bathroom is. When you go someplace new, make a point of taking your child in to use the potty before he starts playing so he can see where it is and get used to it. Also, monitor kids engrossed in activities for signs that they need to go, like fidgeting, holding themselves, and irritability.

✳ *Helplessness—or excessive independence.* Some kids will use the potty—as long as you do all the real work, like remembering, pulling their pants down and up, wiping them, etc. (Not to be sexist, but this tends to be a male problem.) You can gradually build some independence by picking *one* problem behavior *that you are sure your child really can perform himself* and using an incentive plan to encourage the skill. See also pages 28–29 for more tips on handling dependence.

✳ *Bed-wetting.* It's incredibly common and mostly not under your child's control. I wouldn't worry about it too much until the end of the preschool years, and then only if it bothers your child. Then you might want to talk to your child's pediatrician about tactics like mattress alarms. Meanwhile, limit drinks before bed, take your child to pee before you turn in, and arrange things for easy changes (like having a laundry basket and a sleeping bag handy). Or just convince your child to wear Pull-Ups at night.

There's a Sucker Reformed Every Minute

✻ ✻ ✻

Helping Your Child (and You) Give Up Bottles, Pacifiers, Thumbs, and Other Habits That Suck

There are good reasons to help a preschooler wean from whatever she sucks on. Sucking may harm her teeth (although this is less true for orthodontic pacifiers), interfere with speech and language development, make her seem like a baby to her peers, delay learning more mature ways to soothe or occupy herself, and become linked to other health or behavioral problems. For example, prolonged use of bottles is associated with higher risk of obesity, and thumb and pacifier sucking tend to be circularly linked to TV watching. These tips may ease the transition:

The Basics

Before you get started breaking bad habits, think about these key points.

✻ *Involve your child.* One of the great things about preschoolers is you can reason with them—sort of. Tell them why you're weaning them and discuss ways to offer support during the difficult time.

✻ *Decide on a gradual or cold-turkey approach.* Which is best depends on your child's—and your—temperament.

✻ *Provide oral and tactile substitutes.* Offer thick liquids to suck through a straw, crunchy foods, bubbles to blow, or the occasional lollipop or Popsicle. Thumb and finger suckers need things to keep their hands busy too—a short length of silky ribbon to run through their fingers, worry stones or beads, or squeeze balls.

✻ *Offer other self-soothers.* Make a picture list of comforting things—like hugging, playing with water, rocking or swinging, snuggling with a blanket or stuffed animal, reading a book, playing with toys, or deep breathing.

✻ *Reward success.* Simple praise may be enough. Otherwise, reward your child with special time with you, a new stuffed animal or snuggle blanket, or another relaxing object or activity.

✳ *Be patient and understanding.* Expect whining, clinginess, irritability, etc.

Popular Approaches

These strategies have worked well for other parents.

✳ *The sucking room.* Limit your child to sucking in one place (usually her room). This approach is especially useful with thumb or finger suckers. Many parents also restrict sucking to certain times, such as the Arsenic Hour (just before dinner) or naptime and bedtime.

✳ *Nuisance laws.* Anything you do to make sucking inconvenient or bothersome will reduce its occurrence. Try telling your child to run around the room three times or assemble a puzzle before she starts to suck, have her give you a token or ticket to suck (you can also limit the number of these she has per day), have her wear a finger puppet or mitten which she'll have to remove prior to sucking, or require her to give up some other desired treat in exchange for sucking, such as watching TV.

✳ *The yuck factor.* Personally, I never liked this approach, but many parents swear by it. You can dip the sucking object in something that tastes bad (e.g., pickle juice, vinegar, commercial preparations) or, snip away at a pacifier so it goes flat and doesn't work right. (Just be careful that there are no loose parts for your child to choke on.)

✳ *The pacifier fairy and other substitutions.* Some parents have their child put all their pacifiers under their pillow—and in the morning the child discovers that the Pacifier Fairy has replaced them with some big-kid item the kid wants. Or they may offer an open trade for some desired big-kid toy or treat.

✳ *The big day.* Set a date for giving up sucking. Many parents use a birthday or similar occasion for this, but I think those days usually have enough stress all on their own. Some families throw a party to mark the occasion.

✳ *Lost and forgotten.* "Forget" the pacifiers when you're going some place or coming home from a vacation—and just don't replace them. Or taper off a sucker naturally by not replacing pacifiers as they wear out or get misplaced.

✳ *Throwing them all away in the midst of a sleep-deprived temper tantrum.* Well, this may not be a *popular* approach, but it worked with my kid. (I'm *not* recommending this method! I'm just telling you about my bad-mommy moment so you'll feel better if you don't manage to be as patient and understanding as you feel you should during the withdrawal phase.)

It's Not What You Say, but How You Say It

✳ ✳ ✳

Strategies for Minimizing Crying, Whining, Bossiness, and Baby Talk

Following a weekend visit to our house when my kids were small, a childless friend asked if there were ever days when no one cried or whined. And that's when I realized it had been *years* since I'd gone twenty-four hours without wishing for earplugs. Fortunately, crying decreases during the preschool years; unfortunately, it's replaced by whining and other verbal torture techniques, like bossiness and baby talk. Minimizing—forget eliminating—these behaviors requires a multipronged attack.

Prevention: The Usual Suspects

Structured routines, consistent rules, good nutrition, calm parenting, etc., really do minimize whining and crying, as well as other problem behaviors.

Identify the Source

Likely causes include: fatigue, hunger, frustration, sensory overload, boredom, the mere existence of siblings, and pain or illness. Many kids whine when they can't perceive or communicate what they need. Name what your child is feeling, and then ask, "What's a *better* thing to do when you're _____ (tired, hungry, etc.)?"

Only Reward the Behavior You Like

Okay, be honest. Do you sometimes give in and buy your kid candy at the store when he whines? And do you *never* buy candy when he doesn't? Instead, offer a reward when he uses his pleasant voice.

"I Can't Understand You When You Use That Voice"

It's a little more honest to say something like, "I'll listen when you use your big-boy voice (or nice voice or whatever)," but I'm not opposed to the occasional white (or even gray) lie when dealing with kids.

"Please Use your Gila-Monster Voice"

Same technique—but with a dose of silliness to lighten the mood. Ask your child to tell you his problem with a French accent or like a robot. Or have him whisper, sing, or quack what he has to say. Almost *anything* is better than whining or baby talk.

Make the Sign of the W

Cub Scouts hold up two fingers as a signal to be quiet—and in my house, three fingers (American Sign Language for the letter *w*) means, "You're whining and I need you to stop it before I go stark raving mad and start throwing Tinkertoys everywhere."

Give Your Child More Control in His Life

Helpless people of all ages are more likely to whine. Make sure you give your child chances to make decisions (between two choices) or to do things himself as much as possible.

"A Sock for You! A Sock for Me!"

✳ ✳ ✳

Ways to Foster Your Child's Independence

I'll be honest: *it is always easier to do any task yourself than to let a preschooler do it for you.* Which is why many of us fall into the bad trap of doing everything for our kids—and then being thoroughly annoyed with them when they act helpless.

Childproof and Child-Enable Your Home

Busy daycare and preschool teachers set up the physical environment to make it both safe and easy for kids to help themselves. You can too. The bare minimum you should provide: a snack shelf in the fridge and a kid-tableware drawer, drinking water in sports bottles or other dispensers your child can work herself, a cubby or basket for outdoor clothing, toy bins on low shelves clearly labeled with pictures, and a step stool in the bathroom. And you can pray your child's clothing obsessions involve garments she can manage herself.

Teach Your Child the Skills She Needs

Preschoolers can learn to do an amazing number of things *if* you teach them, breaking down the task step by step and offering both encouragement and praise. Whenever possible, let your child work alongside you with her own equipment. It takes a lot of energy to do this teaching, and you won't see good results for a *long* time with most skills—but it does work and it's worth it.

Promote a Sense of Competence

Kids who feel strong, coordinated, and knowledgeable are more likely to seek independence in a variety of areas. Preschooler playground skills—climbing the ladder and sliding down; hanging from the monkey bars; throwing, catching, and kicking a ball; pedaling a tricycle or small bike; or pumping a swing—are important not only for helping your child make and keep friends, but also for helping her feel like a capable person who can also put on her own coat or set the table. Not sure how or when to teach these skills? Watch other kids on the playground (and encourage your child to do the same) or check out websites like www.teachkidshow.com.

Job Share

Do you have a child who resists doing things she's capable of? Agree to do half the job for her—she puts on one sock and you put on the other.

Build in Extra Time

A good rule of thumb is to triple the amount of time it will take a three-year-old to do a given task herself (like putting on her own coat), and double the time for a four-year-old.

Distinguish between "Hurry Times" and "Take-Our-Time Times"

Warn your kid when it's a "hurry time" and explain that you're going to help. Just take care to provide plenty of "take-your-time" opportunities, too.

Offer Choices Often

Two is a good number of choices for most preschoolers: "Would you like to wear the stained dinosaur shirt or the torn Spiderman one?" "Pick up your toys or brush your teeth first?" "Wear your underwear on your head or on your bottom?" Choosing can be hard work for kids—use humor, clear ground rules, and an occasional break to keep kids from getting frustrated or overwhelmed.

Minimize Hovering and Smothering

All kids need to learn to take *reasonable* risks, even if it sometimes scares their parents. They also need chances to make mistakes and learn on their own. They need to feel their *own* sense of pride and accomplishment. Show your kids how to do tasks properly and safely and then back off!

Isn't Child Labor Wonderful?

✳ ✳ ✳

Putting Your Preschooler to Work

Our family policy is "Everyone pitches in, even if some people don't feel like it, plus their legs hurt, and the sun is in their eyes." This rule minimizes parental resentment, sort of—and forces you to teach your kids skills they'll need to know. It also builds family cohesiveness, since the underlying message is that everyone matters. These tips may encourage more effective and persistent work from the smallest helpers.

Have Realistic (i.e., Low) Expectations

Preschoolers cannot go into a messy room and clean it up. But they can pick up all the Barbie heads and put them in the Barbie-head bin. Other jobs a preschooler can learn to do (badly) include the following: make his own bed (use just a comforter—no top sheet), care for his own body (brush his teeth and hair, get dressed himself, wash himself, maybe wipe after using the toilet), fetch and carry unbreakable objects that are not sharp, sort and fold some laundry (e.g., socks and towels), be a cleaning or fix-it assistant (favorite jobs include anything involving spray bottles—fill his with warm water and a splash of vinegar or a dash of baking soda), prepare and clean up after a snack or simple meal (like cereal and milk, or peanut butter and crackers if you can bear the inevitable mess), set the table, wipe up spills (sort of), and perform outdoor chores like picking up sticks before you mow. Preschoolers are also good at operating the TV remote for the family, or any other job that involves pushing buttons, including yours.

Scale the Job Down

A preschooler may not be able to carry a full bag of groceries, but he'll feel very strong lugging in one bag "filled" with a box of cereal and a carton of yogurt. Or have him scrub the hubcaps when you wash the car.

Give a Clear Job Description

Break the task down into steps, and be sure to describe what constitutes being "done" (e.g., *no* Barbie heads left on the floor, not even bald ones). The Montessori method is particularly good at breaking down almost any task from closing a drawer properly to slicing apples. See Shu-Chen Jenny Yen's Montessori Album site (http://www.ux1.eiu.edu/~cfsjy/mts/_link.htm) and click on "Practical Life Album" for fabulous instructions for teaching your child many tasks.

Add an Appealing Title

Want your four-year-old to empty all the pockets before you do the laundry? Make him the Official Pocket Master for the family. He might like a hat or at least a badge.

Provide Cool Tools

It's much more fun to empty the wastebaskets when you're dumping them into a box that you pull around in a wagon *in the house*. Kid-sized tools are popular too. My kids loved helping me do laundry by washing one item in a dishpan with a little Woolite.

Add an Element of Fun

And, as Mary Poppins says, the job's a snap! There are a number of easy ways to up the pleasure quotient of any task. Boppy music always helps move things along. Add a dash of suspense: assign chores by pulling out a slip from a job jar. Many kids adore a competition, even if it's just to see if they can pick up all the Barbie heads before you corral all the plastic dinosaurs. Treasure hunts rarely fail. For example, you can hide small rewards, like pennies that can be discovered as a child dusts the furniture. (I learned that technique from Sydney Taylor's classic chapter book ALL OF A KIND FAMILY.) Or have your child work toward a small reward for himself or for the whole family.

Offer Work That Matters

Build pride and self-esteem by making sure some of your child's jobs contribute to the well-being of others. Perhaps he can earn money for a charity by completing jobs. Or have him assist when you do volunteer work. My daughter used to collate papers when I volunteered in her big brother's classroom.

CHAPTER TWO

Whoa, Baby!

* * *

Busting New-Sibling Bothers

One day soon after we'd brought child number two home from the hospital, I was sitting on the sofa nursing the baby while my firstborn played on the coffee table with the contents of several board games that he'd dumped out. After a few minutes, he said, "Look Mommy!"

I peered over to see that he'd arranged some tiles from the shape game Tangoes. He'd placed two large triangles side by side, nestled a small triangle against one of them, and put a medium-sized one next to that. Trained psychologist that I am, I smiled at the lovely family he'd created. "How nice!" I said.

"This one's the daddy, and this one's the mommy," he said, not realizing that I had a degree in this and didn't need to have it explained to me, "and this one's the baby." He then held up the medium-sized one for me to see, saying, "And this one's the big brother."

I started to say, "Oh, just like you!" when he began smashing and smashing it against the tiny triangle until the "baby" fell off the coffee table and tumbled under the sofa! He then nestled the medium-sized one up against the mommy one and smiled.

Well, even if you haven't taken so much as Psych 101, you probably can tell what was going on.

This kind of reaction to a new baby is pretty common, though by no means as universal as many experts would have you believe. (I know I've waited patiently on several occasions for a friend's older child to finally show some malice toward her new sibling, thereby forcing that smug mother to join the Bad Parent Club with me, all to no avail.) And some kids whine about the new baby, but don't get so…well, *violent* about it.

Hmm, it's just occurred to me that this story might have you thinking that I'm hardly qualified to give advice on helping older siblings adjust to the new baby. But get this—both boys are still alive and the vast majority of the younger one's scars have come as the result of his own follies, like balancing on top of a basketball in the driveway when his brother was nowhere in sight. Plus we went on to have a third child. And she's still alive too.

So anyway, this chapter is about coping with a second pregnancy while helping prepare your first child to welcome the new one. I've included tips for everything from how to tell your child the Big News and answer her questions about reproduction to suggestions for dealing with the old, used baby (who, like an old, used vehicle, tends not to smell as nice as a new one). Plus I've added ideas for supporting your child during the birth period, and helping her if things don't go as planned.

One last thing. Even if your child is "unenthusiastic" about the newcomer, remember that reaction isn't destiny. You *can* shape your kid's behavior and feelings to help him develop a normal, loving sibling relationship with his brother or sister. (As long as you understand that "normal" includes lots of wrestling and quarreling over who gets the last of the cookie-dough ice cream.)

Congratulations!

Breaking News! We're Having a Baby!

✳ ✳ ✳

When and How to Tell Your Preschooler

Expect as much unasked-for advice about this issue as you will about every other aspect of your pregnancy—and people will have *strong* opinions. But ultimately, the right thing is a judgment call—*yours*.

When to Share the Big News

With a toddler, or a kid who is "less perceptive," wait until three or four months before the baby is due. That leaves you plenty of time to prepare her (and the nursery), and it's not the eternity that nine months is.

With a preschooler, though (especially a kid who is sensitive to your moods or who's the little-pitcher-with-big-ears type) tell her about the same time you either start barfing regularly or sharing the big news with the rest of the world (and not before, or your kid will share the news for you). Most kids sense that *something's* up, and their anxiety may be lower if they know the reason for the excitement and tension at home. And you really don't want your kid to learn about this big change in her life from the checker at the supermarket or by overhearing a phone conversation.

How to Break the News

I've talked to parents who actually *apologized* to their kids for getting pregnant! THIS IS NUTS! Okay, there *will* be times when your kid insists you've delivered The Demon Escaped from Down Under, but during these blissful pre-reality days, you might as well build rosy (though somewhat-realistic) expectations. Make the announcement at the family dinner table. This gives your kid time—but not too much—to mull over the new idea prior to bedtime when you can answer her awkward questions about reproduction in the safety of the dark.

What to Tell

Kids are most interested in how *their* lives will be affected by any change, so frame your first remarks that way. Let your child know how her status will change, give her a kid-friendly sense of the timing, and a brief overview of the process by which this change will take place (i.e., pregnancy and birth or adoption). Some parents give their kids a small relevant gift at this time. Good choices are a doll or stuffed animal with baby-care accessories, a set of family dolls or puppets, a "pregnant" doll or stuffed animal, or something that only big kids can have.

Keep in Mind

Don't overwhelm your child with details. You have months to provide information.

Plan to repeat everything. Pregnancy is an abstract idea that's hard for concrete preschoolers to grasp. Just think how many times you've had to tell her not to flush socks down the toilet—and it will take much longer to see the results of pregnancy.

"Why Did You Eat the Baby?"

✳ ✳ ✳

A Preschooler's FAQs about Pregnancy and Birth

After the first blush of excitement, your preschooler's busy brain is going to generate a million questions, some of which will be hysterically funny. Reading books about pregnancy and birth may answer some of his questions, but expect that he'll come up with some intriguing issues no author anticipated. Some common concerns:

How Did the Baby Get in There?

Wait until your kid asks questions to offer information. When he does, give honest but *little* answers—if he needs to know more, he'll ask. In general, younger kids want less information than older ones. A three-year-old may not ask this question at all, and most fours will be satisfied with something like, "A seed from Daddy joined with an egg from Mommy to start the baby growing."

No matter how accurate and honest you are, preschoolers tend to hold tight to their misconceptions. Many will persist in believing that you ate the baby or a special seed to start it growing (and they may have hopes or fears about starting a baby themselves by swallowing a seed or other food).

How Will He Get Out?

Common misconceptions include beliefs that Daddy will unzip Mommy's tummy, that the baby will come out Mommy's belly button, or that Mommy will vomit up the baby (which may make your morning sickness even more exciting or distressing). Threes often want no more information than "The midwife (or doctor) will help the baby come out when it's time." Four- and five-year-olds may want to know about the baby's trip down the stretchy birth canal or vagina. Persistent ones may ask whether it hurts, how long it takes, etc. Just remember to keep giving little direct answers.

Can Daddy Have a Baby Too? His Tummy's Fat. Can I Have a Baby Too?

Preschoolers have lots of questions about who can and cannot have a baby. Many are distressed not to be able to grow their own babies, and some boys may even contemplate a sex change. Don't get worked up if yours does—it's a passing phase. Reassure them that they can help care for the baby, even if it doesn't grow in their bodies.

What's Going on in There?

Curiosity about the developing baby is very common. Many preschoolers enjoy listening to the baby's heartbeat at your checkups and seeing sonogram pictures of the baby. Areas of particular interest: how the baby eats, drinks, breathes, and poops; what the baby is (not) wearing; how big it is and what parts are developing (a development calendar, also available online, or pictures in a pregnancy book may fascinate your child); and whether the baby can hear sounds and see light from outside. Many will also notice and be interested in the changes in Mommy's body.

How Will My Life Change When the Baby Gets Here? What Are New Babies Like?

Not that they'll ask in so many words. This is one area where you should anticipate worries, even if your child doesn't voice them, and provide specific information and gentle reassurance. He needs to know that the baby is an addition, not a replacement for him; where the baby will sleep, and whether where he sleeps will change; that the baby won't be allowed just to take over his toys and things; that he will still be loved and needed; and that he can still be little and you will take care of him too. You will also need to start talking about the realities of having a baby in the house as the birth draws near, so he isn't shocked by how small and helpless (and no-fun) a new baby is, and so he's prepared for how busy and tired everyone will be. If you'll be nursing the baby, talk about this process too. Finally, discuss things unrelated to the baby that he'll be doing after it comes, so he maintains a sense that his own life will continue.

Waiting Ways

* * *

Activities for Anticipating

These activities help preschoolers mark the seemingly endless time until the baby arrives—and maybe even help them develop a positive attitude toward the creature.

Baby Advent Calendars

Advent calendars work just as well for "How much longer until that stupid baby?" as they do for "How much longer until I get a million presents?" Count off *weeks* until the baby; months are big chunks and counting down the days will put too much emphasis on the event for everyone. And remind your child that no one knows exactly when a baby will come. Some calendar methods:

  * *Chain links.* Make a chain with links for each week of pregnancy. Let your child snip off one as each week passes. Or make a chain from wrapped candies. (Just make sure to avoid choking hazards.)

  * *Surprise packages.* Give your child a weekly surprise, like a library book to read about puppies being born, a "coupon" for a trip to buy new shoes now that she's growing so big, or new art supplies. The last box can be a gift from the new baby.

  * *Like money in the bank.* Let your child transfer money or

another token from one see-through container to another as each week passes. This way she can see how much time has passed and how much remains. And after the baby's birth, she can use the money for a special outing for *her*, since the poor baby will be too little to go anywhere fun.

You Can Bet on It!

I know it seems a little…well, bad, to teach a preschooler how to gamble. But having pools and making bets about various things related to the baby will help pass the time, foster math and estimating skills, and teach your child important information about babies to boot. We bet on things like birth date, time of day, gender, weight (exact weight, or an over-under kind of thing, like "more or less than a sack of sugar plus a bunch of bananas"), hair or no hair, looks more like a monkey or like an old man (poll all the visitors to determine the winner), etc. You can also bet on whether the baby will kick or not in the next five minutes (If it does, everyone gets ice cream!), which side it will kick on next, whether Mommy will throw up today—the possibilities are endless.

> ### LITERATURE LINKS
>
> Here are some good books that discuss pregnancy, preparations, and what a new baby will be like: WAITING FOR BABY by Harriet Ziefert, HELLO BABY! by Lizzy Rockwell, the lift-the-flap BEFORE YOU WERE BORN by Jennifer Davis; and for older preschoolers who can handle more graphic images, the classic photo-essay A CHILD IS BORN by Lennart Nilsson.

Prenatal Science Experiments

Try "experiments" like having your child push *gently* on your belly and then seeing if the baby pushes or kicks back (which is a documented tendency). Another great experiment is to have your child recite a nursery rhyme or sing a song to the baby daily for the last several weeks of your pregnancy. Then, after the baby is born, have your child recite or sing her selection to him, and see if he appears to recognize it. (Tell your child he'll show this by opening his eyes, seeming to listen intently, or turning toward her.)

Belly-Button Conversations

Get in the habit of lifting your shirt so your preschooler can converse with her sibling via your belly button. You're in charge of talking back for the baby, using a squeaky, yet worshipful tone. Have your child tell the baby about highlights of her day, ask questions about baby's life, offer words of wisdom, tell jokes, etc. The baby in turn will admire his big sibling's many impressive skills, be a little jealous of the fun he's missing out on, express affection, and generally be silly and endearing.

Baby-Prep Assistant

Older siblings *may* like to help you set up the nursery, test out baby equipment (a good idea since it probably needs to be sturdy enough to support them too, if you know what I mean), and shop for tiny clothes. These activities clue kids in about how little a new baby is—and what a big deal. I also had my kids pick out photos of themselves and our pets to hang in the baby's bassinet at the hospital, and we made a welcome sign. Foolishly, I let them consult on names. I wanted to name our daughter Elly or Megan—but she's Sara because my oldest insisted on naming her after his favorite dinosaur in *The Land Before Time.* (Fortunately, I think he was right—the name suits her.) This brings me to an important warning: Only involve your child in matters where you're willing to accept *her* choices, which will probably involve garish colors, inappropriate cartoon characters, and other tacky tastes. If you reject what she wants for the baby, you risk not only hurting her feelings but also creating resentment toward the new sib to boot.

Nurturing the Nurturing Urge

✳ ✳ ✳

Activities to Elicit Interest and Skill in Caregiving

Although many preschoolers are naturally interested in babies, nearly all will benefit from a little explicit encouragement of this interest—and all need help in learning the ins and outs of caring for those who are young and helpless.

Observe the Miracle of Creation!

Seeing a new life begin, even if it's just the emergence of a weed's cute little baby leaves, often sparks a child's interest in life and helps him develop an urge to care for other beings. Here are some easy ways to help your child be present at a birth, hatching, or sprouting.

✳ *Grow a new plant.* My favorite method is sort of an ant farm for seeds. Take a few large seeds (dried beans from the grocery store work great). Get a small jar and cut a piece of sponge to fit inside it (rolled up). Dampen the sponge, and slide a few *intact* beans between the wall of the jar and the sponge—then keep an eye on them. Within a couple of days you should see a root curl down and a pair of leaves push up. Keep the sponge damp but not soggy. Move the plant to a pot with soil when it has a couple sets of leaves and some good roots.

✳ *Watch a birth* ...of critters! Guppies and mollies are live-bearers and prolific breeders. Even if your child doesn't see the actual birth, the new tiny baby fish will elicit much excitement. We also had some interesting discussions about why parents might be tempted to eat their own young. Visit www.aquarium.net for information. Other options include visiting science museums like the Carnegie Science Center in Pittsburgh to see chicks hatch, or finding videos on YouTube of a wide variety of critters hatching or being born (search for "hatching" or "birth" plus whatever critter you're interested in, but be sure to preview to make sure the clips are kid-friendly).

Pretend to Care

Imaginative play can teach your child both the attitudes and skills of good caregivers.

✳ *House.* Preschoolers play house in many different ways—with props, small figures, or puppets. Good props and a little prompting from you or another playmate will also boost the quality of play.

✳ *Good guys and superheroes.* Superhero play is the ultimate parenting play. You *can* steer play toward nurturing themes as opposed to aggressive ones. Just jump in with requests like, "Guys! Help! Lard Man has put Baby Binky up in the tree."

Teach Caregiving Skills

Remember how awkward you felt the first time you changed a diaper? We all need a little explicit instruction and practice to learn how to anticipate and meet the needs of those smaller than us.

✳ *Creature care.* Daily care for a pet, even if it's just a colony of potato bugs living in an old diaper-wipes box on the kitchen table, will give your child some sense of the relentless needs of helpless creatures—and the pride and satisfaction that can come from meeting those needs.

✳ *Poopy-diaper school.* Many hospitals offer big-sibling classes, where they teach tots to hold babies, diaper a doll, etc. If yours doesn't offer one or it doesn't fit in your schedule, teach your child yourself. Include lessons on what new babies look like (kind of ugly), why they cry, how parents take care of them, etc. If possible, borrow a real baby for some show and tell. And speaking of show and tell…

✳ *Show and tell.* One of the best ways to foster your child's interest in babies is to remind him of his own babyhood. Get out the old photos and videos and tell funny stories about how he did things like pee in your face when you changed his diapers.

Making Womb

✳ ✳ ✳

Managing Your First Kid and Your Second Pregnancy without Everyone Barfing

In one of those cruel tricks that Mother Nature likes to play, your second pregnancy is likely to be more physically difficult than your first. Part of this is because everything was stretched out by the first go-round, so you show earlier and have bigger hemorrhoids and varicose veins. And partly it's because you have no time or energy to take care of yourself, since you're chasing an active child. And now that you don't have enough time or energy for said active child, you can add guilt to the mix. What fun! But these tips can help everyone make it through in one piece and maybe even strengthened by the challenges.

Promote Your Child to Morning-Sickness Manager

Relax rules and let your little guy climb in bed with you to share a snack while you watch TV. (Not Barney, though—that may make *your husband* feel like barfing.) Try dry saltines for you and something that isn't so crummy, like raisins, for her. When you go on outings, your child will like being in charge of anti-barf supplies, like ginger snaps, sour gummy candies or lemon drops, pretzels, and ginger ale—all of which you will share with her for being so helpful.

Teach Your Child the Maxim "Mom Helps Those Who Help Themselves"

Time to make your home tot-friendly and promote your child's independence (see pages 28–32 for more tips). Save your back and avoid lifting your bulky preschooler; instead, have her climb on a chair. Buy step stools so your child can reach things herself. Most preschoolers can also learn to scramble into their car seats, even if they can't manage the final buckling. Finally, get your child comfortable with having someone else help with her bedtime.

Phone a Friend

For your kid, that is. Friendships, perhaps more than any other buffer, help older siblings cope with the birth of a new sibling. This is also a good time to enroll your child in ONE class or activity that will continue after the baby comes.

Be Partners in Good Health

Although you won't have the time or luxury this pregnancy of caring for yourself the way you did the first time, if you make a commitment to good health practices for your older child, you can reap the side benefits. Make a chart for everyone to post stickers for each serving of fruits and vegetables eaten, aiming for five per day each. Exercise daily, whether it's a long walk around the neighborhood, a Mommy and Me yoga class or DVD, or just dancing in the family room. Nudge bedtimes earlier and insist on a daily afternoon rest. Your preschooler probably won't sleep, but she can learn to play quietly for forty-five minutes (see tips in FUSSBUSTERS AT HOME). Finally, make a point to laugh *hard* at least once a day—even if the experts turn out to be wrong about the health benefits of laughter, at least everyone will have had fun.

When It's Not the Way It's Supposed to Be

✳ ✳ ✳

Supporting Your Preschooler During Complications and Crises

If you're facing complications with your pregnancy or delivery, you're probably preoccupied and tired. Add an older child to care for, and you're at high risk for becoming overwhelmed—which in turn will stress out your child. These strategies minimize stress contagion.

General Strategies

Whatever the difficulty, these basic tactics lessen anxiety, increase closeness, and promote coping.

✳ *Maintain routines.* Write out your child's routines so that substitute caregivers can keep him on track if necessary. At a minimum, strive to keep wake-up, meals, and bedtime the same, and have your child continue to attend daycare or preschool.

✳ *Provide age-appropriate, honest information.* Preschool children need to know the basics, especially information about how the situation will affect them. Keep repeating information and adding details as your child requests them. If sad outcomes are likely, such as death or disability, prepare your child for the possibilities, while continuing to offer hope.

✳ *Keep in touch.* Schedule regular cuddle times, as well as outings or projects, to maintain the closeness that you both need. If you're hospitalized, talk on the phone daily and exchange photographs, notes, and gifts. Many children appreciate a chat a half hour or so before bedtime or other difficult transitions.

✳ *Provide outlets for feelings.* Gather art supplies, musical instruments, dolls, or puppets to help your child to play out his feelings. Be accepting of his emotions, even if they seem odd or uncaring. Many preschoolers will either ignore the baby or express anger toward it for disrupting life. Your child may also be angry with you or the doctor. Reassure your child that the baby's problems were not his fault— young children often feel irrational guilt.

✳ *Increase soothing.* Expect regression, tantrums, physical symptoms, sleep or eating disruptions, and other signs of stress—and combat them with extra TLC, such as a "rest bath" in the afternoon, play with sensory materials (like finger paints, sand, beans, or button jars), and exercise opportunities. Try hanging balloons from the ceiling just out of your child's reach, and giving him a paper-towel tube to bat them as he jumps. Also make a point of using pleasure touches—like back scratches, gentle tickles, stroking, and massage— with your child.

How to Rest in Bed without Everyone Getting Exhausted

You wouldn't think that *resting* could be so tiring, but having a mom on bedrest absolutely stretches the resources of families to the limit. Boost energy in these ways:

✳ *Enlist help.* Active preschoolers need a substitute caregiver to meet their needs—don't be tempted to get by on your own for more than short periods of time. Arrange play dates if you can't afford other regular childcare—and offer payback whenever a spouse or other caregiver is available. If possible, splurge on home and yard care help.

✳ *Get bed-set.* Arrange your own environment to make yourself as comfortable and mentally stimulated as possible—otherwise you'll just transfer your frustration and depression onto your child. Include items to help you stay connected and effective in your family, like a phone, computer, writing supplies, or an intercom system.

✳ *Be visit-friendly.* Lively preschoolers won't understand your physical limitations and will try to crawl and bounce all over you; cushions or a beanbag chair can provide a cozy spot to sit *next* to you instead. Have your child join you for quiet activities like reading, non-messy crafts (pipe cleaners are great), doing stretching exercises, watching a DVD or TV show together. Be sure to touch your child often, rubbing lotion on him, or playing tickle-me games (especially good as an end-the-visit ritual). Here's a new one to try:

One, two, three,	*Trace numerals on child's back.*
Buzzy, buzzy tickle bee.	*Use finger to "buzz" and tickle all over.*
Four, five, six,	*Trace numerals again.*
Stacking up sticks.	*Spread fingers and tap child from base of spine to shoulders.*
Seven, eight, nine,	*Trace numerals.*
A ziggy-zaggy line.	*Make a long lightning bolt on child's back.*
That leaves TEN,	*Write number ten or big X.*
Hug! Kiss! The END!	*Hug and kiss your child.*

Where's Baby? How to Help Your Older Child if the Baby Is Hospitalized

Having a new sibling in the hospital can be scary, sad, lonely, aggravating, and even surreal—all at the same time.

✳ *Visit the baby.* Many hospitals allow older siblings to visit. Prepare your child ahead of time for what he'll see, hear, and smell. (Photos can be a great discussion starting point.) Practice an activity he can do with the baby, like singing a quiet song or showing her a puppet.

Plan to keep the visits *short*; if possible, bring along another adult who can accompany your child to the snack bar or waiting room to play while you have a longer visit. No visits allowed or possible? Record baby's day in photos or videos. She still won't seem quite *real* to your preschooler, but at least he'll be less shocked when she finally does come home.

✳ *Help your child brag.* Every baby is a miracle, and all new siblings deserve congratulations. Buy a snack like lollipops for your child to hand out at preschool or to friends. Make a brag book for him to show around too.

> ### LITERATURE LINKS
>
> For more tips, try MOMMY HAS TO STAY IN BED by Annette Rivlin Gutman, as well as THE PREGNANCY BEDREST BOOK: A SURVIVAL GUIDE FOR EXPECTANT MOTHERS AND THEIR FAMILIES by Amy E. Tracy.

✳ *Exchange sibling gifts.* Your child can choose pictures and items to decorate the baby's bassinet, as well as clothing like tiny hats to keep her head warm. He may want to donate a shirt he's worn (so baby can get used to his smell), make a recording of songs or stories, or put together a collage of photographs to help baby get to know him. The baby can also "give" something special to her big sibling.

✳ *Spend time together.* Put aside your worries and focus on your child *every day*. Time at a playground (indoor or out), a long collecting walk, or another physical activity will relieve stress. Have your child make three wishes each night when you tuck him in; his desires give you a window to see how he's coping. Finally, a token from you may help your child feel connected even when you're at the hospital—consider a mini photo album, a special coin to keep in his pocket, or a small cuddler like a cloth hankie, a ribbon, or tiny stuffed animal.

Multiple Birth Sibs without Multiple Problems

Even if you don't end up on bedrest or the babies don't arrive prematurely, you'll need to take it easier during your pregnancy. Stock up on activities you can do with your child while resting on the sofa, and start talking about life with twin siblings. Your resources will be stretched especially thin after the babies arrive—and the reality is that visitors and strangers give multiples extra-special attention, so you'll need to be vigilant to keep your child's stress in check.

Pregnancy Tech Support

There are lots of useful resources for challenging pregnancies on the Internet. For more tips and support, check out some of these websites:

✳ *http://www.twinslist.org/bedrest.htm*
Although this site is intended for women expecting multiples, it has lots of practical tips for any mom on bedrest.

✳ *www.sidelines.org*
Sidelines is a large organization that provides information and tips for every aspect of a high-risk pregnancy.

✳ *www.marchofdimes.com*
This site has information on birth defects, prematurity, and helping families cope with babies that have difficulties.

✳ *www.multiplebirthsfamilies.com*
Nice site with tips for helping singleton siblings cope with your pregnancy and life with twin (or more) sibs.

Avoiding the Delivery Gloom

✳ ✳ ✳

Easing Separation Anxieties and Other Birth Day Concerns

Because the events surrounding the actual birth may set the tone for an older child's initial adjustment to her sibling (or even her lifelong crabby attitude), it pays to prepare. And, because Murphy's Law seems to apply in spades to Big Events, you should *doubly* prepare.

Teach your child how to dial 911 and talk to a dispatcher, so she'll be able to summon help for you in an emergency—a useful skill for any child, pregnant mom or no. Post a sign with the number near the phone, and practice on a toy phone. You might also want to program auto-dial on your phone and show her how to call your husband or the doctor if you should need them too. Be sure to tell the story of THE BOY WHO CRIED WOLF, though, while you're at it.

Nest, Test, and Rest

While making final preparations, review for the hundredth time what your child knows about babies—and about what will happen on the day of the big event. Retell the story of her birth, and then read THE THREE LITTLE PIGS so everyone can practice huffing and puffing with you. Shop for and wrap gifts—for your child to give the baby, for the baby to give your child, and for you to give yourself (because you'll need a little pick-me-up during the first few days home). Stock your freezer with a week's worth of meals and remind those friends who have offered meals that you're counting on them. Your child can make a "focal point" for you to look at during labor, and choose the pictures for the new baby's hospital bassinet. Finally, be sure to increase rest times during this period, so everyone can build reserves for the stressful postpartum period.

Separation Preparation

Make plans for *everything* and talk through them with your child. Preparations should include:

✻ *Choosing good substitute caregivers.* Notice I said caregivers— make sure you have at least one backup, since you never know when Grammy will slip on the ice dashing out to her car and end up at the hospital with you. In addition to grandparents, consider neighbors or friends with young children—it may be easier for them to provide distractions. Make sure you and your spouse have all phone numbers for potential subs, as well as plans for delayed transfers (e.g., a neighbor who can watch your child until Gram arrives).

❋ *The book, part I.* Assemble a notebook with information for your child's caregiver, including the following: your child's routine in excruciating detail (e.g., she needs to sleep with Puppy Pee Pee who has usually slipped under the bed but has occasionally been left outside in the playhouse); what she will and will not eat; strange idiosyncrasies she's developed in the last week, like only going potty with the Snoopy night-light on; MapQuest directions or GPS-programmable addresses to school, the supermarket, and friends' houses; phone numbers for doctors, dentists, etc.; how to operate the remote and the DVD player, especially if it's stubborn and has to be smacked with your slipper first; and other details of daily life. It may seem over-the-top—but whoever is stuck trying to soothe an overwrought child will greatly appreciate this Child Bible. The book is also useful for sitters AB (After Baby) and is a cool thing to tuck into your child's own baby book later.

❋ *The book, part II.* This book—or collage—is for your child. Include pictures of you and your spouse, the substitute caregivers, a photo of the hospital (perhaps from brochures you've gotten), pictures cut from magazines of new babies, a photo-map of your child's day so she knows what to expect, and anything else that will make life more predictable while you're away.

❋ *Tricks and treats.* Assemble a basket with a new book (especially something like a WHERE'S WALDO-ish book or a story featuring a good relationship between siblings), a DVD, a treat food or two, and a game or craft activity—it will be appreciated by everyone should tough moments arise in your absence.

Labor Relations

Chances are you'll spend your early labor at home with your older child. *Do not blow your bonus energy on ambitious activities with her*—save it for the work ahead. A stroll around the block, a stack of books to read, or simple play with materials like Play-Doh or bubble soap can keep you both distracted. If you feel irritable, explain your feelings to your child and apologize for snapping at her.

The Quick Good-Bye

Tell your child you'll say good-bye when you leave for the hospital—and *keep that promise*, even if it's the middle of the night and she doesn't remember in the morning. Keep it short, sweet, and casual—prolong the good-bye and you'll breed anxiety.

Checking In and the Big News

If labor is taking a long time, have someone phone to let everyone know how things are progressing. Funny details like "Mom is wearing a lovely gown with little frogs on it" will keep the tone light and optimistic. And when the baby does arrive, place a call regardless of time of day again—you want to at least give the illusion that your child was the *first* to know—even before Grandpa. (Also, keep in mind that it is considered very bad form to lie about things like birth weight so that you win the pool.)

Home-Birth Notes

If you choose to have your baby at home, you'll need to prepare your older child for the experience. She'll need an adult who can focus just on *her* during labor and delivery, regardless of time of day or night. Attending the birth should always be the child's option, and she should be free to change her mind at any time. Prepare her for sights and sounds by reading books and watching videos. If you have complications or even just an exceptionally hard labor or birth (which *can* happen even after an easy first birth), your child may need to leave home for a while. Issues to discuss with her include blood, noises you might make (try playing growling and grunting games), your being in pain (from your muscles working so hard, not the baby hurting you), nakedness, and being emotionally unavailable to her—this last one may be the hardest of all for a young child.

Welcome Matts!

✳ ✳ ✳

Safe and Satisfying Ways for Siblings to Meet and Greet

I'll never forget the look of *shock* on my middle child's face when he saw his new sister for the first time. We'd thought he understood when we talked about the expected baby, but clearly he didn't get it until that moment. He buried his face in a pillow and refused to look at her. When we encouraged him to hold her for a photo, he backed away warning, "HOT!" (toddlerese for "absolutely do not touch!"). I tell you this because you can't predict how a sibling will react initially—and to remind you not to get too upset by a less-than-warm reception; within days, Eric was more solicitous than any of us toward the colicky newcomer, even sharing his beloved "plugs" with her when she cried.

Empty Arms Opened Wide

This is the correct stance for greeting the new big brother or sister. The best place for the baby to be is alone in the bassinet, with a gift for big sib hidden under a blanket. Spend a few minutes focused on your child before even mentioning the baby. You'll be amazed at how big, gangly, and dangerous-looking he has become overnight—this reaction is normal. Try to avoid crying when he asks why your tummy is still so fat. Then tell him—*don't ask*—to come "check out your baby sister." Have someone hold him up or prop him on a chair. Unwrap the baby so he can examine her cool features, like her teeny tiny toenails and that gross-but-fascinating umbilical stump. Then bundle the baby back up, commenting that she's so incompetent she can't even keep herself warm. We liked to give a little demo of all the things the baby can't do, like sit, walk, and eat candy (while handing a piece to the big guy who can).

The Gift Exchange

Have your older child bring whatever gift he's selected for the baby and "give" it to the baby by unwrapping it for her. Then point out the present tucked under a blanket for him *from her*. Naturally you will have chosen something he wants badly, though by now you'll be wishing that you hadn't picked something that could be used as a lethal weapon.

Photo Ops

First take a picture of your child alone—it's a nice reminder for everyone that he's still an interesting person in his own right. The second photo can be of him and the new baby. To help him hold the baby without the adults suffering heart attacks, either nestle the big kid in a grown-up's lap and then put the newborn on the kid's lap, or get the camera and photographer ready, place the child on a pillow *on the floor*, position the baby, and shoot. Few preschoolers really understand the idea that the baby can't support its own head, so arrange his legs to support the head and be ready to leap in and save the baby when he's had enough (about five seconds usually). Or, opt for some great shots that boost big-kid esteem while protecting baby. Try a shot of the baby's tiny hand curled around your preschooler's huge finger; a side-by-side comparison of their bare feet; a snap of the older child sticking his tongue out at the baby and the baby imitating her big brother (this shot takes an alert baby and patience); one of the big sib wearing an item of baby's clothing (like a bonnet) and baby wearing something of sib's; or a photo of big sibling holding a photo of himself as a newborn next to the new newborn.

Post-Visit Decompression

Immediately afterwards, provide a way for your child to let off a little steam—a stop at the playground, a splash at the pool, a visit to a fast-food restaurant with a play area, a romp at a friend's house—anything where stress will be low and physical activity will be high.

The Welcome-Home Birthday Party

Although it's probably the last thing you feel like, your preschooler will love throwing a little family party for baby, complete with cake, hats, and a few favors. (Avoid noisemakers at all costs. And definitely no clowns either.) *Dad gets to make all the arrangements.* Your preschooler will have to eat baby's cake for her because baby has no teeth.

Birth Announcements and Birth Gifts

I confess I feel a little sad every time I get a birth announcement that makes no mention of older siblings. And I like the ones that include stats about the big sibling (his current height, weight, eye color, batting average, etc.), as long as no one gets carried away and wants to put Mom's stats on there too. Your child will appreciate his own announcements to hand out to his buddies. Something involving candy is good.

When visitors come, let your older child be the one to show off the new baby and share the glow. Thoughtful visitors will bring a gift for the big kid. Really thoughtful ones will bring pizza for everyone. Your preschooler *may* want to open the boring gift for baby, or you can stall and open it when he's out of the room.

Adopt-Able

✱   ✱   ✱

Coping with the Special Concerns of Welcoming an Adopted Sibling

At its core, helping your preschooler prepare for and welcome an adopted sibling is pretty much the same as helping her get ready for a birth sibling, so for the most part you can simply use or make small tweaks to the other suggestions in this chapter. That said, adoption does typically involve some unique circumstances and issues not faced by birth families. For example, birth mommies and daddies rarely have strange ladies popping by for visits to determine whether they'll be fit parents. These tips and discussions may help you make decisions as you navigate some of the more common sticky adoption situations.

Wait-y Matters

The wait for an adoptive child tends to be both longer and more variable than the wait for a birth child, making it extra tough to pinpoint the optimal moment to tell your older child the big news. Tell her too soon and you're in for months and possibly even years of pestering and anxiety; wait too late and you'll have to fast-track the preparation process and multiply everyone's stress as you gallop about getting ready. In addition, there are situations in which the newcomer's status remains uncertain even after being placed with you; it can be hard to know what to tell your child if, for example, you're fostering a child prior to possible adoption or you're adopting from a state or country that allows birth parents a grace period in which to change their minds.

There's no perfect approach to these scenarios. My general advice is to start talking hypothetically about adding to your family around the time your application is approved—or when some situation, like a home visit, raises questions—and to be honest about the tentative nature or timing of your family expansion. "Maybe some day…" is a useful phrase to sprinkle throughout your discussions. Similarly, phrases like "probably" and "we hope" are helpful when you're talking to your child about an uncertain placement. Some parents describe their family as babysitting while the birth parents decide whether they're able to care for the baby.

Meanwhile, begin preparing your child for the realities of big sib-hood in a general way by casually noticing and admiring babies, teaching ordinary nurturing skills, and chatting informally about brothers and sisters so that you have a foundation to build on in case you do get a sudden placement. If you stock up on baby supplies before you actually have a placement in sight, do so casually, explaining it's "just in case," and store everything out of sight until it's needed.

'Twas the Night Before the Home Visit

The experts who conduct home-study visits uniformly insist that they won't disqualify you if your home has that "lived in by young children or possibly a pack of rabid wolves" look or if your preschooler has recently started using "you old poop face" as her preferred term of endearment; the home-study folks consider such things to be the sign of a normal, well-adjusted family. This is probably true, because families with preschoolers do manage to adopt second and third children all the time.

Nonetheless, your nerves might feel less jangly if you talk with your child a day or two before the visit, explaining what will happen and the kind of behavior you expect from her. If you haven't mentioned the possibility of adoption to her yet, present the home visitor as an ordinary guest who's interested in what a nice family you have. (Make sure the home visitor knows in advance about your youngster's ignorance, and remind her when she arrives.) Either way, let your child know that the visitor will probably ask her questions about his room and toys, her family, and so on and remind her that she should answer politely, like she does with other adults she knows. (You can also try advising her to wait until *after* the lady leaves to call you "old poop face"—but she'll probably forget.) Then read page 170 from chapter six about how to do an emergency tidy-up before showing your house, carelessly leaving a few classic educational toys and some nice wholesome books scattered about. Just make sure not to leave them where someone might accidentally step on them in the dark and say the very bad "S" word not once but three times right in front of a preschooler who would then repeat the "S" word to the nice adoption lady, along with her favorite term of endearment.

"Why Do You Want Another Kid When You've Already Got Wonderful Me?" and Other Tricky Questions

Some of these questions, including the one above, are questions birth siblings sometimes ask too—but they're questions that seem to come up even more frequently in adoption situations, perhaps because to young kids adoption is more likely to seem voluntary. (Pregnancy, as we all know, happens by magic or by accidentally swallowing a watermelon seed.) Here's a cheat sheet of responses to a few of these tough questions, as well as to other questions that may be hiding behind them. Keep in mind that you will probably need to answer all your child's questions in small bites and return to them multiple times.

   ✳ *Why would you want another kid when you've already got me?* Your child may not ask this in so many words—but you can answer it proactively anyway, with a message like "Families come in all different sizes. We're lucky that our family has enough love and time to give to more than one kid. And we're super lucky to already have a wonderful kid like you who will be such a fabulous big sister." Follow up with words and actions that reassure your child of your undying love and commitment. This does not involve using your credit card.

✳ *Why didn't the baby's other mommy and daddy want him?* This question requires an answer that is honest at its core—because it's what you'll tell your adopted child later too—and which also addresses your older child's fear that you could abandon her. You'll have to tweak your response to fit what you know about the newcomer's history and the certainty of his placement with you, but you'll probably say something along the lines of "The new baby's birth mommy and daddy *do* love him, but they just can't take good enough care of any baby right now. So we will be the baby's forever family, just like we're your forever family."

Some children wonder about whether the new baby will be sad to leave his other mommy and daddy, and this is a good opportunity to begin your discussions about both how the baby may act in the first weeks, especially if he's at an age where he will be stressed by the transition, and to begin talking about how all people have mixed and complicated feelings—a subject you'll revisit many times over your children's lives.

✳ *Where did I come from?* Whether your older child is a birth or adopted child, retelling her own birth and family story is a good way to help her connect with her personal history *and* to spark further discussion about the new baby. If you haven't already done so, make a book or poster with photos and mementos to help her understand her background and family connections. Many adoption experts recommend making a Life Book for your adopted child, to help him preserve a record of his background before he came to your family as well as his life going forward. (Learn more about making a Life Book at www.foreverparents.com). Involving your older child in making this book can help her examine the similarities and differences between her background and the baby's. Some families find it helpful to trace every family member's history, even—or perhaps especially—the family pet's (who, after all, has been adopted too). This helps children see that everyone's life is a series of arrivals, departures, and reunions to which everyone adjusts.

Questions about reproduction often follow questions like these, so make sure to address that topic too if needed; read up on talking to your children about conception and sex on pages 36–38.

Standing on Ceremony

Undoubtedly you'll want to usher your new child into the family with the same kinds of celebrations you'd have to welcome a birth child—a shower, christening, welcome party, whatever—and so you should. And as with any new baby event, you'll find ways to involve your older child, marking her change in status and helping her feel proud of becoming an older sibling. But many families also like to throw additional special celebrations when a child is adopted—perhaps a big party to celebrate the final adoption, an annual adoption day or "gotcha day" party in addition to the child's birthday, or, in the case of an open adoption, an entrustment ceremony where the birth parents formally transfer their responsibilities—and trust—to the adoptive family.

If all your children are adopted, these extra events are nothing but wonderful (though you'll save yourself hurt feelings and resentment if you're thoughtful enough to limit the number of times you expect friends and relatives to bring gifts, send cards, make congratulatory phone calls, and send singing telegrams; for example, the annual events can be immediate-family-only celebrations unless people have explicitly asked to be included and you're reasonably confident they actually like parties that involve Dora the Explorer and fruit punch and they're not just saying so to be polite). But if your kids' backgrounds are mixed, you'll want to figure out ways to equalize the parties (and especially the treats and gifts) so you don't fan the flames of sibling rivalry. One nice way to celebrate one child's adoption each year without making the others feel left out is to mark "family anniversary days" instead, to note the occasions when your family grew or changed, with goodies and rituals for everyone. For example, your adopted child can receive a present to mark his arrival, your birth child can receive a gift for becoming a big sister, and you and your spouse can get a nice restaurant gift certificate and a babysitter to commemorate all the additional sleepless nights, runny noses, and toys with small plastic parts you've taken on. And then everyone can jointly light some candles on a cake, sing "We Are Family," make a big wish, and blow the flames out together—because after all, what you're really celebrating is being together and helping one another out as a family.

Announcements and Introductions

Just as with a birth sibling, your older child will likely get a kick out of sharing the big news with neighbors, friends, and classmates, especially if she's armed with popularity-boosting pink or blue lollipops and fancy cards featuring her picture and stats along with the new family member's. And just as with a birth sibling, she'll benefit from some coaching and practice about exactly what details to share (or not) with the curious.

Your child will especially need help figuring out what to say and how to say it if the adoption was sudden or unexpected (to others), or if the newcomer looks different from the rest of the family, is well past the newborn stage, is a set of mixed-age siblings, or is otherwise not what people expect in new baby. Yes, many people, even those plenty old enough to know better, will ask your preschooler the same silly questions and make the same insensitive or even cruel comments they do to you.

And while it's fine for *you* to squelch inappropriate comments with a silent stare or a withering look, it's not okay for your preschooler. She needs to respond respectfully to other adults because she's too young to tell when someone's mean-spirited or just uninformed and because young kids just have to be respectful to adults—and of course he needs to be helpful and informative to other youngsters who may simply never have encountered adoptive families before. That's why you'll help her explain to folks who ask her if the baby is her real brother that yes, he is; his skin and eyes just look a little different because he's adopted and his birth parents were Chinese. She'll tell everyone earnestly the same things that you've told her: that families are formed in many ways, but they're just as real and important and forever however they come to be. In the long run, this firm-but-open approach will strengthen your whole family, prepare your child to deal with clueless or unpleasant people in many situations, and maybe even shame some of the unkind. Or not. *Sigh.*

International Adoption, Part 1: The Facts and Fantasies of Fetching #2

For many parents adopting internationally, one of the first thorny issues is whether to bring their older child along to collect the new one. I can't tell you what to do—there is no one-size-fits-all right answer—but I can list some considerations to weigh in making your decision, and I'll warn you that international travel with a young child is nearly always a challenging experience, even without the complications of a momentous family change.

 * *Money.* In addition to the airfare, you'll have to pay for other travel expenses like a passport if your child doesn't already have one and a visa if it's required by the host country—as well as all the other usual costs of traveling abroad with a child. In addition, many families opt to bring an extra adult to watch the older child while they deal with paperwork or devote time to a needy, confused baby; obviously, doing so will multiply your costs.

 * *Your child's personality and readiness.* Is your child an easygoing, adaptable sort who enjoys traveling—or is she more the sort who melts down after a simple overnight at Grandma's? Have you had an opportunity to prepare her both for the experiences of traveling and for her new sibling or is everything happening in a rush? How does she feel about becoming a big sister? How long will you be away—and how might that affect your child in terms of her relationship with you or her comfort with his usual routines and relationships?

 * *Practicalities and safety issues.* Do you have satisfactory childcare options (and a backup plan) if your child stays home? (If not, you may fret the entire time you're away.) Do you have childcare support abroad? There are likely to be situations that will be difficult with an extra small child in tow, and there may be times you aren't even permitted to bring your other child. Ask yourself whether you can

juggle all the equipment and supplies needed for two young children, which will likely include two car seats in addition to clothes, diapers, toys, snacks, etc.? How good are you at remaining calm while being barfed on by two small, screaming people at the start of a fifteen-hour flight? What are the sanitary conditions where you'll be traveling, and is there adequate health care if your child gets sick? Finally, do you have adequate lead time to get your older child's travel documents and immunizations, as well as qualify for lower airfares?

✳ *Preferences, fantasies, and realities.* Are you more likely to regret missing out on a chance to focus on the new baby, or to feel wistful about missing out on the chance to rejoice in being together as a family right from the start? How will you feel if your older child is fussy, rejects the new baby, or is so clingy that it interferes with your ability to connect with the new baby? Or what if your older child is so angry at being left behind that she spoils the homecoming by pushing you and/or the new baby away? How will you feel if five years from now your older child has *no* recollection of going to get the baby (likely for younger preschoolers—though obviously you can document and discuss the trip repeatedly and preserve the experience that way)? Or if she pouts through her whole adolescence because you were too mean to take her to China when she had a chance to go?

Okay, by now you may be sensing (even though I was trying so hard to be fair and balanced) that I think it's usually best to leave your older kid at home. I do know of a friend of a friend whose family traveled together to pick up their baby and who recall the actual journey as being as filled with sweetness and light as their pre-trip fantasies were. But my sense from the experiences of other friends as well as families I've read about is that more often picking up your new child is an exhausting, overwhelming event, especially for the new family member—*and that's who deserves a few days of your undistracted attention and energy.* Your older child can have a memorable greeting with her new sibling at home, which might even be more comfortable for her since it will take place on her home turf, and she'll likely recover soon enough from the separation (though probably more slowly from the reality of having a new sibling). But feel free to ignore my advice— you'll have to get used to ignoring lots of well-meaning advice anyway.

International Adoption, Part II:
Promoting Cross-Cultural Bonds

In the early years of international or cross-racial adoption, many experts urged parents to discard any links to the child's past as quickly and thoroughly as possible, so that the child would be forced to assimilate to his new culture and family. Now, however, most agencies recommend (and some may even require) that you preserve familiar elements of your child's birth culture and language to benefit him, both in the short run and the long term: first to ease him through the transition from one home to another, and later to help him develop a more complete sense of identity. Doing so also benefits your whole family; one of the advantages of adopting cross-culturally is the opportunity for everyone to develop or deepen an understanding of, respect for, and emotional connection to people from a different background.

There are plenty of fun ways to help your older child connect with her new sibling's background—many of which may have the bonus of making her a champ at soothing him in the early weeks.

✳ *Now you're speaking my language.* And singing it. Or signing it too. Even if the new family member is too young to talk, he's accustomed to the sounds and rhythms of his native language and hearing them may calm him. Your older child can practice traditional baby songs or rhymes to share with the newcomer, as well as learn everyday words (like the words for family members, animals and their sounds, and familiar activities like eating, bathing, and sleeping) and terms of endearment. Some good starting points for tracking down songs, words, and games include: www.mamalisa.com, which has lyrics and melodies for children's songs from around the world; www.thelullabyproject.org, which seeks to collect lullabies from every culture and has several CDs available for purchase, and the BABY'S FIRST WORDS IN… series by Living Language.

I also recommend having the whole family learn some baby sign language, especially if you're adopting an older baby or toddler. For many babies, signs are acquired more easily than oral language and can act as a bridge between two spoken languages. Older siblings seem to be especially effective sign language teachers, and being the family sign-language expert will boost your older child's big-kid pride while helping the siblings feel a special connection to one another. You can find descriptions and demonstrations of basic baby signs at www.babies-and-sign-language.com and www.signingbaby.com.

✳ *Book binding.* Folktales, contemporary stories about children from your adoptive child's homeland, and nonfiction picture books, as well as quality films and children's TV shows, can introduce your older child to her new sibling's culture of origin and position her to teach the baby about it as he grows up. Make an effort to discover traditions, like birthday celebration rituals, that your older child will enjoy learning and sharing.

✳ *A taste for each other.* Preparing and trying some dishes from the baby's native land has many potential benefits. Cooking together helps you bank quality time with your first child before she has to share you daily, and provides relaxed opportunities to talk about life with a new baby. In addition, the process of getting used to new smells, tastes, and textures offers you a chance to help shape how your child approaches the many new experiences and challenges she'll face once the baby arrives. In addition, because smell is closely linked to the primitive emotional centers in the brain, the scents of familiar spices may later help the new baby feel more comfortable in his new home.

✳ *All dolled up…* Try to track down a doll with a similar appearance to your expected baby's for your older child to care for in advance (and later in parallel). Fortunately, it's easier than ever to find baby dolls, as well as fashion dolls and dollhouse dolls, who aren't just blond, blue-eyed, and fair-skinned. African and Asian dolls, and increasingly Hispanic dolls too, are available from nearly every major doll manufacturer. If you can't find an appropriate doll at a local store, try online sellers; www.sleepysoft.com specializes in dolls for adopted children, including dolls that resemble different Asian nationalities.

❋ *...And all decked out.* As you update babyproofing in your home, have your child help you tweak your decorating to include crafts or color schemes that are traditional in the new baby's homeland. (Decorative items for your child's room make good gifts from the baby or souvenirs from your trip to pick up the baby.) And have her help arrange the baby's nursery to resemble the room he's had, at least at first, even if it's very plain. Hang faces, which babies love to study, that resemble people from your new child's homeland.

While working together, talk about how hard it must be for the baby to get used to so many new things; these conversations will make it easier later for you to remind your preschooler to tone down her behavior around the baby without making her feel overly scolded or rejected. Finally, involve your child in picking out or making a holiday ornament that reflects the baby's culture to commemorate his first celebrations with your family—and to signal his ongoing presence in your family.

If Things Don't Work Out: Disrupted Placements

It takes my breath away even to mention this, just as it does to discuss the death of a baby, but sometimes a planned adoption doesn't work out, and unfortunately it does happen with a greater frequency than the death of a baby. Even if you've prepared your child for the possibility, she'll likely react with a young child's grief, confusion, and anxiety (which may look nothing like an adult's responses to these emotions). Please read about coping with loss in the earlier part of this chapter as well as about talking to your child about death and living with grief on pages 207–210 and 259–264. Professional support may ease everyone's path through this difficult time; don't feel you must shoulder all your child's pain yourself on top of your own.

A Final Note

Despite the doom and gloom you've undoubtedly encountered while doing your homework on adoption, most of the time families expanded through adoption work out well for everyone involved, just like families increased by birth—which is to say they have ups and downs, joys and challenges. But as you may have gleaned while reading these notes on just the welcoming phase, adoption is usually a more complex way to make a family, which means there are greater chances for big swings in the ups and downs, for complications that you haven't anticipated, or for situations that seriously tax your resources or test your family's strength. In fact, I haven't even touched here on many of the potential adoption scenarios that might affect your new child's homecoming and how your older child responds to it (like if one child has an open adoption and the other doesn't, if you adopt out of birth order, if you adopt multiple siblings, or bring home a child with orphanage/third-world-related conditions ranging from lice or intestinal parasites to severe malnutrition or reactive attachment disorder—and more).

That's why I'm urging you to look beyond this book as you move forward with your family. Continue to educate yourself, to keep up with emerging research, and especially to connect with other families like yours.

LITERATURE LINKS

Although there are tons of children's books dealing with adoption, there are relatively few that help kids prepare for an adoptive sibling. For the youngest children, I like two books that feature animal characters: A MOTHER FOR CHOCO by Keiko Kasza, told from the point of view of a little bird who joins a large multi-species family, and ALL TOGETHER NOW by Anita Jeram, which showcases the differences and similarities of the three Honey children, a birth-child rabbit and his adopted siblings who are a duckling and mouse. For families welcoming a second child through international adoption, there are a number of nice options, mostly featuring Asian adoptions: MY MEI-MEI by Ed Young about an adopted Chinese girl and her wait for a sister from China (and also just a nice tale of how siblings bond), WAITING FOR MAY by Janet Morgan Stoeke and THINGS LITTLE KIDS NEED TO KNOW by Susan Uhlig, both about birth boys and their adopted Chinese sisters. For families adopting older children, try three humor-laced easy readers pitched at a slightly older audience: EMMA'S YUCKY BROTHER by Jean Little, PINKY AND REX AND THE NEW BABY by James Howe, and A NEW BARKER IN THE HOUSE by Tomie dePaola (about a dog family).

Once Upon a Time There Was a New Baby

✳ ✳ ✳

Just-Right Strategies for Soft Spots and Hot Spots

During the first few weeks, your little princess may take on a variety of less delightful fairy-tale roles: a Goldilocks for whom nothing is just right, a Wicked Witch who schemes to turn her rival into a toad, an Alice whose curiosity gets her into one jam after another, or even a sorcerer's apprentice whose efforts to be helpful go horribly awry. I can't of course promise "happily ever after," but these tactics, in addition to the usual strategies like maintaining routines, may nudge your child closer to a fairy-tale beginning with her new sibling.

Do Be a Do-Bee

Kids are more likely to do what you want them to if you phrase your requests in a positive way. So instead of telling your child, "Don't push on the baby's soft spot!" say "Protect the baby's soft spot by stroking her head this way." And show your child how to hug a baby *softly* by demonstrating on him.

Howl at the Moon

Start a tradition of going outside with your child to howl at the full moon—or create another ritual that allows your child let off steam. Vigorous helpful activities like shredding those annoying credit-card offers, or stomping leaves onto the compost pile can make your kid feel useful and appreciated while releasing tension.

Redecorate—Add a Wild Room and Hidey Hole

Push the furniture aside in the den or rec room for some good romping room, and clean out a closet you can furnish with pillows and books for cozy privacy. This will give your child places to play without being constantly reminded to be careful or quiet.

When-You-Were-a-Baby Tales

Retell all those stories about funny or cute things your older child did as a baby to help him understand the newcomer and give him a dose of vicarious babying. Other good stories to tell include tales about how you or other family members reacted to new babies and made-up stories about animals or other characters who had new siblings. For example, what might happen if Baby Bear had a new little sister and Goldilocks came to visit? Let your child jump in with plot ideas too.

Nursing—But You Hope Not a Grudge

Nursing intrigues some preschoolers, annoys others, and grosses out or alarms a handful. Talk about what you're doing, which may not be obvious at all to your older child. Many moms use nursing time to snuggle or read to an older child, and that's a great way to reduce jealousy. My kids were so keen on this routine that sometimes they'd suggest I feed the baby just because they wanted a story. Work in the occasional new baby book, like SMILE, LILY! by Candace Fleming, about a nice big brother.

Many preschoolers want to try nursing themselves. You can let them experiment—they probably won't be any good at it. I just gave my kids some expressed breast milk to taste-test. (Fortunately, they thought it was nasty.) Don't worry that your child will be scarred for life either way—just be calm and matter-of-fact in how you handle their questions.

Baby Talk

Make the baby more interesting and likeable by having her be witty and self-deprecating—in a goofy high-pitched voice. She can say flattering things like, "Ooh, I can hardly lift this rattle! You must be as strong as Superman because you can carry that heavy box!" or "Ow! I just smacked myself in the head again. How do you control these arm thingies?" You can also teach your child "parentese," the way that parents instinctively talk to their babies (high-pitched, slow and exaggerated, face-to-face) so that baby will be responsive to him.

Finally, expect baby talk—and bed-wetting, clinging, tantrums, and other immature behavior—from your normally big kid. Regression's a pain in the butt, but it's normal. It'll usually disappear soon if you don't turn it into a big issue.

Infant Scientist

Put your preschooler in charge of checking for emerging milestones (e.g., baby raising her head for five seconds, smiling, following a moving finger) and help him record them on a chart for everyone to see. You can also have your child perform little "experiments." Does baby like barking or meowing better? Looking at the black and white mobile or the picture of the pink elephant?

Diffuse your child's reactions to the baby's crying by taking bets on what will stop it (feeding, changing diaper, nap, holding, talking, etc.). If necessary, cheat so your child wins lots of times. Your preschooler may get surprisingly good at recognizing different cries.

Help Your Kid Be Helpful

Offer a pretty basket or a sturdy dump truck to make fetching supplies more appealing, and narrate silly scenarios to get your child to do what you need him to without sounding dictatorial. ("And then the Super Kid leapt off the tall tower and flew over to the door. Using his super strength he yanked it open and held it until the poor lady with the little baby made it through safely. Naturally she thanked him with a mushy kiss, and he was so brave and tough he didn't even wipe it off.") And remember to provide explicit limits on helping, like "Only hold the baby when a grown-up is there to help you," or "*Always* check with me before you climb in the crib with the baby."

Protect your preschooler from her own worst impulses by childproofing your newborn. *Never* leave her unsupervised with the baby, and expect her to "forget" rules and appropriate behavior regularly. Make use of gates, baby monitors, and other equipment.

Entertaining Your Child on Auto-parent

* * *

Activities for Tired Days

After staying up half the night with a fussy newborn and a bed-wetting, nightmare-having preschooler, only to discover that you're running a fever yourself, first try Plan A: The Dump (i.e., call a good friend who will ignore the gook oozing out of all your kid's orifices and let her come over and play all day anyway). If that doesn't work, go for Plan B: TV. And if TV has lost its magic, or if you've had so many bad days during the past week or two that you're afraid Child Protective Services will show up to charge you with neglect, try some of these low-energy activities.

The Great Hundred Hunt

Lounge on the sofa while you send your preschooler in search of one hundred objects—ten at a time. I'd send my kids to look for ten stuffed animals, ten socks or shoes scattered around the house, ten tiny toys that might hurt the baby, ten pieces of garbage, etc. When the mission's accomplished, struggle off the sofa and take a photo of your kid with her impressive collection—then offer a special treat, like ice cream, for putting everything where it belongs. Brain not working well enough to think of stuff to look for? Scatter pennies around the room and send her looking for those.

Read-a-Rainbow

Lounge on the sofa while you send your child to fetch a book with a red cover for you to read to her while nursing the baby. After the red book is done, send her in search of an orange one, then a yellow one, etc., until you've assembled a nice rainbow pile of books beside the sofa and a hoarse voice.

Mommy's a Mountain

Whenever I felt under the weather, my kids felt compelled to climb all over me. I finally realized if I briefly gave in to their need to manhandle me,

I could reclaim my body afterwards. This game often did the trick. Roll off the sofa and curl up on your hands and knees. Have your child climb up on the "mountain" (your back) and sit quietly—until suddenly the volcano erupts (you rise up)! And she falls off! You can do lots of variations on this game—for the five minutes until the timer rings. Then she has to play with her toys while you lounge on the sofa with baby, a cup of tea, and the heating pad.

Tickle-Me Mommy

Shhh. This game's really a sneaky way to get your kid to give you a back rub. Lie on your stomach, with a pillow to cushion your head. Tell your kid to "make thunder" on your back (i.e., gentle pounding with her little fists). Then she can make rain or play the piano (i.e., tap with her fingertips) all over your back. Or draw rivers from your neck to your bum—whatever creative descriptions you can come up with to describe what will feel nice for you. The baby can lean on you and drool for a little lubrication. You can also vary commands for a face rub if you have a headache (but the drool is less appealing for that).

The Command Circle

Make a circle or other shape on the floor (trace it in the carpet with your finger or use a long loop of string). Then lounge on the sofa while you give your child commands like "Hop three times in the middle of the circle and six times outside it!" or "Balance on the line all the way around." Most preschoolers will play this indefinitely.

Rockin' the Day Away

Gather everyone who needs to be on you into the rocker. Rock while you count out loud to 100. Then sing a song or play music ("Rock Around the Clock" is good) while you rock in time to it. Rock slowly. Rock fast. Try a syncopated rhythm or a chant. Maybe someone will fall asleep. If not, maybe she'll get restless and go play with her blocks while you close your eyes and keep rocking.

Beyond Newborns

✳ ✳ ✳

That Bothersome Old Baby

The charming and competent older baby may bring out the Green Monster in your older child even more than the boring new one did. Plus, bigger babies get into bigger trouble—they pull hair, knock over blocks, interfere with social plans, and generally annoy. These strategies can help a frustrated older child cope, while protecting the baby *and* keeping you from pulling out whatever hair remains after your post-pregnancy shedding!

Tactics to Tame the Toy Wars

Walk a mile in your child's Blue's Clues sneakers and remind yourself that your preschooler's desire to protect his art projects and special toys is not unreasonable. Try these ideas:

✳ *Send the Big Kid to the pen.* The playpen, that is. Older babies hate being confined in playpens, but before you sell yours (the pen, not the baby) on eBay, try corralling your older child and his special toys in it. (Those play-yard-style pens provide even more spacious and flexible accommodations.) I baby-gated my older child off in the hallway or dining room.

✳ *Reverse the possession flow.* Expect your older child to become insanely possessive of baby toys he has not shown any interest in for two years the moment you try to pass them along to the baby. Counteract the jealousy by asking relatives to give the baby toys appropriate for your preschooler (or cheat and buy some "baby gifts" yourself). Then tell your preschooler that the baby "wants" to let him use the toys until she's old enough for them. Or maybe she wants to negotiate a trade…

✳ *Schedule Lego hour.* Let older kids get out the Danger Toys and Projects when baby's not around, like during her nap or after she goes to bed. You can also have one parent take baby on a walk or other outing while the other stays home to play Teeny Tiny Pirate Guys yet again.

Balance the Attention Seesaw

The cute factor, coupled with the older baby's demands for attention, may leave your older child feeling shut out.

✳ *Nursing without cursing.* When the baby reaches five or six months, you may no longer be able to combine feeding the baby with cuddling your older child. Older babies may be distracted too easily to feed properly with siblings at hand, or may insist on having your attention too. Occupy your preschooler during nursing with easy-grab kits (like shaving cream and a tray for finger painting, or marsh-mallows and spaghetti noodles for building structures). *And* make sure you schedule a big-kid cuddle time just before or after your nursing session.

✳ *Teach your old dog new tricks.* Are visitors captivated by baby? Help your older child capture some of the limelight with cool tricks. My boys learned to climb up the door frames by pressing their hands and feet against the sides and shimmying up—a stunt that never failed to command attention from nervous visitors. Other less death-defying tactics work too—songs and dances, puppet shows and other artistic expressions, jokes, intellectual mastery like counting to a hundred (try the good trick method—"I can count to one hundred—one, two, skip a few, ninety-nine, one hundred!"), and assorted athletic feats can all give big guys acceptable ways to show off.

✳ *Don't abandon the dating scene.* All their lives, kids benefit from special outings with you—without their siblings. Also continue to help them form other friendships with relatives and friends that let them escape the sibling rumbles.

Reset Your Roughhouse Comfort Zone

Later-born kids are often both tougher and more tolerant—and you'll discover why if you don't rush to protect your baby every time she romps with her big brother. I used to be horrified when I saw my older nephews "playing" with their baby brother. But before long, I realized that not only was Scott unharmed, he was loving the rough-and-tumble play and actively seeking it out. Today he's a champion high-school wrestler. Monitor play for both safety and pleasure, but take care not to step in too soon.

Also, remember that your older child may need to be protected from the baby's accidental roughness! Empathize while showing him how to respond appropriately (e.g., telling baby "NO! That hurts me!" rather than punching) when the baby hurts him.

Avoid the Comparison Pitfalls

As your baby develops more and more of a personality, you'll be tempted to compare him with his older sibling. *Every other parenting expert will warn you not to do this, under any circumstances.* Not me! For one thing, it's simply not possible for most parents. For another, comparing can be good—it may even alert you to developmental problems in one child or the other. The key is to avoid comparisons that belittle or create resentment, as in "Why can't you ___ like your sister?" Instead use comparisons that are not judgmental.

✴ *Delight in differences.* Notice those differences that make your children unique and special—and help them understand themselves better. Saying things like, "Your sister likes to jump into new situations and learn while she does things, but you like to sit back and watch first so you're ready when you try something" just puts a fact into words without making one child look or feel bad.

✴ *Celebrate the similarities.* Comment on ways your children resemble each other to build a bond between them and to reinforce family loyalty. Do they both love booger jokes? Have the same problems with unruly hair? Like to jump on the beds when you're not looking? Great!

CHAPTER THREE

Skip into School!

* * *

Cha-Cha into Childcare!

Sit down on your mat and put your listening ears on. I'm going to tell you two stories about preschool. Once upon a time, a long, long time ago, I went to preschool. (Only it was so long ago that it was called *nursery school.*) I went three times a week for nine months. And the *only* things I remember from that year are 1) my teacher always wore nylons with huge holes and long runs in them, and 2) one time when I was getting ready to go on the seesaw with my friend, this stupid boy named Christopher ran up and slammed my friend's end down to the ground and my end flew up and smacked me in the chin and I cried and then I was really embarrassed that I'd cried in front of everybody and I didn't want to go back the next school day but my mom made me. Then I grew up and lived happily ever after. The End.

Now for the second story. Once upon a different time, not very long ago—in fact just a couple of weeks ago—I was standing in line at Wendy's with my sixteen-year-old daughter because it was dinner time and I hadn't managed to get to the grocery store in a while and there was nothing edible in our house except low-carb Special K. And who should be standing right in front of us but Sara's old preschool teacher! She was delighted to see us, and Sara chatted with her in a friendly way about her current activities and our dog and all those things that your old preschool teacher might like to hear about. And then Mrs. Nave left with her salad, and Sara leaned over and whispered to me, "Who was that lady?"

"Who was that lady?!" I shrieked, "*Who was that lady?!!!!!*"

It seemed inconceivable that my daughter hadn't recognized the woman who had been her idolized preschool teacher for two solid years. For those two years at our house, it was always *Mrs. Nave this* and *Mrs. Nave that.* We were constantly being ordered to do things the infinitely superior Mrs. Nave way. (I didn't mind the sharing and passing out napkins at snack time, but I really didn't think I should have to raise my hand and ask permission every time I went potty.) We also have reams of photos from Sara's preschool days, some of them actually in albums, and one even framed and hanging *right next to her bed.*

Sara shrugged. "The only thing I remember about preschool," she said, "is playing dogs with Colleen and Jenna. And that weird kid who cried all the time." Sara has not grown up yet, so I can't swear she'll live happily ever after, but I think she will. The End.

Okay, hands up—who knows why I told you these stories? Anybody?

Well, I'll tell you. First, it's to make you marvel at the fact that there was ever a time when preschool teachers actually wore nylons to school! Is that weird or what? Second, it's to give you a heads-up that no matter what happens at preschool or daycare, good or bad, there's a very good chance that years from now your child won't remember any of it.

This is not to say that your child's early school experiences don't matter so you don't have to bother to read this chapter. As a former preschool and daycare teacher, the sister of a preschool teacher, the daughter of a former kindergarten teacher, and even the next-door neighbor of a preschool teacher, I firmly believe that early childhood education is good stuff. Kids learn crucial lessons in preschool and daycare, like the best way to pass out napkins and how to talk to adults who aren't their mommy or daddy, and these experiences smooth their way, not only in grade school, but probably even in grad school, long after the face of their wonderful teacher has faded from their memories.

Before you start reading this chapter and figuring out to handle separation blues or prepare your kid for kindergarten, though, the first question you'll need to ask yourself is whether you're even going to send your child to preschool or group daycare. Not all kids are ready at three or four or even five. Or you might prefer to homeschool your kid, or no-school her, which can be fine choices.

At any rate, for kids to enjoy school and not be the weird kid who cries all day, they should 1) be interested in meeting and playing with other kids, 2) be able to separate from you for at least a few hours, 3) have the flexibility to adapt to different rules and expectations, and 4) be able to communicate with people outside their families. Many programs have additional requirements, like being potty-trained, and you should be reasonably confident your child will meet these requirements by the time school starts or the whole thing could end up being ridiculously stressful for everyone.

If you do decide to send your child to school or group daycare, the next question to consider is which school to choose. This can be a daunting task—kind of like trying to decide which of the ninety-three choices of mustard to buy at the grocery store. Only worse, since it's not like your sandwich will cry and carry on or not get in to an Ivy League college if you accidentally choose the wrong one. Lucky for you, I'm going to help you out with this decision. The main things you should look for in a preschool or daycare center are 1) it's safe and attractive and has plenty of nice, smiling teachers who don't wear nylons, or if they do, they have lots of runs in them from kneeling on the floor, 2) it's reasonably clean, 3) it fits your budget and it's near enough to your home or work to be convenient, and 4) (this is the most important one) it emphasizes play and social skills over academics.

Yes, I know the kids down the street have lessons in Japanese and analyzing classic children's literature at their preschool, and you don't want your kid to fall behind. But backed by the vast wealth of research on early childhood development and oodles of experience with little guys, I can promise you your kid will catch up quickly in Japanese and literary analysis after she starts big-kid school, but if she doesn't figure out taking turns on the swing set or how to help the group out by being the napkin passer, she may really struggle in kindergarten and first grade and may never even get into a good college, let alone grad school. Heck, it's probably more important during the preschool years to learn how to paste dried pasta onto a construction-paper heart for a Mother's Day gift than it is to learn the ABCs.

Before you start freaking out about the new SATs, I'm not saying your kid shouldn't learn about letters and numbers and shapes and things at school. I am saying that for the most part, she should learn those things casually, while she's playing with sticky spaghetti noodles on a tray, passing out napkins, or building a castle in the block corner.

Okay. Good listening. You can put your hand down now and go potty. Don't forget to wash your hands!

3...2...1... PRESCHOOL!

✳ ✳ ✳

Preparing Your Child for a Successful Launch

The more you can see this beginning from your child's viewpoint, the more successful you'll be in helping him adjust. Not that this task is as easy as it seems. For example, by the time I was preparing my second child for his first day, I felt like an old pro. I'd taken him to the school many times, we'd played school at home, he'd selected a token to keep in his pocket, etc. But it turned out I'd neglected to tell him that he had a different teacher from his brother's (and apparently they all looked alike to him). For the entire first semester he persisted in calling the very tolerant Mrs. O'Connell "Mrs. Walker." Before long he had all the other kids calling her by the wrong name too. After much work on my part, I finally got him to shift closer to her name, and she finished out the year as Mrs. O'Walker. So take a deep breath, have your child practice his teacher's name, and try these other tips to get him ready for school.

Read All about It

My family jokes that if I decided to become a brain surgeon, my first impulse would not be to attend medical school but to head for the public library. I admit that I'm biased toward reading as a way to acquire knowledge—but books *really* are a gradual, nonthreatening way to introduce your child to what life is like at preschool or daycare. Over time, read a variety of books and reread your child's favorites, pointing out the ways in which his school experience will be similar or different.

Library School and Other Sort-of-School Experiences

Attending story time at the library, playing on a little-tyke soccer team, or taking a Saturday art class will give your child some sense of the demands associated with being part of a group of children and listening to an adult outside the family. Even just going to friends' homes without you will boost his skills and confidence in adapting to new situations.

Pretend School

Furnish supplies like dolls or stuffed animals, books, chairs, art supplies, etc., so your child can play school. Join in at first so you can introduce new concepts, like circle time and raising your hand, and reinforce more familiar ones, like taking turns, asking for help when you need it, and making new friends. Playing with your child (or listening in) will also alert you to your child's worries (like will he be allowed to bring Puppy Pee Pee?) and help you address his concerns before school starts.

A Letter of Introduction

Craft a letter to help the teacher get to know your child (who will nonetheless turn out to be a somewhat-different person at school from who he is at home). Writing this letter is kind of like writing one of those holiday letters: too positive and the recipient sees you as bragging or lying or both; too negative, and the teacher might start out hating your child. Nonetheless, a letter is usually worth the risk and effort. It puts the teacher on notice that you care (*okay*, and that you're a little neurotic), which will probably make her pay a little extra attention to your kid the first few weeks. We liked to include a photo and a "letter" from the child in question. Try making a list of sentence beginnings like "My favorite thing is _____" and letting your child fill in the blanks with your help (and a little editing should he decide his favorite thing is eating his boogers).

The Visit

About a week or so before school starts, visit the classroom. Try to time it for when the teacher will be there, but not too many kids. Don't forget to check out *all* the facilities—cubbies and bathrooms may rank higher on your child's list of concerns than the classroom itself. Take your camera too, and promptly assemble an album, PowerPoint presentation, or video so your child can revisit the school as many times as he needs to before the Big Day.

A Gift for the Class

We usually took a token present for the classroom or teacher when we went to visit. Taking a present gave a reason for the visit if my kid was dragging his feet, made him see school as a place we valued and loved, and meant that there'd be at least one familiar thing in the classroom on the first day. Gift suggestions include a book (naturally), nonperishable snack foods, stickers or other art supplies, or a plant (nonpoisonous). (Note: No experienced teacher needs any more apple-themed knickknacks.)

Phone a Friend

If you don't know anyone who will be in your child's new class, ask the school if you can have a class list so that you can schedule a play date with a future classmate. They may even be able to suggest a good match for your child. Having one familiar face in the room can be a big help during those first anxious minutes.

Adjust Routines

About two weeks before school starts, begin shifting your child's bedtime and wake-up hour to the school-year schedule. Work on establishing other good school-year habits, like laying out your clothes and having the breakfast table set the night before.

LITERATURE LINKS

There are dozens of books about the first day of school. Although many of these titles are aimed at kindergarten rather than daycare or preschool, most address the major worries of a youngster just getting started. I love FIRST DAY JITTERS by Julie Danneberg (about a case of nerves—for the teacher); the classic WILL I HAVE A FRIEND? by Miriam Cohen; STARTING SCHOOL by Janet and Allan Ahlberg (for kids who love detailed illustrations); the wordless delight CARL GOES TO DAYCARE by Alexandra Day; and my kids' all-time favorite, OFF TO SCHOOL by Ann Schweninger (out of print but still easy to find at libraries).

The Grand Entrance

✱ ✱ ✱

Squashing First-Day Jumpy Jitters

Will I be able to find the classroom? Will the teacher like me? Will I do everything I'm supposed to—and nothing I shouldn't? Relax—your worries will largely evaporate after the first day! And so will your child's! Plus, you can lessen everyone's first-day anxieties with a few easy tactics.

'Twas the Night before School

Do some vigorous running around the afternoon before to wear your kid out, and plan for a longer, gentler bath time. If shampooing is a major battleground for your child, skip it on this nervous night. Probably no one will notice if her hair's a little gamy. Follow your child's lead in deciding how much to talk about school; some kids need to talk through their worries or review the game plan, while others prefer distraction. Lay out backpack and clothes so you'll have one less worry in the morning (and make that a habit). Maybe the school fairy will come during the night and leave a little something for your kid to put in her backpack, like a teeny-tiny stuffed friend.

Clothing

Let me make a few suggestions before you drag a crabby child to the mall. Although the classic tradition calls for new, fancy clothes for the first day, most preschoolers will be less stressed wearing something familiar and comfy. And for the rest of the year, preschool and daycare teachers everywhere beg parents to dress kids in clothes that can get dirty and that they can handle themselves at potty time (i.e., elastic waists instead of zippers and snaps). Finally, avoid buying too many new things until your kid has had a chance to check out how everyone else dresses—the urge for peer conformity starts young.

The New-and-Improved Morning Routine

If you followed my earlier suggestion to adjust to a school-year schedule, everyone should be waking up with plenty of getting-ready time. And since you have a few extra moments, you can add *one* new pleasant ritual. (No, it cannot involve turning on the TV. No TV on school mornings.) Instead, try something like reading a joke and having your kid learn to tell it. Or you can sing "Ain't No Mountain High Enough" or something that gets everyone energized and giggly. Then do it every day, even if you have to do it in your Oscar the Grouch voice on some difficult days.

First-Day Traditions

Rituals to mark this annual transition make an unfamiliar day a little more predictable, though if this is your child's *first* first day she won't have that benefit. Still, it's never too early to start! Photograph your child, of course, or record a few seconds of video for a file you'll reserve for first days. Then someday you'll be able to watch and hear her grow up before your eyes and ears. For best results, snap or tape her at a consistent distance with an object that won't change, like her special stuffed animal, a favorite piece of furniture, or the front door. You might want to record other important stats like height, weight, or distance she can throw a stale bagel. We always have a "real" breakfast on the first day (i.e., eggs or pancakes) since nerves wake everyone early enough for this indulgence. Some families picnic together at the bus stop or first carpool stop.

Plan to Arrive Fashionably Early

That's early, but not too early—being first is a lot of pressure for most kids, but you'll want to get there before the teacher is distracted by a crowd and all the other kids are already engaged. Most preschools have a shortened first day, and many schools and daycares invite parents to stay for all or part of the time. Do your best to back off and fade into the woodwork, acting as a secure base where your child can check in if necessary.

Sweetening the Sorrow

Parting, especially that first time, is hard for most kids—and wrenching for their parents. Rehearse the good-bye in advance if your child often balks at separation. In any event, talk to your child beforehand about the game plan (keeping it short and sweet) *and follow through.* You must appear to be trustworthy on this day of all days! Having a good-bye catch phrase like "Ciao, bella" or "I'll be back, Jack" makes it easier for everyone to recognize the end point. And don't forget to remind your child when you'll be back, using a kid-time anchor, like "right after story time." *Make EVERY effort to be early for pick-up for the first few weeks.* Finally, many kids benefit from taking along a transitional object. Some schools will let kids bring favorite stuffed animals or blankets, but most discourage items like these for fear of loss or damage. Instead, laminate a family photograph your child can clip to her backpack or hang in her cubby, or give her a tiny token to stash in her pocket and rub when she feels lonely. Or read THE KISSING HAND by Audrey Penn and tuck a smooch in your kid's hand.

A Month of Muchness

✳ ✳ ✳

Support during the First Weeks

It takes four to six weeks to adjust to a major change like starting school. No matter how much your child has been looking forward to going to school, the first month may leave him grouchy, tired, clingy—or worse. Some kids are cheerful for a few days or weeks and then collapse completely, leaving you wondering if something has happened at school. Most of the time, though, the problem is just that your child has used up his initial adrenaline. These activities may help smooth over some of the rough patches.

Routine Stress Relief

Adapt routines to give your child extra physical contact and rest while his body adapts. Try things like reading a book under the dining-room table after school (with a pillow and blankie—maybe he'll snooze), pulling him in a wagon, playing tickle or knee-bouncing games, and shifting bedtime a little earlier. Sucking helps many kids too—provide lots of Popsicles, lollipops, and drinks with bendy straws. Finally, make an effort to reduce demands and be tolerant of more immature behavior.

Pretend Stress Away

Imagination will remain one of your most powerful allies for the next several years. Themes that seem to be especially powerful for school-stressed kids include:

✳ *Baby.* Especially good for kids who are already acting helpless, whiny, or otherwise babyish. Hold them, feed them, burp them, and serenade them with a lullaby while you rock in a rocking chair.

✳ *Mrs. Teacher.* Any pretend school theme is good, but many kids have an especially strong need to turn the tables and be the one in control. Select this theme for a child who seems exceptionally demanding and impatient after school.

* *Kitty Doctor.* Vet or doctor play provides opportunities for you to touch your child in a loving and protective way and reassures him that you are still taking care of him even if you're not together as much. Some kids may prefer to be the doctor, usually inflicting pain in the form of shots. This kind of play lets them release aggression and feel in control.

* *Superhero or Wild Animal.* This is especially alluring if your child's school does not allow superhero or "wild" play (a mistake, I think). Don't be alarmed if your child prefers to be the bad guy or the fierce animal; he may be encountering some bad guys and tigers (or at least people he doesn't understand) at school and needs to step into their shoes for a bit.

Many kids will relish chances to play with puppets, small dolls, stuffed animals, or other multi-character toys so that they can work out interpersonal issues that have arisen at school.

When-in-Rome Games

One of the most taxing issues for new students is learning different rules and expectations for school—while still following the old ones at home. Games that teach flexible thinking and behavior may make it easier for your child to bend without breaking.

* *Change the Rules.* State a rule like "Clap your hands every time I snap my fingers." Then perform a series of actions, giving your child a point each time he remembers to clap at the right time. Then change the rule—"Now you have to stomp your feet when I snap"—and see if he can adjust. Don't forget to switch places, and let your child give the commands too.

* *I'm Snorking.* Make up a word for an action and when you do it, tell your child the name of the action. Like sticking your tongue in and out really fast might be *snorking*, but wagging it side to side is *borking*. See if he can snork and bork too—and then he can make up some new things for you to do.

* *Jump in the Circle, Stomp in the Square.* Use sidewalk chalk to draw several shapes in the driveway, and agree on actions to do in each

shape. Then call out a shape. Your child moves to that shape and tries to remember and perform the correct action. Make the game easy enough so that he has a *high* rate of success. When you switch places, make mistakes and show him how to recover from goofs by laughing at yourself, asking for help, or apologizing for being confused.

In Teacher We Trust

Establishing a trusting relationship with a different caregiver takes time—and that's basically good. Make it easier for your child to feel comfortable with his teacher, though, by showing him how much faith you have in this other person. Smile, make eye contact, and chat with the teacher in your child's presence. Don't let him leave at the end of the day without saying good-bye and thanking her. Help him select objects to show her, think of stories to share, or bring small gifts (bouquets of dandelions or a picture he's made would be perfect). And don't get worked up when he gushes over how wonderful she is—teacher love is not the same as parent love.

Help! I Think My Kid Is Made from Superglue

✳ ✳ ✳

Handling Persistent Separation Anxiety

After two weeks of prying my son's fingers off the car-door handle so that I could haul him into preschool (he wouldn't walk), I admit I had my doubts about whether he was ready. Two weeks later, though, he was trotting into the classroom under his own steam most mornings. What changed? Not much—mostly he just needed more time to adjust. We also made some small tweaks, like arriving early and waiting in the car for his new buddy to get there so they could walk in together. If your child is struggling with good-byes, try some of these ideas—and seek help from the teacher or director. I promise you it's a problem they've seen many times.

Balking at separation, though uncomfortable for your child and for you, is not a major problem, *as long as she settles in and is able to participate once you're out of sight.* Check with the teacher (and maybe peek through the window) to see how she's doing. Also, don't forget to give her a month to adjust. If after that, she's still miserable, you should try a different arrangement.

Ease into the School Routine

Your farewell routine should always be brief and consistent—and for a child who has a hard time with sudden changes, the first school days can be short too, going just an hour or two at first and extending as your child feels comfortable. You'll need cooperation from the school and a flexible schedule of your own for this to work. Start small and gradually lengthen school time until your kid's going full time. *Make sure you return when promised!*

Other adjustments to the routine, like arriving a little earlier or a little later, may help. Also try enlisting help from a special teacher to stay with your child, giving your child a helping job (like setting out supplies or caring for a class pet or plant) as she comes in, or deciding on a first activity before she arrives at school.

Scale Back...

Temperamentally sensitive or already-stressed kids may be overwhelmed by long hours in group care. Consider reducing the time your child spends in school or daycare (filling in with "easier" care, like a sitter, if necessary) if after four to six weeks she is still crying long and hard or being unable to have fun at school. Occasionally, a child may just need another six months or so of growing up before she finds school to be a delight instead of a torture.

...Or Scale Up!

Paradoxically, some kids have less separation anxiety if they go to school more often or for longer hours. For example, in a typical two-day-per-week program, kids have four days off between school days, which is enough time for many to forget how much they enjoy it. If your child is consistently anxious on Tuesdays but fine on Thursdays, you may want to increase her schedule.

Some kids may just need a timing change, like attending the afternoon class instead of the morning one if they're slow starters.

Be Boring at Home

If home life is too full of fun things like outings, treat foods, and electronic amusements, your child may balk at the demands and routines at school. (I've always made a point of being especially dull if my kids are staying home with suspicious ailments.) This means no TV, no special treats, no fun outings or new toys—just your usual routine, including a few chores if your child isn't running a fever or throwing up all over the place.

Nurture School Friendships

Even one buddy can make school an inviting place. Have kids over to play after school or on weekends if your child needs extra assistance in cementing relationships. You might also consider a carpool, since many reserved kids find it easier to separate with a buddy in hand.

Tell Success Stories

Some kids just need reassurance that there is a light at the end of the tunnel. Remind your child about other times she's been nervous about changes but then adapted successfully. Stories about yourself as a child, as well as books about kids who initially had reservations, may ease her mind too.

Also, make sure to give your child lots of opportunities to be successful at mini-challenges she undertakes, whether it's helping to stir some stiff batter, wipe fingerprints off the woodwork with a baby wipe, or try the high slide by herself. Nothing breeds success like success!

Play at Separating

The games that help younger children feel comfortable parting from caregivers work for preschoolers too. Try games like peek-a-boo, hide-and-seek, chase and escape games, pretending to leave and return, etc.

Stay Linked—Metaphorically

Make him a picture schedule of what you'll be doing and where you'll be when you're apart. Or exchange love tokens—try an old key on a chain, a laminated photo or a locket with a picture, a "magic" polished stone, a toy cell phone or beeper, or a heart charm pinned under her shirt.

Did You Know Bullies Could Be So Little? And Cute?

✳ ✳ ✳

How to Support or Intervene with Bullies and Other Tough Social Situations

I'll never forget the day my four–year-old came home from the Teddy Bear Picnic at his preschool, slammed his beloved Pooh Bear into a wastebasket, and announced he was *never* going to school again. Turned out the "cool boys" had not brought their teddies to school—and had spent the picnic making fun of those who did. The next several months were torture for my son, who continued to endure belittling and harassment from these miniature bullies despite the best efforts of the teachers. Things got a little better over time, but the problem never disappeared. In retrospect, I wish I'd switched my son to a different class—but it's not easy to know what's the best thing to do in these difficult situations. Here are some approaches to consider for problems your child might encounter.

When Your Child Is the Victim

It will be so painful for you—and so hard not to charge in with sharpened sword or at least some fierce words. But it's really better to try a multipronged approach like this.

✳ *Stick up for him.* Alert the teacher to what's happening. Has she observed the problem? Something else? What is she trying to make things better? Also check out the school rules—all daycares and preschools should have policies about including anyone who wants to play, using kind words, and not hurting. Finally, if your child is ignored or rejected by peers, the teacher may be able to boost his status by giving him desirable helper jobs or simply paying extra attention to him. (This strategy is less effective after the preschool years.)

✳ *Help him stick up for himself.* With coaching, your child may solve the problem better than any adult can. Use puppets or action figures to role-play a variety of coping strategies, like saying, "That hurts my feelings," ignoring mean comments, finding other kids to play with, or playing near a teacher. Watch for victim behaviors, like strong emotional responses to teasing, and talk about other ways he might react, like laughing it off or just shrugging his shoulders. Finally, help him make a friend who can be an ally.

✳ *Invite the bully to tea.* Preschool-age bullies are rarely *real* bad guys. Often the problem disappears if the two kids can just get to know each other better in a calmer environment. Plan some structured cooperative activities for the visit. If nothing else, you may get a more accurate picture of the problem your child is facing, which may help you plan your next move.

✳ *Empower your child at home.* Create opportunities for him to feel powerful in his play (e.g., superhero play; pretend play as powerful adults like police officers, firefighters, and teachers; or large-scale construction play with oversize cardboard blocks, rolled newspaper tubes, and large mural supplies). Also give him chores and teach him grown-up skills, like cooking or hammering. In addition to keeping his morale up, these activities may lead him to seem more confident at school and thereby make him less of a target.

Even Worse—When Your Child Is the Bully

You don't get to hide your head in the sand, so matter how badly you want to. Remind yourself that even good parents have kids who show bad behavior at times—and then be a good parent by confronting the problem and helping your child work through it.

✳ *Believe the teacher.* The vast majority of preschool teachers are nice people who aren't out to "get" your child or any other—and they've had lots of experience observing kids. At the same time, don't condemn your child (or let the teacher pigeonhole him)—*all* preschoolers are "innocent." They need and deserve patience, understanding, and support.

❋ *Do a stress check.* Is something going on in your child's life that's stressing him out, like a new baby, an upcoming move, ill grandparents, or tension between his parents? Even if you think you're hiding a problem from your child, he may be sensitive to the mood at home. Also, rule out physical problems, like allergies, poor nutrition, too little sleep, or chronic illnesses, such as diabetes.

❋ *Teach social skills.* Most of the bullying that occurs at this age disappears when kids learn more acceptable ways to get what they want. Get out the puppets and dolls again and role-play different situations, like how to obtain a wanted toy, respond to kids who want to join in, or get people to notice you. Also, invite children to play one-on-one at your house while you supervise. It may be easier for your child to learn social skills from a slightly younger child.

❋ *Help your child learn to read.* Facial expressions and body language, that is. Call his attention to faces in books, on TV, or around you. Ask him what the characters are feeling and how he can tell. Have him act out different feelings using his own face, body, or both. Talk about cues he can notice to tell him whether people like what he's doing or not. Make picture charts showing different emotions and have your child point out the one that matches his feeling or the feeling that someone else is showing.

❋ *Foster impulse control.* Teach your child to stop, look, and think before he joins in a game or responds to what he sees as a tease or provocation. (Many aggressive kids misread innocent behavior as an attack.) Also teach him to notice signs of tension building in himself. Try a technique like having him push his "magic button" (belly button) to calm himself down when he starts getting worked up.

❋ *Teach the golden rule.* Empathy is just emerging in young kids—but that's what will ultimately help kids to behave well toward others. Have your child stop often and think about how he would feel if someone treated him a particular way. Do this in a calm, curious

way—not in a way that's angry or shaming—and you may begin to
see results in a matter of weeks.

　　* *Work with the teacher to implement effective consequences.*
Brainstorm about what seems to work. Does he calm down after a
hug? Can the teacher ward off brewing trouble by offering him a few
quiet minutes in a tent or the book nook? Does he need someone to
help him figure out better words to use? If the school seems overly
harsh or blaming, pull your child out. No child this age should be
made to feel like a bad person.

When the Teacher Is the Problem

　　Don't automatically assume your child has a lousy teacher because he
complains about her. First, talk with other parents, arrange to observe the
class in action, watch for symptoms like disturbed sleep or potty accidents,
and do a gut check. If you do decide your child has either a personality conflict or just a bad teacher, you have several options.

　　* *Talk to the teacher.* Make an appointment, and bring your
spouse if you need an ally. Describe the problem calmly and con-
cretely, avoiding blaming words—teachers are people too. Ask for her
ideas and offer yours. Make a plan for changes and set an appointment to meet again in a few weeks. If you don't feel satisfied, take
your concerns to the director. If that doesn't work…

　　* *Yank your child.* When your child is older, you'll want to help
him figure out how to cope for a year with a problem teacher—but
that's too much to ask of a preschooler. You may be able to switch him
to a different class, or you may have to find a new school or other
childcare arrangement.

You Can Kiss That School Good-Bye!

* * *

Tactics to Ease Vacation, Caregiver, and End-of-the-Year Transitions

Given that many preschoolers struggle with the weekend/weekday shift, it's hardly surprising that many feel overwhelmed by long vacations or changes in who cares for them. Summer vacation may be especially trying for young children. Most relish the school routine, buddies, and activities, and they usually feel a strong attachment to their caregivers. You probably won't be able to eliminate vacation discombobulation, but these tips may smooth some of the bigger bumps.

Paint the Big Picture

Okay, *you* know that spring break starts in two weeks. And that it will last one week and then your kid will return to school. But does your *child* have a clue about all these upcoming changes? Quite possibly, no. At least five days before any long vacation, start talking about the changes. Make something like a sticker calendar, showing remaining school days, the number of vacation days, and when she'll return. Discuss what will happen during the break, especially if you'll be filling in with alternate care arrangements or going away. When summer vacation is coming up, make sure she realizes that she'll be attending a different class in the fall with a different teacher and different kids (if that's the case), and alert her to other changes in the works. Finally, before long breaks or caregiver changes, predict your child's likely emotional reactions for her to reassure her that her discomfort is normal and temporary ("You'll probably feel a little sad and lonely for your friends at first, but soon you'll be busy with other fun things and feel happier.").

Build Bridges between School and Break and School Again

Invite a school buddy or two to play, sing songs learned at school, and (especially for a vacation of a week or less) stick to your school day schedule for waking and sleeping. A day or two before going back, chat with your child about what she likes best about school (reminding her if necessary). When she returns to class, she might want to take a souvenir of her holiday, even if it was just an ordinary stay-home vacation. Some kids who had previously given up transitional objects (like a stuffed animal or family photograph) may need to take one again for a while.

Capture Kodak Moments

A scrapbook can be especially comforting when a beloved caregiver leaves. One moment to capture is a ritual you develop for long good-byes—like literally kissing the school good-bye. A friend's kid actually did this before weekends as well as longer holidays—and she's a pretty normal, well-adjusted teenager now.

Plan Something Wow

For many years, we celebrated the last day of school with an egg drop. I provided the kids with materials to fashion a cushioned craft for an egg they decorated as a character and then we (meaning "I" until they were old enough to be trusted near open windows) dropped the contraptions, passengers and all, onto—I hoped—the plastic tablecloths spread across our cement driveway. Occasionally the eggs survived. But good feelings *always* did, and the event lessened the sting of change back in the days when kids were sad about the end of school. You don't have to be as nuts as I am—a class picnic or a trip to the ice cream store for sundaes instead of cones will suffice. One more tip. *Do not give in and do a watermelon drop*, even if watermelons are on amazing Advantage Card special and everyone assures you they'll help with cleanup. Years later we still have sticky red goo in the crevices of the garden wall. (It was really, really cool though—all the liquid blasted out of the melon on impact, leaving the rind filled with dense, and supposedly-still-tasty-though-I-refused-to-try-it flesh.)

Where's Ms. Waldo? Special Tips for When a Caregiver Leaves

Losing a beloved teacher can occasion real grief. Your child may regress (sleeping poorly, having potty accidents, being clingy and easily upset), so give her extra TLC until she settles in with the new caregiver. Be honest and direct about the change, taking care not to promise ongoing contact if it's unlikely. Most children will appreciate having a mental picture of where their teacher will be and what she'll be doing. A good-bye party on the last day gives kids a chance to express some of their bittersweet feelings, especially if you make a gift for the teacher (like a card, poster or T-shirt) on which the kids fill in blanks in sentences like, "I'll miss my teacher because _____." *Don't forget to talk about the change with your child, emphasizing all the things that remain the same even when the caregiver leaves.*

Finally, you also have to plan a welcoming hello for the new caregiver. Ideally, caregivers will overlap for a few days, so kids can see that their familiar one likes and trusts the new one. Help your child prepare a small gift and think of other ways to show the newcomer that the child is glad she's there.

Graduations and Good-byes

Many preschools and daycares have a ceremony or picnic to mark the end of preschool. Some tips for making these occasions enjoyable:

* *Follow your child's lead.* Don't force a child to participate in a ceremony if she doesn't want to. Many kids prefer to watch from the audience.

* *Invite the ants as well as the aunts.* Most preschoolers enjoy picnics more than formal ceremonies. Offer to help set one up, even if your school has a ceremony.

* *Good-bye blocks, good-bye smocks.* Do say good-bye to the school. Try a GOODNIGHT MOON approach, saying a formal good-bye to all the people and places that have mattered to your child, including to favorite toys, the bulletin boards, his cubby, etc.

* *Be memorable.* Let your child leave something of himself behind. Many kids fear being forgotten. A donation to the school (as small as a book or as grand as a tuition scholarship) will ensure that she'll be remembered.

✳ *Stay in touch.* Don't say good-bye if you don't have to! Maintain relationships through visits and memory books. (My sixteen-year-old still pals around with her best buddy from preschool even though they attended different elementary schools for six years.)

Ready! Or Not?

✳ ✳ ✳

Is It Time for Big School?

The transition from the relative coziness and small size of preschool to the hustle, bustle, and crowds of kindergarten and the beginning of formal education can feel overwhelming—though often it's harder for parents than kids. Here are some ideas to soothe anxieties for everyone.

Around January of the year your child turns five, you'll need to evaluate whether he will be ready for kindergarten—and the beginning of "real" school—in September. Why so early? Because preschool sign-ups are about that time, and if you don't register your child then, it may be impossible to find a slot in the school you want in August. If you're on the fence about whether to send your child, here are some factors for *you*—not your mother-in-law or the neighbor with the perfect kids—to consider:

Your School District's Policies

Most districts have a cutoff date for an entering child's birthday. Some allow testing of too-young children for early admission, while others do not. You should also consider the district's style of kindergarten (all-day or half-day schedule, social or more academic emphasis, class sizes, rates of retention in kindergarten and first grade), *and* look ahead at what is expected of kids in first grade. You should also talk to other parents and find out what really happens; in many areas, parents tend to hold back younger fives, so the average age in kindergarten may be closer to six.

Your Preschool Teacher's Recommendation

Assuming you have a competent, experienced teacher (and one who is familiar with your district), I would give a lot of weight to this person's recommendation.

Your Child's Gender

It is a *fact* that boys are slower on average to mature and more likely to have trouble meeting the demands of early schooling than girls of the same age. And even though the current trend is to encourage parents to send any child who is old enough, I would recommend holding back *most* younger boys (i.e., those whose birthdays are within two months of the cutoff).

Your Child's Readiness

The Internet is brimming with readiness checklists, and your school district probably has one aligned with its curriculum. All areas of readiness—cognitive/language, physical, and social/emotional—matter, and though few kids meet every standard, if your child is significantly immature in any of the above areas, chances are he'll struggle in kindergarten (and quite possibly beyond). If you have a bright child who has already mastered many school skills (maybe he's even reading), this judgment may be especially difficult—but trust me, you'll regret sending a child who lacks maturity in other areas.

Future Projections

The hard part. Even if your child doesn't seem ready for kindergarten right now, will he be nine months—or a year—from now? If your concerns relate to matters of temperament (e.g., he's quiet and shy), your child may not be any different even a year later. If he has tended to lag behind his peers in other developmental milestones, you might make a guess that he could use some extra growing-up time. Also, project your child ahead to middle school. If your family tends to go through puberty early, it's probably better to send a child on the young side (so he won't be the only fifth grader shaving the fuzz above his lip), and vice versa if your family tends to mature on the late side. Size also matters, even though we wish it didn't. Ask yourself whether your child is likely to end up either the smallest or biggest in his class—both are hard for most kids.

What His Friends Are Doing

You shouldn't count this factor much, but of course you will because it's impossible not to. And it can matter. An anxious child can receive a real boost from entering a bustling kindergarten room with his best buddy in hand. But—and this is important—there is probably no way to guarantee that they'll be in the same class. And while you may worry about a blow to your child's self-esteem if he sees himself as falling behind his peers, these issues will probably persist (and be much harder to face) when you have to confront them again after kindergarten or later.

Get-Set Games

✳ ✳ ✳

Competence- and Confidence-Building Activities for the Summer before Kindergarten

If you're foolish enough to be comparing your kid with others who will be entering kindergarten with her in the fall, you may be starting to panic. Some will be tying their shoes with macramé knots while yours can't consistently manage her Velcro closures; others will be reading FAUST while yours can't remember whether her name starts with *B* or *V*. Chill out— most kids have islands of incompetence when they start school. For example, those kids probably can't burp "The Star-Spangled Banner" like yours can. And *that's* a far more useful skill in kindergarten. Still, it doesn't hurt to spend the summer helping your kid brush up on some of the skills that will make her feel competent as she strides through those big kindergarten doors.

Practical Matters

Kids who can manage basic self-care will seem more competent and likeable to both other kids and their teachers. And as a bonus, your life will get easier once your kid masters these skills.

✳ *Wiping her bum.* Up to now, you may have continued to wipe your child's bottom after she poops, but the teacher won't be able to spare time to do it for her. Skills she'll need include measuring the right amount of toilet paper (have her count out four or five squares, or measure it against a string of the proper length that you've tied to the dispenser). Show her how to fold the paper to keep her hands clean and how to wipe *from front to back* (essential for preventing infection). After she's done, have her wash her hands while singing the ABC song, thus killing two readiness birds with one activity.

✳ *Tying her shoes.* Not essential, as long as you can provide acceptable shoes with a closure she can work (like Velcro, zipper, buckle, or pull-on shoes). Note that many kindergarteners consider Velcro babyish, and schools may prefer or require sneakers of some sort (which may rule out buckle shoes). The book Red Lace, Yellow Lace by Mike Casey provides instruction and bicolored laces for practice tying using the bunny-ears method. You can also help your child make her own bicolored laces by folding hers in half, and then coloring each half with a different colored permanent marker. (Two-tone laces make it easier to give verbal instructions to your child.) If you and your child have the same dominant hand, practice with her sitting in your lap; otherwise, face her for instruction. I recommend teaching all kids to double-knot their laces; today's laces seem to be especially slippery.

✳ *Knowing her left from her right.* Several techniques help with this. Casually comment on which hand or foot is being used as you help your child or she performs actions, sing "The Hokey Pokey" and other action songs with a strong left-right emphasis, or put a sticker or stamp on your child's left hand every morning until she has the feel of the "sticker hand." (Ask her to guess which is the left each day before you place the sticker.) Also, if she knows her capital letters (and doesn't reverse them, as many young kids do), have her hold up her hands in front of her in a "stop" position with thumbs extended: the left hand will make an *L*.

* *Miscellaneous skills.* Play games like Office to work on useful skills like slipping papers into a folder *neatly* (which will increase the likelihood of her schoolwork coming home unrumpled) or talking in a nice "grown-up" voice that other people can understand. Also, start doing things like raising hands for a turn to speak at the dinner table, and having sit-still contests. (You should lose much of the time.)

Fine-Tuning Fingers

Fine motor skills are essential for accomplishing many important school tasks, like learning to read, write, and do arithmetic. These games will help you judge your child's physical maturation (to help you decide whether she's ready for school tasks) as well as boost her competence and pride.

* *Holding a pencil.* Teach this skill in the context of pretend play too. Websites like http://drawyourworld.com/grip.html and www.handwritinghelpforkids.com (click on parent tips) provide detailed instructions for helping kids use proper form to hold pencils. I did not do this with my kids, and the school didn't really teach it formally—and boy, are we sorry now, as both my boys struggle with terrible handwriting and writer's cramp. If you have a lefty, visit www.handedness.org for tips (like positioning paper to the left of the midline) for teaching writing skills. Games like Pick-Up Sticks or Jenga, and activities like modeling with clay, stringing beads, or doing finger plays like "Five Little Monkeys Jumping on the Bed" will build deftness and finger strength.

* *Tracing.* This skill continues to be emphasized in kindergartens because it helps teach letter formation. Start by teaching your child to trace around large, real objects, like say, people lying in the driveway (use chalk and then color in your own body with interesting spaceman outfits or princess gowns). Progress to a smaller scale, like tracing silverware, plates, and glasses onto a piece of heavy paper that can

be used as a place mat. (Tape the paper down and either fasten the objects in place with adhesive or hold them for your child.) We also played games like Connect the *B*s on a page torn from a magazine or newspaper (good for waiting in restaurants) and had kids use the ever-popular tracing paper to make copies of beloved cartoon characters—just make sure you tape everything down.

✳ *Cutting (not running) with scissors.* This is another old-fashioned skill that's still needed—your kindergartner will probably encounter lots of tasks requiring her to cut along a line. If she can't manage scissors at all, start by showing her how to place her fingers and open and close the blades like a snapping alligator mouth. Then practice cutting easy things like ropes of Play-Doh, grass or dandelion flowers in the backyard (sorry, she'll take too long for you to get out of mowing), or hair (pretend hair, of course, made from paper you fringe and paste loosely around a drawn face). Next, teach her to cut along a line by drawing simple shapes (like *V*s on a folded index card) and having her cut them out to make crude snowflakes or have her cut along a spiral you've drawn on a paper plate (which makes a snake that will spin nicely when hung by its head).

The Pre-Three Rs

You don't have to be a certified teacher to start gradually introducing the basics kids need for formal learning—and the subjects will seem familiar and undaunting when she encounters them in school if she's known them already in a casual and playful environment at home.

✳ *Recognizing letter shapes and sounds.* Point out letters in books as you read. Most kids learn the letters in their names first, but some like other letters for their shapes or special associations. In the car, you and your child can hunt for letters—the first to spot five examples of his letter wins. Our favorite sound game was Letter Balloon Bounce. We'd bat a balloon up in the air while reciting the alphabet. If it landed on the floor, everyone had to think up a word that started with that letter. Also play rhyming games in the car (*What rhymes with* bat? *With* toilet?), and pause for your child to fill in the missing word when you read rhyming books (like Dr. Seuss stories) or recite funny poems.

❊ *First writing games.* ALPHABET ART by Judy Press has instructions for crafting a beautiful alphabet from paper plates and ordinary materials, as well as information about reinforcing forming and learning the sounds of letters. Many kids find it easier to write on vertical surfaces like chalkboards and dry-erase boards. Practice writing letters in sand or cornmeal sprinkled on a cookie sheet, and take turns "writing" letters on each other's palms or backs—it's educational *and* soothing!

❊ *Number play.* Teach your child to count one-to-one by having her count out forks as she sets the table or drop M&Ms into the numbered compartments of an egg carton as she counts out loud. Games like Sorry or Chutes and Ladders also encourage one-to-one counting. Teach relative value with card games like War, or have your child guess which small pile of crackers or pennies has more.

Playground Smarts

I know lots of teachers who swear that this kind of "intelligence," which includes social-emotional abilities as well as physical ones, has the biggest impact on a child's enjoyment of the school environment.

❊ *Physical feats.* Over the summer and early school year, work on big-kid skills like pumping a swing (the real trick is to use your arms to pull and push), skipping ("hop, step, hop, step"), or doing the monkey bars (This is hard; many kids don't master this until near the end of the year, but all should be able to hang and many can do one hand-shift).

❊ *Monkey-bar manners.* Your child needs to practice taking turns, helping when someone gets hurt, and not-too-disgusting snack-munching manners. These skills are best learned in the context of playing pretend games and discussing problems encountered by characters in books and on TV. You'll also want to get a sense of her social style and nudge her toward the positive end of her personal spectrum—kindly, competent leader rather than bossy tyrant; cheerful follower instead of pushover wallflower.

✻ *Kindergarten-baby skills.* In preschool, your child was the big kid. Get her used to being the little guy again by having her play around older kids and learning how to handle good-natured teasing. For example, she can learn to respond to rhymes like "Kindergarten baby, stick your head in gravy!" by ignoring the speaker or by dishing out a little just-for-fun sass to the cool first graders, like "First is the *worst,* second is the best, but kindergarten's the one with the treasure chest!"

✻ *Bus-savvy…*or walk-ready. Have your child take practice trips along her bus or walking route, learning to recognize important landmarks. Discuss what-if scenarios with her, like what if she fell asleep on the bus (as my husband did coming home from the first day of kindergarten) or missed her stop? And take time to teach bus safety! Find kid-friendly tips at http://www.aboutschool.com/busstop.htm.

CHAPTER FOUR

Friends and Festivities

* * *

Without Too Many Hissy Fits

I rank making friends slightly above potty training on the scale of essential things to teach your young child how to do. And I think potty training is crucial.

It's not just that you won't have to play so many games of Hungry Hungry Hippos if your child has a buddy to play with him instead. Making friends will make him happy in a way that nothing else will. From the time newborns peer blearily at one another while whacking each other with their little flailing fists, kids know that there's something different and special about other people who are just their age. And they're right—research has documented that friends provide different kinds of healthy support and pressure than what we get from our families. Lucky people have lots of time with both friends and family.

So during his preschool years, it's your job to make sure that your child has plenty of opportunities to hang out with other people just like him who like to wear Peter Pan tunics while debating whether dogs should be allowed to drive cars. It's also your job to make sure your child acquires core social skills, like using the magic word when he wants something (*please*, not *abracadabra*—unless it turns out he's not a Muggle) and squabbling *nicely* over the rules of a game. Why? Because research suggests the preschool years are a "sensitive period" for socialization, and it gets increasingly harder for kids to learn basic friend skills at a later age.

Another thing you'll want to teach your preschooler is how to be a party animal. Knowing the ins and outs of celebrating a variety of occasions from family birthdays to Halloween trick-or-treating will smooth your child's passage through life, at least for the first ten or twelve years. Especially if he learns to open presents without whining, "But this isn't what I wanted!"

In this chapter, I offer advice on how to be to be your own Emily Post for the small-fry set. There are tips on everything from what play-date pick-up lines to teach your child to how to (*shudder*) handle that annual rite of passage known as "The Birthday Party." I've also included suggestions for helping your child handle those tricky social situations, like peer pressure, crowded threesomes, and "disagreements" over whose turn it is to pick between Hungry Hungry Hippos and Candyland. So phone a friend—well, two friends (one for you and one for your kid)—and kick back and laugh together. *With* my advice, not *at* it.

Social Engineering, Part I

✴ ✴ ✴

Helping Your Child Make Friends

If your child is more of a social caterpillar than a social butterfly, these solutions to two common obstacles may help her find her wings.

Whine! There's No One to Play With!

Undoubtedly one of these days we'll see singles ads for the preschool set: *Wanted: SF to dress Barbies, share teddy-bear tea parties, and jump on the sofa with me.* Until then, things to try:

✴ *Take a daily walk around the neighborhood.* Chat up families you see along the way. Tote play-as-you-go toys, like sidewalk chalk or binoculars so your kid can engage others immediately (if a caregiver is present). Exchange phone numbers or make a date to play.

✳ *Join a playgroup.* Or start one yourself. Or sign your kid up for a class. Then keep your eyes peeled for kids whose interests, energy level, and playing style match your child's. It's a bonus if you like the other parent too, and if you live close enough for easy exchanges.

✳ *Look for unexpected opportunities.* If your child is socially immature, match her up with a playmate who's younger than she is. Also, don't forget while you're "shopping" for buddies that the preschool years are a great time to introduce your child to friends who are different from her—you'll never have a better time to dispel prejudices and promote openness. Many young children can become good buddies to children with special needs, especially if you're accepting and answer their questions. Finally, remember that a relationship with an older neighbor, a favorite aunt, or even a pet can *help* fill a child's yearning for friendship.

✳ *Seek the services of a matchmaker.* For example, your child's teacher can probably suggest a good potential buddy. Ask for her help in pairing the kids while they're at school, and then invite the potential friend to play at your house. (It often works best to invite parent and child for the first visit.)

✳ *Visit a kid hot spot on a consistent schedule.* Spend Friday evenings at the local park or school playground, attend library story time, or even just frequent the supermarket on a regular schedule and you'll notice that you see the same kids over and over.

✳ *Teach pick-up lines.* Use puppets or little figures to teach your child how to approach a child she'd like to play with. Keep it simple, like, "My name's ____. I like to play ____. Want to play with me?"

✳ *Make your home a kid magnet.* Install a great climbing structure, permit lots of messy play, or just have a stash of something cool—like great dress-up clothes or supplies for making forts—and kids will flock to your home. This strategy can be especially useful if you have a child with special needs.

Stuck on the Fringes

Joining a group in action is hard for many kids; some hang wistfully on the outskirts; others barge in and get rejected. These tips can help your little one ease in more gracefully:

✳ *Help her look for an opening.* The best times to join a group are 1) before it gets going (so arrive early to school or playgroup), 2) when there's a break in the action (like when kids are ending one game or getting ready to start something new), or 3) when the group needs help working out a problem. Act out various playtime scenarios with your kid, notice them in books and TV shows, or stand with your child to help her catch opportune moments to join in. Another good strategy to slow down an impulsive kid is to teach her to count to three before she joins in—naming things the kids are doing as she counts.

✳ *Give her an entry.* This can be as simple as teaching her what to say and do. A good formula (at any age) is smile, offer a compliment (like "You're a fast runner!" or "That looks like fun!"), and suggest a way to contribute (like "I can be the little sister in the family" or "Can you catch me too?"). An alternative is to give your child something to add to the play. For example, if a group is playing T-ball, your child might offer bases or cones to mark the home-run line. Be careful with this approach though, since many kids are either overprotective of their stuff or they end up disrupting the game in the process of making their offer and thereby end it for everyone.

✳ *Coach from the sidelines.* While it's tempting to join in yourself and drag your child along, this strategy rarely works in the long run. Instead, agree on hand signals or code words to remind your child of desirable behaviors while she plays. Also, give advice before or after she plays with the group, so you don't disrupt the flow of the play.

Social Engineering, Part II

✳ ✳ ✳

Helping Your Child Keep Friends

Some kids have a series of one-date buddies or even casual playmates, but don't seem to be able to form lasting or deeper friendships. To a large extent, this pattern is typical of the preschool years when friendships are often situational and fluid; nonetheless, most preschoolers are happier when they have one or more "special" buddies. Fortunately, you can help your child improve his friendship skills by teaching him the three things a good friend does: care, share, and be fair. Talk with your child about these skills when you're doing things like riding around in the car, sitting at the dinner table, or giving him a bath—and definitely have refresher discussions before a play date. Keep in mind that it's generally best to work on *one* skill at a time.

Care

Here are some age-appropriate ways your preschooler can demonstrate that he cares about his friend:

✳ *Ask his friend questions and give compliments.* Everyone likes to talk about himself. And everyone likes to hear nice things about themselves. Help your kid brainstorm some questions he might ask, and work with him on waiting for his friend to answer before talking himself. Also discuss compliments your child might offer his friend.

✳ *Use a friendly body and voice.* Just as many kids need to be reminded to use "indoor voices," many preschoolers need help remembering to use their "friendly bodies" or "friendly voices." Practice appropriate touching (which may or may not be very gentle depending on the friend), and talking in a way that's upbeat, not too loud or too quiet, and not whiny or aggressive. Some kids also need help with personal space issues. (Tell your space invader to imagine something like a giant rabbit standing between him and his buddy.) Other kids need help fine-tuning their body language, or even just remembering to stay *with* their friends during most of the visit.

✳ *Say sorry.* If your child hurts his friend's body or feelings, *even if he didn't mean to*, he should tell his friend he's sorry. He may say it very quickly and in an I-don't-really-mean-it voice, but that's okay; he's just learning. Talk about and rehearse other ways to make up after disagreements.

✳ *See his friend often.* Sounds obvious, but it still bears mentioning. Young kids have short memories; a friendship is more likely to stick if the kids get together at least once a week.

Share

Preschoolers who are good at being friends share their toys (at least some of the time), and they also share ideas and secrets and reveal vulnerabilities. Both kinds of sharing are "emerging behaviors" during the preschool years, so don't panic if your kid isn't good at them yet. Try these tips to promote the skills:

✳ *Prewarn and prepare.* If your child struggles with sharing possessions, empathize with him about the fact that it's difficult, but also talk about how good it will make his friend feel to share—and how he'll feel good too. In the end, though, make it clear that sharing is just something you do whether or not you want to, like brushing your teeth before bed.

✳ *Put away special toys before a visit.* Limit the special toys to five objects max or you'll be packing up your kid's entire toy collection.

✳ *Acquire a stash of play date toys.* You need things that 1) only come out when a friend is over (and aren't your child's personal possessions), 2) are playthings that invite sharing, like blocks or art supplies, and/or 3) are multiples of highly desirable objects, like ride-on toys, dress-up clothes, action figures, etc.

✳ *Force the issue.* When you have a treat for the kids, give both to your child, asking him to hand one to his friend. Or distribute the materials for an activity by giving *all* the vinegar, for instance, to one kid, and *all* the baking soda to another. If necessary, challenge the kids to solve the problem. Then praise the kids for doing such a good job of sharing.

✳ *Encourage your child to share ideas and experiences.* Suggest things he might talk to his friend about, like the big umbrella that scared him, or the new kitten Grandma got. Help him think of follow-up questions for his friend, like "Are you afraid of umbrellas?"

✳ *Help him notice when he's the share-ee.* Say things like, "Wasn't that nice of Nick to let you use his Barbie-smashing tool? Sharing is such a kind thing to do."

Be Fair

It's hard for preschoolers to be fair—in large part because they don't really notice when they aren't being fair. Few have any real ability to put themselves in another's place, which means you will need to encourage this kind of thinking over and over by saying things like "Let's pretend you're [friend's name]. How do you think you would feel if _____ happened?" Even more useful in the short run, though, is teaching matter-of-fact rules for behavior in certain situations, like what your kid can say when he loses or wants to have a turn. Here are some fairness skills preschoolers can start to acquire.

✳ *Play by the rules.* To some extent, arguing about what the rules are and changing them midstream is the point of preschool games. But if your child is constantly being rejected (or opting out himself) because of rule disputes, help him figure out ways to reach compromises with his buddies.

✳ *Take turns.* This is a good policy both for the bossy, pushy kind of kid and for the shy, pushed-around kind. Apply it for deciding who gets to choose an activity, as well as for making sure that everyone gets a chance to do things like be the good guy or play with Sammy Slug. Timers can be a BIG help in regulating turns. Keep several handy and teach the kids how to set them.

✳ *Be a good loser.* A script comes to the rescue again! When your child loses a game, teach him to say, "Good game. Let's play again!" (or "Let's play _____ now!"). Also adjust your kid's expectations, so that he doesn't start off thinking he should win every time. Explain that if there are two kids playing, he will probably win only every other time or so; if there are more kids, he will win even less. A final alternative is to avoid competitive games as much as possible (though I've noticed that the worst losers are usually the kids who are most drawn to competitive games—and the ones who are most likely to transform every situation into a contest).

✳ *Be a gracious winner.* Being a good winner is as difficult for many kids as being a good loser. We taught ours to say something like, "You played great! What do you want to do now?" (Okay, I admit I am *still* repeating all these phrases to my highly competitive oldest child—who's twenty—but I really think he's starting to get it. Don't give up!)

Play Date-iquette

✳ ✳ ✳

How to Help Your Child Be a Happy Host or a Great Guest

For most of us, the days when you could just send your kid over to the neighbor's—or even better, just open the back door and shoo her out for the day—are long gone. This means you'll need to schedule play dates for your child. You need to do this even if she's attending daycare or preschool, and even if you've provided her with perfectly nice siblings, because having a friend over (and visiting one) is a different—and important—experience.

Anatomy of a Play Date

Teach your child how to make her own phone calls to arrange dates. You and the other parent will still have to firm up the details, but initiating the conversation is a good first step toward teaching your child to be her own social secretary. (Supervise dialing carefully if you don't have unlimited long distance.)

First play dates work best as one-on-one affairs, so limit the number of kids you invite over. Keep the dates short at first and schedule them for a time of day when your child is relatively energetic and no one will be too rushed on either end.

Many kids fare better if a parent accompanies them for the first date or two. After that, plan to have kids stay by themselves; this arrangement builds children's ability to separate, often improves the quality of play (and even the behavior of both kids), *and* most importantly (at least from *my* perspective), gives one parent a much-needed break. Let your child know what to expect.

A loose structure makes the date more comfortable. You might start with a semi-planned activity (like making "potions" from nontoxic supplies you've put out), followed by some time for the kids to play actively at something they choose themselves, then a snack (and potty break), and finally another "quiet" activity, like making baking soda-and-vinegar volcanoes, while you wait for pick-up. After *many* repetitions, the kids may impose this kind of structure all by themselves!

On Your Mark, Get Set…

A little preparation goes a long way. Make sure your child knows that the play date's coming up (a step I've overlooked on occasion)! Involve her in planning an activity to start with and a snack. Talk about fun things the two of them can do. Make sure she knows that it's *her* job to help her friend feel welcome and comfortable. She should let her guest go first, choose first, etc., and she should always offer her friend food or drink if she has some herself.

If you haven't done so already, make a sign with your house rules. Keep it simple and leave it up all the time. Two good rules to include: "We try not to hurt anyone" and "We take care of our things." (You can use the sign during a date as a neutral way of reminding the guest and host of appropriate behavior.)

If your child will be the guest, review expected behavior, like following house rules, asking before getting something to eat, etc. While you're getting ready or are en route, casually review good host or guest etiquette.

Help Your Child Put out the Welcome Mat

Good greeting manners can get everyone off on the right foot. Teach your child to greet her guest at the door. Give the guest a quickie tour, showing the kids where they may play and eat, and, of course, pointing out the bathrooms. Ask if anyone needs to go now. Get the kids settled with a welcome activity as soon as possible. Stay nearby for the first few minutes.

If you're the one dropping off your child for a play date, make your good-bye short and sweet, like you do at preschool. Let her know about when you'll be back. If she has trouble separating, your child may find the transition easier if she brings something, like bubble soap to play with or a favorite snack to share. Be sure she knows where the bathroom is.

Make It Fun

Provide for a variety of play activities that kids can do on their own or with minimal adult help. I think pretend play is the number-one best choice—provide props, little figures, costumes, etc., but also offer some energy-burning options like swinging, dancing or driveway games, as well as games, puzzles, science projects, or arts-and-crafts choices.

Don't allow any TV or other electronic media, except in emergencies. I really mean this. The point of having a friend over is for the kids to learn how to play together, work out disagreements, burn off some kid energy, etc.—none of which will happen if they're both zombied out in front of a screen.

Discuss in advance how your child should handle likely problem issues, like whether siblings have to be included, what your child should do if his friend is breaking a house rule, or if someone gets hurt.

And then…butt out. This is your kid's date, not yours. (Eavesdropping, though, I encourage. How else will you know that they've decided to play hairdresser using real scissors?)

Now Stop!

The end of the play date can be tough because kids have used up many of their resources. Having a routine and knowing how to act can stave off some ugly scenes. Warn the kids fifteen minutes before pickup time. I think it's good for *both* families to agree to have visitors participate at least nominally in tidy-up.

A stash of good-bye tokens like stickers, seashells from your vacation, bottles of some stinky potion the kids made, etc., can ease good-byes. This strategy can even sometimes circumvent those awkward borrowing-a-favorite-toy situations.

The Peer-Pressure Cooker

* * *

How to Let off the Steam—Or Cook with It!

When someone mentioned "peer pressure," I used to think two things: teenagers and *bad*. But once my kids came along, I discovered that a) peer pressure began before they were even out of diapers, and b) at least half the time, it was a good influence! In fact, it was due to peer pressure that my kids got *out* of diapers—and found the courage to put their heads under water at swimming lessons, and learned to like, or at least sometimes pretend to tolerate, the taste of broccoli. And lots of other good things! These ideas can help you and your child make the best of the power of her friends.

Minimize Bad Influences

Genuine hooligans are rare in this age group, but it's also a rare child who doesn't have at least one buddy who makes you wish his parents would accept a job overseas. To some extent, you should be glad to have the opportunity to walk your child through coping with a bad influence at an age when the stakes are a lot lower than they will be in the teen years. But if you're tired of the "I don't care what _____'s parents let him do, in this house we don't_____" wars, try these strategies.

* *Check IDs.* Steer your child toward playmates who are the same age or slightly younger. Older peers are more likely to encourage behaviors that are a problem simply because they outstrip your child's maturity.

* *Introduce Jiminy Cricket.* Your child's conscience is developing. Choose a metaphor, like Jiminy Cricket, a little voice inside, a funny feeling in his tummy, an angel on his shoulder, etc., and talk about how it can help him make good choices.

✳ *Play What If?…a lot!* If he offers a "bad choice" as the option he'd choose in a hypothetical situation, talk about drawbacks of the choice and ask questions like, "What would be another thing you could do?" Keep discussing his "power" to make good choices.

✳ *Teach the phrase "That's against our rules."* Rehearse a variety of ways to "just say no" when something's a bad idea. Making Mom the heavy is a face-saving way out of uncomfortable situations for kids of all ages.

✳ *Eavesdrop, corral, and supervise.* The bottom line is that preschoolers do not yet have good internal controls. *You* have to provide the voice of reason when they're deciding whether umbrellas or blanket parachutes work better for jumping off the garage roof. So get out the baby monitor, double-check your childproofing, park yourself nearby, and limit playing to "public" areas.

✳ *Keep your reactions low-key.* The more you openly despise a buddy, the more intriguing he'll be to your child. (This principle gets truer the older your child gets, so keep reminding yourself of it through adolescence.)

✳ *Say, "Darn! We're busy that day!"* Avoiding playmates you dislike should be a last resort. But sometimes, the best choice just is to have a "prior commitment" when the Bad Egg issues or demands invitations.

Maximize Good Influences

Maybe you'll be lucky and your child will befriend Little Mr. Perfect all on his own. Or maybe no more appealing playmates will live nearby and your child will be forced to hang out with the kid you want him to imitate. But in case some choosing is involved, here are some ways to encourage friendships with kids you like.

✳ *Play matchmaker.* At this age, you still have influence over who your kid spends time with—so exercise it. Keep your eyes peeled for prospective playmates who relish green vegetables, share nicely with their younger siblings, and call you "Mrs. Joey's Mom" instead of "Mrs. Booger-Face." Invite them over and keep your fingers crossed.

Of course, there's no predicting whether these sweetie pies will be a good influence on your kid—or yours a bad influence on them.

✳ *Build the bond.* Help your child cement his healthy friendships. In addition to inviting "desirables" to play, take them on outings, and include them on special occasions. Your *actions* should say, "I support this friendship."

✳ *But keep your words low-key.* Just as criticizing a buddy can make him desirable, so can overpraising one make him despicable. Above all, never say, "Why can't you _____ like _____?" tempting though it might be.

✳ *Be a good role model.* Talk with your kids about how you try to emulate your friends' best qualities. And let them see your words in action.

✳ *Let little kids be little kids.* Watch the messages you send to your child. Make sure you're letting him know that you're happy that he and his buddies are immature, naïve, sweet. Many peer pressure problems actually stem from adult pressure to act prematurely cool or sophisticated.

Handling the Keeping-Up-with-the-Joneses Issues

If you think preschoolers are immune to concerns like wearing the right clothes or watching the right TV shows, think again. Although designer tags may not matter (and tiaras may), most preschoolers want to resemble their buddies. And they definitely want to watch the same Cartoon Network shows their best friends do.

Although I agree it's important for kids to dress something like their peers and to be generally familiar with kiddy pop culture, I also think your own values and budget matter too; you have to find a balance and it may take some adjusting before you achieve it. For example, when my son was small, I didn't let him watch the Teenage Mutant Ninja Turtles; we were more of a PBS family. But once he started school, he felt left out when the other kids talked about Raphael and Leonardo. So I took him to the art gallery. Okay, not really. I caved in *some* and let him rent Turtle videos on the occasional babysitter night. This exposure was enough to keep him in the swim at school without having Turtle TV dominate our lives.

Friends Who Fight

✳ ✳ ✳

Unscrambling the Squabbles

It's completely normal for preschool buddies to fight. It's even normal for disagreements to escalate occasionally to name calling, shoving, pinching, and other behaviors typical of pro-wrestling matches and presidential elections. And it's also normal for you to want to rush in and make things right (or else hide your head under a pillow).

Instead, though, wait to see what happens. Because most of the time, kids *will* work things out all by themselves, and that's best. Step in to mediate only if a) the fighting is rough or cruel, b) important property is at risk, or c) they ask for help.

Five Steps for a Fair Fight

You'll have to assist the kids with this process at first, but over time some may learn how to follow the steps themselves! Have the kids count off the steps on their fingers.

✳ *Take a deep breath.* Tell the kids to pretend their bellies have a balloon that they're trying to inflate as they breathe in. Let it deflate as they breathe out. Oxygen helps people think clearly and make better judgments.

✳ *Use words, not bodies.* Young kids should repeat this mantra out loud before "negotiations" begin. While you're at it, add, "Listening ears on!"

✳ *Listen to your friend.* Have your kid zip her lips and hear what her friend wants. Help her repeat her friend's desires as a check that she understood.

✳ *Tell your side.* Next your child gets to state what she wants. Again, help the friend understand. (Steps 3 and 4 can be reversed, but we let guests go first.)

✳ *Look for compromise.* Explain that *compromise* means finding an in-between solution to their problem. Like, if they both want to play with Super Slug, they could take turns, both choose different animals, or one could use Smarty Snail instead, since he's slimy too.

When Friends Keep Fighting Even after You've Tried This Great Technique

Entrenched bickering among kids who are usually friendly is probably the result of a "state" problem (one or both of the kids is too tired, hungry, thirsty, overstimulated, stressed out, sick, etc.). Or else the kids are typical four-year-olds. Resolve the underlying problem if possible and let the kids have a go at playing (and fighting) again. Sometimes, though, you either can't fix the root trouble or can't even figure out what it is. And if you're stuck with the friend at your house for another hour and a half, you'll need to try:

✳ *Diversion.* Let the kids play one of the classic stress-busting activities, such as making a mess with water, finger painting with shaving cream all over your major appliances, annoying the baby with flashlights, etc.

✳ *Separation.* One of my most successful ways to separate squabbling kids was to grab a bunch of the stuffed animals that apparently bred under my daughter's bed, and hand half of them to one kid and half to the other. Then I would send them into different rooms and help each hide his critters. Finally the kids would switch rooms to hunt for them, repeating until the other mom came. Sometimes I'd sweeten the pot with some of the leftover Halloween candy I was saving for PMS days, or a handful of coins, or some other treat.

✳ *Desperate measures.* When all else fails, it's time to break out the videos. Have the kids sprawl on separate couches while you sip a nice cup of tea and remind yourself that this too shall pass—and besides, next week the kids are playing at the friend's house.

Teach Kids How to Make Up

Although it's true that most preschoolers will forgive and forget with just the passage of time, if I have to intervene from time to time I get my

LITERATURE LINKS

Good choices for crabby friends include LET'S BE ENEMIES by Janice May Udry, BEST FRIENDS FOR FRANCES by Russell Hoban, THE QUARRELING BOOK and THE HATING BOOK by Charlotte Zolotow, and DUCK AND GOOSE by Tad Hills.

revenge by inflicting instruction in social graces. I teach my kids the rule: "If you have hurt someone's body or feelings *even if you didn't mean to* (and even if the someone is a pesky brother who deserved it), you must say sorry." Expect that nine times out of ten the word will be muttered without a hint of sincerity. The injured party should follow up with something like "That's okay." (Despite years of instruction in this lesson, my kids still struggle with telling each other *sorry*, being more inclined to go straight to arguing their cases, *but* I have noticed they now use the word easily with friends and adults, including me, on occasion.)

More Buddy Bugaboos

✳ ✳ ✳

Handling Threesomes, Leeches, and More

If you thought squabbling was all you had to worry about, think again. The list of potential headaches is endless, but I've picked a few to discuss.

Threesomes and Throngs

Getting three preschoolers together often reminds me of the old puzzle about ferrying a fox, a goose, and some grain across a river—some pairs are more compatible than others, but if you leave all three together unattended, disaster is certain to result. Here are some tips that will probably keep anyone from being gobbled up should you find yourself hosting a trio of "buddies":

✳ *Increase supervision*…because the amount of trouble a group of kids can and will get into increases geometrically. Also, threesomes need a fourth to balance the triangle problems.

✳ *Monitor states.* A single hungry kid can have a catastrophic impact on group dynamics. Plus, taking breaks to eat, drink, go potty, etc., uses up time and distracts kids who are just starting to squabble.

✳ *Choose games for a gang.* Preschoolers will have fun putting on a show, playing run-around tag, or building a fort together if you provide sufficient supplies. I have also had good luck with group art on long rolls of paper stretched across the kitchen floor. Provide LOTS of duplicate *washable* markers.

Lopsided Arrangements

At one point or another, all my kids had buddies who either a) *never* came to our house or b) *only* played at our house. Both arrangements drove me crazy. Okay, the second one was worse. What to do?

The bottom line is that there may be no easy solution to these situations. You may have to just accept an unbalanced arrangement if the friendship seems worth the annoyance. Some ways to encourage alternating:

✳ *Ask directly.* Say something like "I've noticed Peaches prefers to play at her own house. Is there something we could do to make her comfortable enough to try a short visit at ours?" or "I really need a few hours to _____. Any chance Evan could play at your house next Tuesday?"

✳ *Take small steps.* Invite a reluctant visitor to come with his parents, try very brief visits at first, or meet moochers, parent in tow, on neutral territory like a park.

✳ *Put the ball in the other parent's court.* Mention that you have a family rule that friends have to alternate playing at each other's homes, and then wait to see what happens. (Okay, probably nothing. Darn it.)

Leeches

Occasionally, a child your kid dislikes may latch on to him. This situation can be especially awkward if it's a neighbor who barges in constantly.

Again, there are no easy answers, but these strategies can keep you from being sucked dry:

✳ *Set limits.* Basically this consists of saying *no* in a polite but firm way like "I'm sorry Steffi, but we're having family time now. You can come over another day." Or you might have a rule that kids can only come over when invited. You'll need to be consistent but kindly. And teach your child how to say similar things in a polite way.

✳ *Hide.* It can certainly work in the short run, but at a cost. Play in less visible areas, go to play areas away from home, etc. Or you can always move…

✳ *Be kind.* Parasite kids are often needy ones. I know it's hard to spare the energy to half-raise an extra child when you have young ones of your own, but you may be doing a tremendous kindness for an innocent child. And think what a great example you're setting for your own child. Having said that, I'm not advocating being a doormat. For example, you might have a set play date for *just* two afternoons a week. (But if you suspect abuse or genuine neglect, *please* call Child Protective Services; in most states you can make reports anonymously.)

When Your Friend's Kid Isn't Your Kid's Friend

This situation can strain even the oldest, strongest friendships. Here are some tips for handling the problem:

✳ *Require politeness to guests in your home.* And also to hosts when you go visiting. By all means, acknowledge and validate your child's feelings, protect him if your friend's child is too aggressive or intrusive, and give him needed breaks. (Plus read the hysterically funny and charmingly illustrated book, BOOTSIE BARKER BITES by Barbara Bottner and Peggy Rathmann.) But insist that your kid be polite and friendly, just as he would with a visitor he chose to invite.

✳ *Help the kids get to know each other.* Sometimes familiarity breeds friendship rather than contempt. Aim for short but regular get-togethers. Then look for *any* common interest, even if it's just a mutual love of pretending to be birds while eating sour gummy worms.

✳ *Find ways for the kids to be separate when together.* Offer side-by-side activities, such as having each kid play with his own set of blocks. Or take the kids on outings to the zoo, museums, or play-grounds where they can be in the same space without having to inter-act much.

✻ *Nurture your friendship away from the kids.* You shouldn't have to lose out just because your kids don't mesh. Find times and places to get together without kids in tow, or talk on the phone or online chat. I've found it's best to be open and matter-of-fact about the kids' differences while continuing to affirm my own friendship.

Excitement Management 101

✳ ✳ ✳

Celebrating Like Mad without Getting Mad

I'm not sure which is worse: when your kid is so wound up before a special occasion that she's either shrieking and swooshing around the room or melting down on the floor; or when she's utterly blasé about an event that someone has spent hours and mucho bucks preparing. The following tips are intended to help you keep your child's emotional level out of either red zone, at least some of the time.

Celebration Preparation

The old a-stitch-in-time-saves-nine philosophy: what you do ahead of time can pay off in spades.

✻ *Simplify, simplify, simplify.* The bottom line is that whether you're hosting or attending, tweak the occasion so you can meet your kid's needs for rest, activity, amusement, appropriate food, and com-fort—or everyone will regret it. *Do this even if it makes some of the other celebrants cross or disappointed.* Screaming fits won't make them happy either.

✻ *Preset the expectation buttons.* Tell your kid what will happen, the timing, and how she should behave. Look at photo albums and videos so she'll be familiar with the names and faces of other guests. Read books or watch shows featuring similar occasions. Finally, armed with your knowledge of your child's temperament and past reactions, talk about how she might *feel* at different points during the event. Discuss specifically what she can do if she's bored, overwhelmed, or just feeling very, very noisy. Make up a hand signal for her to show she needs your support—and another so you can let her know if her behavior is out of bounds.

✳ *Be present-able.* Sick of last minute trips to the toy store? Try the present-of-the-year method—buy a large quantity of some unisex gift (like a gumball machine, art supply set, or a book-and-toy set) and give it to *every* kid for one year. Another option is to have a "present closet" stocked with ready-to-wrap gifts. On the wrapping front, you can't beat gift bags. Or let your preschooler wrap the gift herself with aluminum foil—no tape necessary, *and* it's wonderfully shiny.

✳ *Teach Merry Making 101.* Rehearse common trouble spots, like getting (and not getting) presents. Pretend to have your child open a present she already has or doesn't like. (A good rule of thumb: think of one nice thing to say.) Present-getting etiquette can be very tricky. My brother once gave my son a game we already had. Everyone could see the wheels turning as Eric, who'd been coached to keep quiet about duplicates, tried to remember how to react. Finally my brother, not thinking, asked, "Do you have that already?" Eric looked stricken for a moment and then blurted, "None of your business!" Other skills to teach are expressing positive emotions appropriately, party-food manners, and how to greet both familiar and unfamiliar guests.

✳ *Get your kid in peak partying condition.* Ideally before a big event, your child will be well rested, well fed, and emotionally nourished. Yeah, right. Well, at least have him run around and burn off excess energy beforehand, and of course visit the potty. And, most importantly, take deep breaths and get your own stress under control; if you don't, your kid will catch it.

The Big Day

Think "coach." And make that image more Phil Jackson (peaceful and positive) than Bobby Knight (volatile and violent).

* *Cling to routines.* A plan accommodating your child's typical meal, play, and rest schedule is the scaffold for success.

* *Issue a* few *reminders.* Hit the big topics in advance but remember that too much input will wipe out your child's entire hard drive.

* *Have the right equipment on hand.* Small, quiet toys for distraction are a must, as are changes of clothing if your child will be wearing something new, itchy, or disliked.

* *Use your hand signals.* And if all else fails, swoop your kid up for an emergency conference in the powder room.

* *Offer time-outs as needed.* Help your child pace eating and drinking, make sure she goes potty regularly, and find her chances to run and jump for a bit. Give her hugs and chances to catch her breath.

* *Praise and encourage.* Celebrating is hard work! Let your child know when she's doing a good job.

Post Party

The fun—or the birthday meltdown—doesn't have to end when the last guest goes out the door! The following tips can act as a merry-making parachute.

* *Always leave everyone wanting more.* So get out of there early, before your kid turns into a pumpkin. A scary, screaming one.

* *Head for the showers.* Well, the bathtub really. Some soothing water play is perfect for helping your child regroup. Or just reduce the stimulation level with mood lighting, peaceful music, and a snuggly pal to cuddle.

* *Prepare for letdown.* Think of something energy-expending or fun for your child to do during the post-party moments, such as playing with a new package of stickers on the way home or squashing pop cans for recycling. And start talking up the next fun thing coming up.

* *Debrief and view the films.* Good coaches will tell you this is a task to save for a few days later—everyone needs a few days to get strong emotions out of their systems. Remember to maintain a praise:criticism ratio of 5:1.

The Birthday Blues

✳ ✳ ✳

Putting the "Happy" Back in Your Child's Birthday

Recently I've been asking adults and teens what they liked best about their childhood birthday celebrations. Interestingly, only one person has mentioned a gift he'd received. But *every* single person I've asked has listed one or more family birthday traditions. Rituals matter for several reasons—they're predictable and thus an anchor in a stressful time, they make families feel bonded to one another, and most have appealing elements of silliness or empowerment. Here are some customs from other families and cultures to try.

Food Stuff

Birthday-cake rituals come to mind of course. In our house, the birthday child also gets breakfast in bed and control over the dinner menu. In Russia, kids get a pie with a message pricked into the crust, and in China they get noodles for lunch.

Decorations

One family I know has a "birthday throne"—a fancy painted chair that's dragged out of the attic only for family birthdays. Other families put out a birthday flag, tie balloons to the lamppost, festoon the birthday child's room with streamers, or spread out a special tablecloth.

Spankings and Stuff

These kinds of customs are common in many cultures—and some kids love them. They're often intended to ward off evil spirits or to symbolically toughen the kid up for the year ahead. In Ireland, the birthday child is held upside down and bumped on the floor, once for each year they've been alive. In Argentina kids get their earlobes tugged.

Special Things for Special Ages

At sixteen you get your driver's license, but at four you're finally old enough to push the buttons on the ATM! In my family growing up, you got your library card at five, your first watch at six, and penny loafers at twelve. I read about a family that gives the kids a new tool for each birthday and then teaches them how to use it. Make up your own special privileges (and responsibilities) for each age.

Power

The birthday child may get to choose his seat in the car, what TV show the family watches, a fun activity, etc.

Weights and Measures

Many families use birthdays as an opportunity to note growth and changes. In addition to the usual height and weight, you might record things like shoe size, handprints (but not butt prints, even though one of my kids thought that'd be a cool tradition), or how much faster they can run from the family room to the kitchen when you open a carton of ice cream.

Altruism

Giving *by* the birthday child, instead of *to* her. My daughter likes to take pet food and toys to the local animal shelter. In my husband's family, the birthday person gives the rest of the family small "unbirthday" presents.

Planning the Better Birthday Party

✳ ✳ ✳

Simple, Short, and Not Too Many Sweets

Birthday-Month Meltdown is a well-known phenomenon. Yes, you read it right: *month.* For the weeks around your child's birthday, pull out all the usual stress-relieving strategies, like reducing demands on her, toning down stimulation (which means less TV and fewer video games, not more), and increasing affectionate touch. Maintain life as usual. Stick to your child's normal schedule and take extra care to see that she's well nourished. Also, remember that the birthday period is not a good time for big changes like potty training

Given that baseline emotional state, you're probably guessing there's no such thing as a perfect party with preschoolers—and you're right—but there are some ways to increase the smiles:tears ratio.

Refuse to Enter the Brat Race

Competitive partying is "in" these days. But having given and attended approximately a zillion birthday parties for little kids *I swear this is true:* the kind of party preschoolers like best is the small, at-home kind with simple games and a slightly mangled cake that they helped bake. If you're dying to give an elaborate party, wait a few years. Older kids are much more likely to appreciate expensive entertainers and elaborate goody bags; party places with costumed characters, flashing lights, and tokens; sleepovers at pricey hotels, etc. All that stuff just overwhelms little guys (and puts their parents' patience in the ICU).

The Guest List

The old guideline is limit the number of guests to your child's age, plus one. That's *still* the best guideline, but you'll probably violate it anyway. Invite kids your child likes, *not* your friends' kids or kids who've invited yours to their parties. If that means your kid gets invited to fewer parties the next year, consider yourself lucky! Also, hold a separate party for the relatives if you must (though they're probably more content than you realize to skip a three-year-old's party). The "guest" I most recommend including is a preteen helper—pay him $10 or $15 and he'll be worth every cent.

Scheduling

The first trick is to hold the party at a high-energy time of day for your kid and you, even if that's breakfast time. The second trick is to keep it short—an hour and a half is *plenty.* And the final trick is not to be limited by the calendar. There's no law that says you have to give a birthday party within a week of the actual date. Two of my kids have birthdays right at the holidays and the third is also a cold-weather-birthday kid. We usually held their "kid parties" in the summer. That meant we could trash the backyard rather than the living room, have some cool themes that didn't work in the snow and slush, and avoid the December party overload. Nobody ever refused to come because it wasn't the kid's actual birthday.

Pick a Kid-Friendly Theme

Themes are really for the adults—keep that in mind if you find yourself up at 4 a.m. trying to sculpt cupcakes into miniature bulldozers. Having said that, a preschooler may be delighted to spend an hour or two focusing on her current passion with her buddies. Involve her in choosing the theme and planning activities and choosing appropriate decorations. Our best theme wasn't particularly traditional (but it was very messy): Things Your Own Mom Won't Let You Do. It really wasn't too bad outdoors. We let the kids do things like shake up pop cans and then open them which was very funny (only no one had sufficient hand strength so we had to open them, which meant *we* got sprayed with pop and that was very, *very* funny). We also let them eat the cake and other refreshments with their hands (and mouths open). Burping was encouraged. In fact, that was one of the activities…

Play Fun Games

At a preschool party, *games should be about doing, not winning.* The same handful of cooperative games can be gussied up to fit almost any theme:

✳ *Musical "chairs."* Or towels, tubs of Jell-O, pretend pirate ships, or whatever. Have the kids double or triple up to fit on the remaining tubs, etc.

✳ *Memory.* Let the kids study a tray of party-themed objects, then remove it and see how many the group recalls.

✳ *Relay races.* Race against the clock or adults who will cheat to lose.

✳ *Stick the ___ on the ____.* You can play this game without a blindfold if the main point is to stick the _____ someplace silly.

✳ *Target toss.* Count up the whole group total or have the kids compete against a klutzy adult.

✳ *Hunts.* These make a good wrap-up activity, especially if you hunt for the goody bag items. Avoid I-didn't-get-as-much-as-he-did tears by specifying a quantity of items to collect, giving out picture-lists of what to find, or tucking the goodies in plastic Easter eggs and assigning a color to each child.

Food

Despite all the fuss about sugar at parties, my experience has been that food is the least interesting part of the party to preschoolers, and most of them eat little if anything. Serve a healthy-ish thing first, like crustless sandwiches, cheese, or fruit kabobs if you must. Then give *small* pieces of cake or mini-cupcakes or something. Skip the ice cream—or substitute it for cake. My only other tip is to make the food an activity—let kids decorate it themselves. It uses up time, saves you trouble, and often cuts down on how much they actually eat. Also, check with parents about allergies in advance and save yourself at-the-party headaches.

Presents

Think of opening them as a learning experience for everyone, and it may make you less crazy. If you have a circle of nice parents, try to get them to agree on a low dollar limit for party gifts—better for family budgets and better for the gettee too. If you have a super-altruistic kid, he might agree to ask for donations to the food pantry or the local animal shelter instead of for more plastic junk for herself. (My own kids were in their teens before anything like that was acceptable—and I think that's typical—but I do hear periodically about saintly children. Maybe they're just urban legends…)

Open presents near the end of the party (just before the goody bags), have a lottery to decide the order of opening, and zip through the whole thing quickly.

I wish we would go back to the olden days when it was enough to thank the giver at the party, but since thank-you notes are de rigueur now, make it easy for your *kid* to do the thanking. For example, snap a photo of your kid with each giver and gift. Later your kid can put a "Thank You" sticker on the back and "sign" his name. Let him stick the stamps on the envelopes too; it will only add another forty-five minutes or so and cost you an extra $2.79 in postage accidentally stuck to the wrong places.

Goody Bags

Keep them simple! My sister's strategy is the best, I think. She raids her bin of fast-food toys, crap from other goody bags, etc., and assembles completely different *opaque* goody bags for each child. Hand these out as the kids leave, and they'll never know they didn't get the same things. And chances are good that your child won't notice how her own goody stash has shrunk because she'll be too busy with all her new stuff!

Party Poopers Should Use the Toilet

✳ ✳ ✳

More Lessons to Teach Your Birthday-Party Animal

Dropping your child off for his first solo birthday party can be nerve-wracking. Will he have an "accident" because he doesn't know where the bathroom is? Tackle his opponents in musical chairs? Show off his skill in farting the birthday song? Relax—he's bound to have a faux pas or two (or ten), but so are most of the other guests! Nonetheless, you can improve the odds of good—well, *adequate*—behavior by teaching him basic party etiquette. And making him go potty before you leave for the party.

Rule One: It's the Birthday Child's Special Day

So it's your child's job as guest to help the birthday child feel special. If he's not sure what to do, like whether he should rip the paper off the gifts or blow out the candles himself, all he has to do is think about what would feel most special for the birthday kid. Okay, that probably won't work. Instead, play What If? for every potential party situation you can think up.

Make a Gracious Entrance

Practice with a pretend present. Show your child how to ring the bell, say "Happy Birthday!" and fork over the gift. It sounds simple—but to a preschooler it's like multivariate analysis. Also, make an effort to arrive more or less on time; it's never too soon to start teaching your child about being punctual.

Use Party Manners

You'll be teaching these lessons repeatedly for the next eighteen years. Practice one new rule at a time. Some to teach:

✳ *Stay in the party area.* If you need to leave it, like to go to the bathroom, tell a grown-up.

✳ *Wait your turn.* Usually the birthday child gets to go first. Maybe once or twice you can go second.

✳ *Win or lose, stay calm.* The point is to have fun playing.

✳ *Let the birthday child open the gifts, blow out the candles, etc.* Let the grown-ups hand out gifts to be opened even though it's hard to wait. Also, the birthday kid gets to *keep* the present you brought.

Playing Let's Pretend It's Cinderella's Birthday Bash! or simply throwing regular Teddy-Bear Tea Parties gives kids low pressure opportunities to learn how to curl their pinkies gracefully or at least to say "Excu-u-u-se me!" when they forget and belch loudly.

Depart Graciously

Practice this too. Show your child how to thank both the birthday child and the adults. Explore what to say if he likes or loathes the goody bag. Talk about why it's important to leave promptly and quietly.

Tips for Special Situations

These are little kids we're talking about, so special situations are kind of the norm. Chances are pretty good that one or both of the following circumstances will apply to either your child or a guest or two at his party.

✳ *Dietary or activity restrictions.* Talk to the adult hosting the party in advance and remind her at the door. But keep in mind that harried adults can forget things despite good intentions, so rehearse with your child what he can say and do if there's something he can't eat or participate in. You might consider offering a consolation prize if he remembers to follow your rules.

✳ *Separation anxiety.* If your child is reserved, opt for attending small parties with a few familiar friends at first. Try to let your child know what to expect (like who else is coming, what activities are planned). Rehearse the party with dolls or puppets, and read stories like ALFIE LENDS A HAND by Shirley Hughes. Some kids may find it easier to carpool to the party so that they enter with a buddy in hand. Toting a security object helps many kids too. Be a few minutes early for pickup if possible.

CHAPTER FIVE

Fighting Fears, Fancies, and Foibles

***

I can almost guarantee that every parent who picks up this book will check out this chapter. That's because the typical preschooler has enough irrational fears, quirks, and bothersome behaviors to qualify as an Official Eccentric, even if she doesn't actually take in dozens of stray cats or insist on storing her urine in glass jars (as Howard Hughes reportedly did). Although she *may*—young children have done far stranger things. In fact, when I looked up clinical definitions of eccentricity for this chapter, I was struck by how much the descriptions of people with significant pathology sounded like those of typical preschoolers. Genius may be next to insanity, but apparently so is early childhood. This fact should make you relax right off the bat—your kid is like every other preschooler and thus completely normal!

Speaking of urine, eccentricity, and preschoolers, when my husband Steve was a tyke, he developed an unusual hobby after the birth of his twin siblings. Long potty-trained, he started taking target practice at a certain spot on the carpet in his room. His mother kept wondering why his room smelled so bad and was cleaning ever more frantically. Then one day, she caught him in the act, and, wise and understanding mother that she was and is, she put two and two together and figured that Steve was expressing his feelings about the newcomers in his life. Even then, after sympathetic discussions, offers of better ways to express his feelings, and gallons of carpet cleaner, his room retained an aroma of ammonia for several weeks until Steve discovered that he preferred sports that involved a ball.

Which brings me to the reasons for this chapter:

While it's comforting to know that your child's behavior is normal and perhaps even sort of rational from the point of view of someone about three feet tall, her oddball practices aren't necessarily something you care to live with.

Knowing why a kid does something doesn't mean you can change the behavior easily. Once kids discover that buzzy bees are formidable foes or become convinced that a monster has taken up residence in their underwear drawer, you're going to be hard-pressed to persuade them that buzzy bees are their friends and that monsters much prefer to live in the cookie jar. Similarly, after kids discover the joys of swearing and nose picking, it can be hard to make them forsake these activities.

Even though change is hard and takes ingenuity and patience, *it is possible.* And that's why I have this chapter full of suggestions on what to try if your child is unable to eat dinner because you bought the wrong brand of napkins or has decided to go pro now that he's getting so good at lying.

In closing, I have one disclaimer: Although I'm willing to guarantee that you'll read this chapter *and* that my ideas are fabulous, I'd be crazy to guarantee they'll work every time. Preschoolers may be nutty, but they're also tricky. Best wishes!

The Fear Factor

* * *

Taming Preschool Phobias

When my kids were small, I thought we lived in the House of Phobia. For example, my daughter required us to take a *long* detour to the children's room at the library so we could bypass the clown mural along the stairway that terrified her; my middle son was turned to gelatin by anything that made loud noises, including the vacuum cleaner, flushing toilets, thunderstorms, and Munchkin soccer teams; and my oldest son had us doing the vigilante thing every night to prevent bad guys from creeping into our house and slithering under his bed. And besides those entrenched worries, we had to deal with more transient suspicions of such scary things as birthday candles and oversized umbrellas.

Chances are good that your preschooler is driving you crazy with one or more powerful fears—perhaps of classics like water, dogs, darkness, doctors, fire engines, costumed characters, separation, or monsters, or perhaps of something quirkier, like ladies' lingerie. Sadly, there's no quick cure for most preschool terrors, but the following tips may ease your mind and keep your kid's quivers to a minimum. And keep this in mind: if your child develops a genuine phobia—a severe, persistent fear that impairs his daily life—seek professional help.

Remember That "This Too Shall Pass"

Most preschool fears are developmentally driven: they emerge as a result of a child's maturing brain and expanding experience, and typically vanish via the same route (though I'll admit my daughter is wary around clowns to this day). Thus you usually can't wish, reason, or hurry your child's fears away. Meanwhile, keep in mind that a preschooler's fears may in fact be healthy and serve useful purposes. For example, it's smart to be wary of outlandishly dressed people who smile too much.

Be Respectful

Forget trying to toughen up a scaredy cat by calling him one or telling him that his fear is silly. For one thing, it won't work, and for another, it hurts his feelings. (Though if you do need to laugh about it—and who can help but laugh about a fear of golf umbrellas—run into the bathroom and pretend you're laughing about something else, like the crazy way Daddy hung the toilet-paper roll.) Acknowledge his feelings, assure him of your support, and let him know that he will overcome the fear in time.

Temper Your Own Reactions

Come on, be honest—do you sometimes shriek when a buzzy bee appears? or at least flinch? Your perceptive preschooler is paying close attention to your emotional messages and believing *them* rather than your reassuring words.

Provide Coping Skills

The most important thing for you to do during these years is not to bust each individual fear, but to teach your child approaches for dealing with his fears; after all, everyone feels irrationally scared sometimes. Here are some of the best coping strategies for preschoolers:

✳ *Talk it up.* For some kids, simply talking about a potentially scary situation in advance is enough to make it manageable. Acknowledge his feelings, suggest coping strategies (like shutting his eyes if an amusement park ride gets too scary), and let him know you think he's capable even though he may still feel frightened. Once he's survived the scary experience, don't forget to praise him for being brave; knowing he got through one tough situation once may also make it easier to handle future ones. However, if thinking about something scary that's coming up just makes your kid an anxious, obsessive mess, skip this strategy until he's older.

✳ *Avoidance.* Contrary to popular belief, you don't usually have to worry about turning your child into a wimp if you let him avoid the thing he fears. Go ahead and provide a night-light to the child who's afraid of the dark, offer a raincoat to the tot who's spooked by umbrellas, and let the clown-o-phobic sort cover his eyes at the circus. Praise your child for thinking up a solution that works. The important thing is to keep offering opportunities to try the feared thing again, and keep reassuring that the fear will pass.

✳ *Hold a hand.* If your child is afraid of something that can't be avoided, like the doctor, remember that everything's less scary when you're not alone. If you can't be right with your child, help him think up a stand-in who can give him courage, like a special stuffed animal.

* *Metaphoric approaches.* A bottle of water labeled "Monster-Away Spray" often soothes a nervous child at bedtime. Try making up magic spells to banish imaginary fears, lighting imaginary candles in the dark, or wearing a cape or something like a St. Francis medal for general protection.

Fear-Busting Techniques

These strategies may speed the rate at which your kid overcomes his fear.

* *Prevent general fearfulness.* One of the best ways to minimize the number and variety of your child's fears may be to monitor media exposure, especially to TV and videos. Visual images from the news can be particularly scary.

* *Gradual desensitization.* Getting used to a feared situation bit by bit helps many kids. If your child is afraid of dogs, read books and watch videos about dogs. Then look at real dogs from a distance. Slowly move closer. Try getting to know a small, calm old dog before meeting a big dog or a boisterous puppy.

* *Peer pressure.* A brave friend can reverse a fear almost magically. Although it may be hard to orchestrate, it doesn't hurt to hang out with fearless buddies.

* *Two steps forward, one step back.* Encourage your child to try a feared situation once, giving him permission to back away again after his brave attempt. Eventually he may garner enough experiences with golf umbrellas to carry one himself!

* *Jump in the deep end.* This technique can easily backfire, so I don't recommend it usually—*especially not for getting over a fear of water.* But sometimes a kid has no choice but to confront a fear. For example, you take your kid to putt-putt, there's a rainstorm, and everyone on the course breaks out golf umbrellas. In this situation, you might as well coax your child under the nearest one and keep your fingers crossed that he has a good experience.

Play-It-Again Sams

* * *

Introducing Change to Children Who Love Sameness

Some people like to leap into the pool. Other people like to ease in gradually. Still others would rather not get in the pool at all. In fact, they'd prefer not to change out of the Spider-Man shirt they've worn for the last week and into a bathing suit. Or get slathered with sunscreen, or climb in the car, or make any of the other changes involved in going to the pool. Given a choice, these folks would just like to stay where they are, contentedly stuffing Legos in the heating vent. These people are called *little kids*.

Not that all little kids resist change. But enough do that people are constantly asking me what to do about their kid who won't eat anything but grilled-cheese sandwiches for lunch or won't wear shorts once winter ends, no matter how hot it gets. These tips help stubborn kids ease into changes.

Minimize Changes

Obvious, but often overlooked. If you have a child for whom change is torture, arrange her day to minimize the number of times she has to make adjustments, and make as many shifts as possible part of the normal routine. For instance, if she hates to change her clothes, have her put on the next day's clothes after her bath; that way you skip both the change into pajamas and the morning get-dressed fight.

Forewarned Is Forearmed

Give five-minute warnings before the end of any activity (use a timer whenever possible), look at next season's fashions in catalogs *before* the weather changes, or casually mention on Sunday that Monday is a holiday so your child will be going to Gram's house to play instead of to daycare. Picture charts of changes help too. For example, make a collage or scrapbook showing all the things that are different in winter, such as the different clothing, activities, weather, etc. Finally, predicting how your child might feel can help. Say something like "You'll feel out of sorts at first when school ends, but then you'll get used to vacation and be happy again."

Educate

Some kids resist change because they don't understand it. For example, if the peanut-butter sandwich is cut in triangles instead of squares, your kid might have a meltdown because it looks different. So you explain that it's the same bread, the same peanut butter, everything the same except the shape.

Ha, ha, ha! Okay, that doesn't work—in the short run at any rate. But over the years, your child will probably internalize your explanations, and *eventually* she'll be able to talk herself through the mis-cut sandwich scenario and choke it down. Of course by then, she'll be old enough to make her own sandwich and cut it however she likes it...

Buy Multiples of Necessities

If your child will only drink her milk out of the pink cup, buy several of them. And buy multiples of preferred clothing or bedding, etc. If your child is SUPER picky about shoes like my middle one was, buy the same pair in several sizes, so you have a replacement ready when she outgrows hers and the style is no longer available anywhere on the planet and she won't wear anything else, so she has to limp around town with her toes curled up and you lie awake worrying about podiatrists and the child welfare folks.

Wait, you say, *isn't this approach just giving in and pandering to a child's foolish whims?*

Yes.

But little kids *are* foolish and whimsical, and consistency helps them feel more secure. Sometimes it works best to see them not as terrorists making unreasonable demands, but as helpless critters needing an anchor or two.

Acclimate and Overlap

Many kids adapt more gracefully when changes are gradual. So a week (or more precisely, six days) before daylight saving time ends, start putting your child to bed ten minutes later each night (It's "fall back," right?), so that by the time the day arrives, he's right on schedule. Or, if she hates the change from long pants to short ones, cuff her pants so they're slightly shorter each day or switch to capris before trying shorts. Or if she insists on listening to the same horrible book about vampire bats every single night, try reading that one *and* a second different one.

Accentuate the Obvious

…which is that change is always happening, and your child is always adjusting. Help her notice, for instance, how her heart rate changes when she goes from resting to exercising and back to resting again. Have her balance on one foot and talk about how she has to shift her weight to maintain her balance. Then praise her for being such an adaptable person. Why, you bet she's the kind of flexible person who could drink her milk out of a *green* cup, if, say, the pink cup got chewed up by the dog. Right?

Relabel Change

Bill something new as actually familiar, in a way. Avoid using words like "new" and instead apply the word "old" liberally, as in "Oh look, here are your favorite *old* pants you wore all last winter. How nice it will be to wear them again!" If her memory's not great, you might not have to be strictly accurate…

Let Me Do It Myself!

✳ ✳ ✳

Living Safely with Pint-Sized DIY-Types

When my oldest was in his can't-do-anything-without-help jellyfish stage, I naively envied the parents of the brash, independent preschoolers I saw strutting about the park and preschool. Then my own kid moved into the DIY stage, and I found myself longing for a return to the jellyfish days. The can-do phase, it turns out, comes with its own annoyances, primarily the need to budget HUGE blocks of time for activities like dressing, eating, getting in and out of the car seat, bathing, toileting, breathing, etc., plus another HUGE block of time to deal with the frustration tantrum that follows when the kid's skills aren't up to snuff. Plus *safety* issues. Because not only will your preschooler want to manage zippers himself, he'll want to climb tall ladders to tackle roof repairs. If your child has a "challenging" temperament, you'll probably find these periods of development (typically at ages two, four, and six) to be particularly taxing. These tips, though, may keep you out of the nuthouse, or at least the emergency room. And for parents of more laidback kids, they can help your child develop competence while minimizing frustration.

OSHA for Preschoolers

Keeping your kid safe at this age means you'll have to both increase childproofing and loosen strictures as your child grows; it's tricky, ever changing, and different from kid to kid, so be prepared to adjust your structure and rules on a regular basis.

Remove, hide, or lock up temptations like matches and lighters, hand and power tools, knives and sharp scissors, *guns and ammunition,* ladders, and other dangers. Remember your child can probably find, reach, and use things he couldn't access at a younger age—you need an extra layer or two of childproofing now. I recommend combination locks.

Arrange your home so that your kid can do as much for himself as possible. You might as well take advantage of his urge for independence.

Set core safety rules like "You always have to let me know where you are." This rule can keep the kid from climbing on the roof and from going off with strangers.

Loosen rules as kids demonstrate competence and achieve milestones. Although your child will be ten before he can cross the street all by himself (really—that's what studies show), around the age of four he can trot across a quiet residential street without holding your hand after *you* check for traffic.

Teach Skills and Provide Safe Opportunities

Many product-safety guidelines and child-safety recommendations are aimed at kids who are either unsupervised or inexperienced. With training and/or close (i.e., touching distance) supervision, most youngsters can participate in at least some activities that would otherwise be too dangerous. Keep in mind that teaching your kids that the world is a dangerous place that they'll never be competent to navigate on their own is as risky in its own way as letting them jump off the roof.

Children can use many seemingly unsafe tools, like hammers and some cooking equipment, provided you show them how to use them safely and supervise carefully. Fire-starting materials and power tools are obvious exceptions.

Look for equipment adapted for younger children, such as rounded scissors, lightweight gardening tools, blunt plastic sewing needles, plastic or flatware knives instead of paring knives, and so on. Keep in mind that these tools will not usually work as well as the real thing.

Provide appropriate classes or tutoring for the DIY types. Or teach them the skills you feel comfortable with. Gymnastics and dance classes, martial arts instruction, and many other sports opportunities are especially good for kids with energy to burn and a desire to try out risky behaviors. Look also for low transverse (sideways) climbing walls for monkey types, as well as traditional swing sets and play structures. Be sure to install adequate cushioning beneath.

Halt Impulsive Kids in Their Tracks— Or at Least Make Sure They Have a Safety Net

Kids who act without thinking are especially at risk during expansive periods of development. Your job is both to keep them safe now *and* to start building internal controls for their behavior for the future.

Fire setting is one of the riskiest behaviors that can emerge during the preschool years. Although most preschoolers never play with fire, it often has disastrous consequences when they do. Having a parent who smokes puts kids at increased risk. Keep all fire materials out of reach and *locked up.*

If you find matches or lighters in your child's room, or see evidence that there's been a fire in a hidden place like a closet, seek professional advice.

Post visual reminders in places where kids are at risk (around play equipment, in the kitchen, driveway, or car, etc.). Put up laminated picture signs to remind them of safety rules. Use driveway cones, chalk lines, colored flags, or other boundary markers to help them stay out of the street or other dangerous areas. And be sure to praise them often and promptly for remembering and following rules.

If you notice your child about to leap into a dangerous activity, say, "Ding, ding, ding! Warning bells!" Have him stop and discuss how (or whether) to do the activity safely. With luck, in time he'll hear his own warning bells in his head and stop himself. Or try a metaphor like a stoplight (teach them to imagine a red light before they decide to do something) or pushing their "magic button" (belly button) to stop and think before acting. You'll have to talk a preschooler through these metaphors *many* times before you see results, but I have known them to help many impulsive kids.

Finally, ask those determined go-getters the right questions: Where is their parachute? Or their safety net, spotter, helmet and knee pads, or lifeguard? Let kids know they can engage in many seemingly risky activities, provided they have proper safety equipment and support, and then consistently enforce rules about using safety equipment and human helpers.

Un-Civil Disobedience— And Too-Civil Obedience

✳ ✳ ✳

Helping Kids Who Won't—Or Always Will

Oppositional behavior, shyness, overcompliance, and gullibility can be the result of your child's personality, her stage of development, or a reaction to pressures in her life (or some combination of the above), and it can be hard to tease out what's a temporary stage versus an ongoing style or problem. Fortunately, similar strategies can help you nudge your child's behavior in a reasonable direction, whatever the causes of her behavior.

The Oppositional Child

This child says, "I won't!" and she really won't. This behavior pattern is developmentally common at the even ages—two, four, and six—and probably worst at age four, which is sometimes described as the out-of-bounds age. These strategies help:

* *Pick your battles.* Save demands and disagreements for safety issues, schedule musts, and major social concerns. Try to let everything else go.

* *Offer two good choices.* Instead of issuing a command, offer two options that are acceptable to you. (Bonus tip: oppositional kids tend to have a pattern of always picking either Choice A or Choice B; once you figure out your child's pattern, you may be able to influence her choices.)

* *Accentuate the positive.* Praise good behavior often (at least five praises per criticism or correction—good advice for all people, really), and promote autonomy so you don't have to direct your child's behavior as much. Also, build your child's attachment to you by touching her as often as she can tolerate (may need to be vigorous touching like bear hugs or roughhousing), smiling at her, and finding things to laugh about together.

* *Use active listening techniques.* Restate what she says to you, and help her label her feelings.

* *Rely on natural consequences.* If she doesn't wear her coat on a cool day, she'll feel chilly but she won't die. But obviously you won't let her discover the consequences of anything truly dangerous the hard way.

The Reserved Child

This style typically has a strong temperament component, though it may fade over time. It's not really a problem to be overcome unless it's getting in the way of your child's learning or ability to enjoy herself. Some techniques that help her:

* *Allow extra time.* Give her a chance to watch others before she attempts something new.

❋ *Lend your physical support.* Let this child hold your hand or lean on you (which will drive you crazy on hot, humid days). For years all my purses had the straps safety-pinned together because my reserved daughter broke them by hanging on them constantly. Try to be relaxed and friendly—these kids are remarkably sensitive to messages from your body—though for me that was easier said than done.

❋ *Be careful with labels.* Instead of thinking of your child as shy or a wimp, call her pensive, private, or considerate, and praise her for looking before she leaps.

❋ *Teach scripts.* Practice what to say or do in new situations, and help her anticipate what will happen or how others might react.

The Overly Compliant Child

Parents and teachers usually love this child. The odd years tend to be more cooperative ages, so a child who's like this at three or five may be just going through a phase. Or you may have a kid who's just a sweetie. But keep in mind that this kid can be at risk compared to her feisty peers; she usually won't stop to process whether it's a good idea to do what she's told. The other concern for me is that this style can be a red flag for an overstressed child; it often emerges during or following a family crisis. These strategies can help keep this child safe and give her the courage to be herself.

❋ *Teach safety rules.* Especially about preventing abduction and sexual abuse. Visit the website for the American Academy of Pediatrics (www.aap.org) and search "prevent child abduction" to obtain the latest recommendations for keeping kids safe.

❋ *Teach kids to question.* Of course you'll praise your child for being so cooperative (and pat yourself on the back for being such a good parent). Then encourage your kid to question authority when her gut tells her something isn't right.

❋ *Help your child know her own mind.* Offer her no-lose choices, reassuring her that either choice is good. Praise her when she expresses an opinion or strong feelings. Use stories and puppet play to support her and teach her it's okay to think for herself, and even to be naughty sometimes.

The Gullible Child

This child is loads of fun for older siblings who are sure to take advantage of her. Being gullible is developmentally normal among all preschoolers; some are just more so than others. These tips can help preserve this child's sweetness while also helping her hang onto her dignity and safety.

✳ *Protect her.* Stop older siblings, peers, and others who enjoy tricking her in mean ways or daring her in dangerous ones. Discourage her from *ever* accepting dares, especially from those who get a kick out of fooling her.

✳ *Play games like Truth or Goof?* Describe something that might have happened, like "An elephant sat on the coffee table last night and broke it!" and ask her whether it might be the truth or it's just silly. Also describe different scenarios and ask whether they're a good idea or "plum crazy."

✳ *Let her check in with you…*and teach her a signal to use when she wants to ask whether something is reasonable or not.

✳ *Help her do a gut check.* Have her stop and ask herself if something feels inside like it's true or a good idea.

Speak No Evil

✳ ✳ ✳

At Least Not with Those Words!
At Least Not in Front of Grandma!

You'll be so proud of your child's expanding vocabulary—until your little angel learns to say the *F* word. Loudly. Proudly. And in the presence of your most sanctimonious neighbor. Try these ideas to keep your child from winning the Annual Longshoreman Colorful Language Competition.

Zip Your Own Lip

…and turn off the telly. And the radio. Even then, short of locking your kid up in a convent, you probably can't keep him from picking up naughty language; he'll acquire it in carpool or from the shopper with line rage at the supermarket. But most of the time, the preschool badword phase passes quickly unless your child is hearing people he admires use inappropriate language on a regular basis.

Be Underwhelmed

Two-year-olds swear because they like to copy grownups. Four-year-olds, on the other hand, swear to shock. Thus, at this age a mild (or even bored) reaction to your kid's language has the greatest chance of eliminating it. (Remember this strategy for when your kid reaches adolescence too.) Meanwhile, if the diarrhea giggles are driving you bonkers, you can also try some of these other strategies.

✳ *Potty talk belongs…*in the potty! Or anywhere else that grownups can't hear it. This excellent rule, repeated frequently, and in a calm voice, doesn't eliminate swearing, but it does strike a balance between a four-year-old's compulsion to say "poop" or "stinky underpants" sixteen zillion times and the rest of the household's desire for a little decorum.

✳ *Dang nabbit!* Using words to drain off anger or frustration actually represents maturation over strategies like hitting or shrieking. Except for those with teenage siblings, most are happy to learn "nice bad words" instead of the X-rated ones. Some to try: *fiddlesticks, broccoli sprockets, pooky, gosh darn it,* and, for the young sophisticate, *zut alors!* Or challenge your child to invent her own naughty phrases. Boost the *verboten* appeal of these alternatives by making it clear that your child should save his "swears" for desperate moments.

✳ *The college-fund technique.* My sister Anna, who has *five* boys and therefore lots of salty language (not to mention noise, action figures, and general insanity) about her house, charges her kids for swearing, varying the amount by age. She deposits the fines in jars for their college funds. If your little one has no money (or is unfazed by losing it) you could fine him in TV time or other privileges instead.

"You Can't Come to My Party" and Other Mean Words

During the preschool years, not only do you have to worry about kid swears like *doo-doo head* and occasional adult language, you also have to deal with words meant to threaten, belittle, exclude, and boast. This kind of verbal aggression is normal, and again, it's really a big improvement over pinching and biting. But it is meant to hurt, and you want to teach your child that hurting—even with words—isn't allowed. Usually, a mild correction and redirection will suffice. Say something like "That hurts people when you talk that way. If you want to play alone with Lisa for a bit, just tell Sam, 'Sorry, I'm busy now.'" If you notice your child is constantly using words to hurt, impose consequences like time-outs until he gets his words under control, and use puppet play and stories to teach him more appropriate ways to interact with others. If that doesn't work, seek professional help. Although serious behavior disorders are rare, many first appear during the preschool years, and they are easier to treat before they become entrenched.

Lies and the Lying Liars Who Tell Them

✳ ✳ ✳

The Truth about Preschoolers and the Truth

Preschoolers lie. I know this from personal experience. For example, when I was about five, I bragged to my younger sister that I'd been on the TV show Romper Room (not true), but she didn't get to be on it too because the host, Miss Nancy, thought I was cuter and smarter than her (doubly not true). This lie was only one of many I told Anna during those years, and I quickly forgot about it—but she didn't! She only learned the truth thirty years later when I overheard her telling one of my kids about the time I was on TV and she wasn't.

Which brings me to the many reasons preschoolers lie, most of which are relatively innocent and benign: because they wish something was true, to boost their status, or to get an interesting reaction from someone. Preschoolers also lie because of their growing imaginations and a hazy sense of the difference between real and pretend. They also might say something untrue because they have forgotten or misunderstood what really happened. Finally, during the preschool period, some kids start to lie for the reasons that upset adults the most: to avoid punishment or get something they want. Understanding the motivation of your junior con artist is important so you respond appropriately, first by not getting too worked up, and second by providing education about the problems and consequences of not being truthful.

Don't Ask, Do Tell

Discourage a habit of lying by not setting your child up to lie. Thus, when you know your child has done something wrong, *don't ask her if she did it.* State what you know and calmly impose reasonable (and usually small) consequences for the misbehavior.

And While You're at It, Don't Say "Liar, Liar, Pants on Fire"

Labeling your kid a liar is likely to guarantee she keeps lying: kids who perceive themselves as liars act accordingly.

Acknowledge the Feelings behind a Lie

It's generally a snap to catch a preschooler who's lying, because most are *terrible* liars. Look for hesitation, eyes shifted to one side, outrageous statements. But rather than getting into an argument about whether he's being truthful or not, just say something like "You wish you hadn't spilled the carton of milk in my underwear drawer." That type of reaction is more likely to help a child appreciate the difference between what's true and what's not—and point her in the direction of the preferred behavior for the next time—than punishing her for lying is.

Help Kids Make Things Right

Reduce the likelihood of future lies by helping your child atone for her mistakes. For example, have her help you mop up the milk out of your drawer. And say she's sorry.

Then forgive her for her misbehavior.

Make Honesty the Best Policy—Most of the Time

Set a good example. This is not always easy, especially since it's often easier to lie to your child than to tell an uncomfortable truth (like, saying that you lost a toy when you actually threw it away). If your child does catch you in a lie, apologize, explain why you lied, and make amends if appropriate.

Reward truth telling by your child or others. Offer mild praise, a hug, or other forms of approval. Incidents with friends or family members, on children's TV shows, and in books give you chances to point out honesty and the good consequences of being trustworthy.

Fun Fooling and Nice Not-So's: For the Rest of the Time

Here's where I break with those who recommend All Honesty, All the Time. I believe there are times when a little dishonesty is fun, kinder, or simply harmless and expedient. For example, fictional stories, magic tricks, silliness, and *gotcha* lies (like when your child tells you Daddy bought you a giraffe for your birthday) are all examples of fun lies. We'd also rather our kid not respond, "It's the ugliest thing I've ever seen and I wouldn't wear it in a million years," when Great Aunt Lulu asks whether she likes the pom-pom sweater she knitted for her, regardless of how true that statement is. Better to teach her to tell a half lie—to find something true yet kind to say, like, "I really like the color" and omit the rest. These are difficult distinctions, and ones you'll need to teach gradually, tolerating many errors in either direction as your child learns.

Playing Fast and Loose with the Truth

Games are one of the best ways to teach the difference between real and pretend, reinforce honesty, and teach the subtleties of trustworthy behavior. Some to try:

✳ *What a Whopper!* When you catch your child exaggerating to boost her status with a buddy, take her idea and run with it! For example, if she says she's so strong she can carry her daddy, smile and say, "Oh yeah? I'm so strong I can carry an elephant! Even ten elephants!" Then give her friend a turn. Continue to one up each other until everyone's exhausted or laughing so hard they're peeing their pants. (Bonus Tip: To protect your own feelings, skip the your-mama-is-so-ugly version of this game.)

✳ *What If?* Great for car time. Describe a situation like, "What if I was just going to sniff your chocolate Easter Bunny a little but then I accidentally ate the ears off? What should I do?" Use this game to have fun, learn how to admit to mistakes or make amends and to underscore times when your child *must* be truthful with you, like if an adult asks her to keep a secret that feels yucky or when she has done something potentially dangerous (like chewed the whole bottle of vitamin gumballs).

✳ *Puppet Government.* Use puppet play to introduce the concept of an "inner voice" that reminds kids of right and wrong. Tote-along finger puppets are especially nice for this job. And if years from now your kid complains that her conscience speaks to her in a high, squeaky voice, tell her you're sorry, you simply can't imagine how that happened...

Cheats and Thieves

✳ ✳ ✳

More Preschool Vices and What to Do about Them

I cheat at games with little kids. Really.

To lose! Geez, what kind of a meanie do you think I am? Sometimes I figure it's better to have me doing the cheating than to tempt little kids to cheat, and sometimes—well, more of the time—I cheat to lose because I'm just not in the mood to handle a frustration temper tantrum.

Which brings me to why preschoolers cheat. Because they want to win. But also because they don't really understand the rules, or even the concept that games should have fixed, fair rules. Or they "forget." They steal for much the same reasons—because they want things and because they haven't quite grasped the intricacies of ownership. So when you try to stamp out cheating and thieving, you have to deal with motivation. Use these suggestions to nudge your child in the direction of virtue and integrity.

Teach Guidelines and Attitudes

A lot of your job during the preschool years is teaching your child rules that seem so obvious to us adults that it's hard to believe we have to teach them. Like *don't lick doorknobs*. And *don't change the rules of games so that you always win*, and *don't take the money you found sitting on the counter at your friend's house*. Most of these lessons, unfortunately, are best taught during the "teachable moments" that occur when your child makes mistakes. Calmly but firmly stop your child, state the guideline, and help him make corrections or amends.

In addition, keep teaching the Golden Rule. Have your child play lots of pretending games, read stories, and talk about incidents so he improves his ability to put himself in another's shoes. Reinforce these values by being a good role model. Have your kid go back to the store with you when you realize that the cashier gave you too much change. Let him notice what a polite fan you are at his soccer games. When you greet him after T-ball, don't ask who won, but whether he had fun. (If winning seems the point, kids are tempted to cheat.) Your kid won't learn the ins and outs of honesty overnight, but your efforts to teach him WILL have an impact over time.

Reduce Temptation

This is just another version of childproofing. Just as you wouldn't leave matches lying around, don't play challenging games that tempt your child to cheat. During the preschool years, you should stick mostly with games of chance (like Candy Land) where he'll win his share of times, or cooperative games, where all the players work together to succeed, or games that fit his skill level (like Concentration). Most kids aren't ready to play formal board games in a remotely fair way until they're at least four, and many perfectly normal kids can't handle the social demands of playing games until six.

In addition, reduce opportunities for kids to take things that don't belong to them. Put the cookie jar out of easy reach, and store your own valuables where it's hard for sticky fingers to take them or leave them covered with Fruit Roll-Up gunk.

But Preserve Some Teachable Moments

Most kids need to screw up and suffer the consequences occasionally. That's why I recommend having your preschooler sometimes play games with siblings and peers who won't let him get away with taking two spins in Chutes and Ladders or rearranging the Candy Land deck. And keep the cookie jar where a little ingenuity or physical prowess puts it within his reach. Just make sure you'll usually catch him in the act.

As with lying, when you know your child has done wrong, don't ask. Just state what he did wrong, and help him correct his mistake. If he keeps making the same mistake over and over, he's probably testing limits. Then it's reasonable to impose a small punishment that fits the crime, like "benching" (being excluded from the action for a period of time), or charging a fine (money, if he values it, or some other important possession or privilege).

Top-Dog Tactics

If you want to cut way down on cheating and stealing, give him opportunities to get what he wants. Give kids ways to earn toys they want, keep a running birthday list, and make sure you present small opportunities to be the chooser or the special guy. You can give each child one day a week to be in charge of decisions, like what you have for dinner, or to pick the video they watch while you have your afternoon tea.

Teach Your Child How To Be Disappointed and Frustrated

Disappointment and frustration are universal experiences—and people rarely die from them. You can help your child learn how to handle these emotions in several ways.

First, offer sympathy without fixing the problem by saying something like, "It feels lousy when you want a candy bar but can't have one, doesn't it?" Show him how to drain strong feelings in positive ways by labeling them, talking about them, and exercising hard.

Next, teach him positive self-talk. Help him attribute his successes to hard work and his failures to correctable conditions. Encourage him to distract himself by moving on to another activity.

Finally, praise him for *any* improvement in how he handles losing or not getting something he wants. (i.e., "I'm very proud of you for staying calmer this time when Phineas beat you at War. You remembered not to throw the cards.")

And While We're at It, Nose Picking

✳ ✳ ✳

Tempering Habits That Drive Parents Crazy

Preschoolers and bad habits go together like fingers and nostrils. Preschoolers are also remarkably inventive (and flexible) about their bad habits, so no sooner have you stamped out nose picking, than hair twirling pops up. Time, fortunately, will take care of many of these "tensional outlets," as some developmental experts euphemistically call them. Meanwhile, you may have some luck with the following approaches to habit taming. (Also see tips for dealing with sucking habits on pages 24–26 and for coping with masturbation on pages 199–201.)

Grit Your Teeth and Ignore It

This is usually the best approach for any habits, like stuttering or hair twirling, that don't constitute a major social faux pas or have adverse health consequences. I'm not claiming it's an easy strategy—but it nearly always works. Eventually.

Set Limits

This technique is easier on parents' nerves while still accommodating kids' urges to do things like pick at their nails or stick their tongues in and out like a snake. Designate a private area (like their rooms or the old refrigerator carton the kids decorated to look like the Goodyear Blimp) as "The Habit Place." When your kid needs to spend a few minutes working on her nose goobers—or you need five minutes to whine about the changes in the tax code—there's an acceptable place to do so.

You can also set a limit on the number of times or minutes a day someone's allowed to engage in a habit. Let's say your kid's habit is flicking your fingernails while she sucks her thumb—you can allot her ten minutes a day to do it, either in small increments or all at once.

Make It Inconvenient or Difficult

Give kids a task to do first and/or make them do something bothersome immediately afterwards. For example, you might make nail biters wash their hands first and nose pickers fetch a tissue. Plus, send the nose pickers to the bathroom to scrub their hands afterward too. Do this every time you catch them, and before long they may conclude the gratification isn't worth the bother.

Similarly, you can reduce habits like nail biting by cutting nails very short. Hair chewers can have their locks shorn or tied back in a hard-to-reach ponytail.

Offer a Reward

If your kid is motivated *herself* to give up a habit, rewards can provide necessary support. You can always use the old sticker-chart-and-treat method. Just start off with modest goals, like only picking her nose three times a day, so she can be successful. Or you can try a technique like "Ten Nickels" (or other incentive). Give your child ten nickels to start the day. Whenever she forgets and does her habit, she forfeits one to you. Whatever's left at the end of the day is hers to keep. Boost success by having her save toward a bigger incentive.

Treat the Underlying Problem

Nose picking, for example, is more common in kids with allergies or sinus infections. Take care of those and the habit may disappear or at least be reduced. Also, kids are more likely to engage in habits when they're anxious, bored, or overtired. Managing stress, regulating their physical states, and keeping them busy with stimulating activities will all help reduce the frequency and intensity of most habit behaviors. Finally, while you're habit-busting, *don't let your child veg in front of the telly*—a situation practically guaranteed to bring on a habit *burst*.

Distract or Provide Alternatives for Reducing Tension

When you notice your child starting to do a habit, quickly shift her into an activity that demands both her hands and her concentration. Exercise is good, and it also reduces tension on its own, thus lessening the need for the habit in the first place. According to guidelines from the National Association for Sport and Physical Education, preschoolers need at least one hour of structured physical activity, and one to several hours of climbing, running, swinging, twirling, etc., *every day.*

Offering other finger or oral activities, like playing with a rubber band, Silly Putty, or a "twiddler" (a ribbon or folded paper scrap or something), chewing gum, a bottle of bubble solution and a wand, etc., can also circumvent habits when they are cranking up.

Code-Word Reminders

If your child has a gross or socially inappropriate habit, talk to her about why she can't do it in public, or at least not in front of your mother-in-law. Then agree on a code word or hand signal you'll use to remind her to stop.

Careful! You're Sitting on Ms. Piggle-Toes!

* * *

FAQs About Imaginary Friends and Obsessions

Q. My son spends hours talking to Ms. Piggle-Toes, an invisible eggplant who is constantly eating all of our chocolate-chip cookies. Is this normal?

A. Yes.

Q. Really?

A. Yes, really. According to one recent study, as many as two-thirds of preschoolers between the ages of two and six have one or more imaginary friends. Although it can freak you out a bit to see your sweetie pie conversing intently with the air, having a pretend friend is usually just a sign of a normal, healthy imagination and can actually help kids' development.

Q. But an eggplant! Ms. Piggle-Toes is an invisible eggplant!

A. Your child seems to have a particularly creative imagination, but that's a skill that will probably serve him well much of his life. Imaginary pals tend to be people or animals, but some kids, especially those who have been exposed to characters like SpongeBob SquarePants, will come up with other variations. Imaginary friends come in all shapes and sizes, and some have magical powers. My son's eleven imaginary friends were miniature, which was handy, because we could hold all of them while he climbed in his child-safety seat, and he could easily defeat them when they played football in the family room. But it was a nuisance when it was time to let the water out of the tub, and we had to be careful that everyone was accounted for on the towel first.

Sometimes instead of creating an invisible friend, kids will assign personalities, feelings, and actions to stuffed animals, dolls, slippers, or other inanimate objects.

Q. Do all imaginary friends eat chocolate-chip cookies? And shouldn't she ask first?

A. Many imaginary friends do seem to exist on diets of sweets or other junk food. And yes, they should ask first. Remind your son of this, and make him responsible if his friend doesn't follow the rules. For example, *he* might have to skip dessert after dinner if *she* eats cookies without permission. And make sure he brushes his teeth.

Q. I don't get it. Why should I punish my son and not Ms. Piggle-Toes?

A. Because Ms. Piggle-Toes isn't *real.* Your son is actually eating the cookies.

If he blames her for other things too, like getting into Mommy's makeup, it's probably because he doesn't want to take responsibility for his own behavior and it's easier to blame someone else, especially someone who can't defend herself. This is normal and understandable for his age, and there's no need to over-react or insist that he 'fess up. If he continues to blame Ms. Piggle-Toes for things he did, though, try saying something like, "You *wish* Ms. Piggle-Toes had gotten into Mommy's makeup. But *you* have to clean it up and tell Mommy you're sorry." If the problem is really persistent, you can insist that the imaginary friend move out, but fortunately that's rarely necessary.

Q. Oh. Well, is it okay for him to have tea parties and play rugby with Ms. Piggle-Toes?

A. Sure. In fact, playing with an imaginary friend is a big help in learning social skills and in keeping kids from feeling bored or lonely when there's no one to play with. Some studies suggest having an imaginary friend also boosts language skills. The only time you should be concerned is if your son consistently prefers to play with Ms. Piggle-Toes instead of real people. Then talk to your pediatrician.

Q. Sometimes Ms. Piggle-Toes is sitting in my recliner when I want to watch the ball game, and I accidentally squash her. My son says I should apologize. Should I?

A. Sure, because it's a chance to model the response you want your son to have when he hurts someone by accident. You may ask her to get out of your chair though, and even lift her out if she refuses.

Many imaginary friends appear to serve a child's desire to spice things up around the house or give them a boost against more powerful older siblings or parents. There's no harm in going along with the "game," but you also don't need to fuel it by letting Ms. Piggle-Toes rule the roost or by doing anything you consider outlandish or unreasonable.

Q. How long do you think Ms. Piggle-Toes will live here? And can I declare her as a dependent on my taxes if she stays less than six months?

A. She probably won't be around long. Some imaginary friends last only hours; others hang around for a year or more. Some come and go or are replaced by a succession of pals. Enjoy this mostly charming stage as long as it lasts.

And you can't declare Ms. Piggle-Toes at all. Remember, she's an eggplant, not a person.

Q. One more question. I always thought Obsession was just a perfume with weird ads. Now my wife informs me that our son has an obsession with dinosaurs. Should I be concerned?

A. Again, not to worry. Most preschoolers go through a series of passionate interests that often border on obsessions. Dinosaurs are a very common passion. Other keen interests include transportation (trains, spaceships, construction equipment), animals (horses, dogs, unicorns, cats, monkeys), superheroes, and other semi-mythical characters like cowboys. Your son will probably want to read tons of dinosaur books, play with toy dinosaurs, and correct you when you confuse T. rex and allosaurus (allosaurus had three fingers; T. rex had only two, among other differences). All this stuff is normal. My only warning is to resist the urge to completely redecorate his room in a dinosaur theme. Spending hundreds of dollars guarantees that his passion will change next week.

CHAPTER SIX

Moving without Mayhem

* * *

Remodeling without Remorse

When I was a child, my family moved fairly often, including a mixture of cross-country moves and around-the-corner ones. I'd lived in seven houses in three states by the time I was in sixth grade. Moving seemed natural and exciting to me, and I continued to move around once I became an adult—my husband Steve and I lived in five different homes in three states before we had our first child.

But it took only one move with kids (actually, more precisely, *one* kid) to put an end to my moving wanderlust. After that move, I swore my next one would need only one box—a pine box for my lifeless body.

That should give you some idea of how much fun I think moving with small children can be! And that's why I've spent lots of time searching the Internet, interviewing friends, reading books, and thinking hard about strategies to help you if you're stuck moving. I've collected tips to help you survive all the steps of the moving process, from breaking the news, house hunting, and keeping your home "tidy" for prospective buyers, to handling your child's grief while he says good-bye to his favorite radiator and the special worms that live only in your yard. Mind you, all these great tips haven't inspired *me* to move or anything, but I think *you* can probably manage it now without having a total nervous breakdown.

I also have suggestions for helping your child adapt to the changes of redecorating his room or cope with the hassles of a major remodeling job.

Now *those* I know about firsthand! Because I refused to move ever again, after we had our third child and no longer fit in our two-bedroom house, we were forced to either put on a big addition or consider moving the kids to a Little Tikes playhouse in the backyard. Doing an addition was a delightful experience. That is, if you consider it delightful to spend a summer entertaining three small children while your entire backyard is a mud pit laced with sharp construction debris. And delightful to share one bedroom among five people, some of whom are decidedly noisy and squirmy at night. And charming to spend days with NO bathrooms except the construction Porta-John and a small plastic potty. Plus, wonderful to discover that the whole project takes nine months instead of the four promised by the builder.

Oops! As I looked over the how-to-keep-your-kid-happy-during-remodeling tips one last time, I realized that I forgot the most important one: hire a builder who's having cash flow problems and so neglects to pay his subcontractors, prompting them to punish him by parking a backhoe in your front flower bed for almost six months. Your kids—as well as every small child for miles around—will sing your praises.

Good luck! Don't forget the Valium! Or at least the triple-fudge brownies!

We're Outta Here!

✳ ✳ ✳

How and When to Break the News of an Impending Move

Moving has enough headaches that it's tempting to avoid another one by just not mentioning it to the kids until everything's over and done with. Unfortunately, that approach usually just creates more headaches in the long run. These ideas will help you fill everyone in without exceeding your monthly Tylenol budget.

Timing

Tell your child about an upcoming move in much the way you'd tell her about a new baby—not so far ahead that she begins to suspect the whole idea is just a hoax, but far enough that she can get used to the idea and participate in the preparations. Similarly, you may need to tell her sooner if you've notified all the neighbors and the mailman, or if you'll be traveling regularly to house-hunt or start a new job. Better to give her a long wait than to leave her imagining all sorts of dire scenarios for the household tension.

What to Say

As usual, you need to tell your child how her life will be affected. Make sure to include the following information:

* *Why* you're moving. (Keep your explanation reasonably positive, even if it isn't. And if you're moving because of foreclosure or other serious financial problems, see the tips on pages 278–286 in Chapter Eight.)

* *Who's* going where and when—and who or what is staying behind.

* *What* changes, if any, she will experience in her everyday life, both in the short run (like having to keep the house tidier than normal) and the longer run (like attending a new school or making different friends).

* *What* the process will be like (house hunting, moving her stuff from Point A to Point B, and joining a new pool and library).

LITERATURE LINKS

Try ALEXANDER, WHO'S NOT (DO YOU HEAR ME? I MEAN IT!) GOING TO MOVE by Judith Viorst (which perfectly captures the quirky regrets and oppositional attitude of many young children confronting a move), MOVING MOLLY by Shirley Hughes (which presents a positive story of excitement and adjustment), ROSA'S ROOM by Barbara Bottner (especially good for the post-move stage), and WE ARE BEST FRIENDS by Aliki (from the point of view of the friend left behind).

What to Play

As always, playing will make it easier for your child to work through her confusion and any strong feelings. Here's a perfect play option that can be adapted for all the different moving stages. Grab two boxes and set up each as a simple dollhouse. Collect an assortment of small gift boxes and some tiny junk like Barbie clothes and accessories to furnish one of them. Add a biggish toy truck or a shoebox to decorate as a moving van. Then have your kid pack everything up and transfer it from one house to another. You can even add extra "buildings" to play at house hunting or exploring a new neighborhood. Or you can furnish both houses to show how the stuff will be moved out of the new one to make room for your things.

House Hunting with Your Child— Without Shooting Anything!

✳ ✳ ✳

It Can Be Done, Sort Of

House hunting with kids in tow is...well, horrible enough to give even mild-mannered folks evil urges. But this plan of attack can minimize the moments of feeling postal for everyone (including the nice real-estate lady who offers to shepherd all of you around in her car, even though hers is the sort that doesn't have peanut butter smeared on the door handles).

Step One: Make Your List

Here's where you can get your child involved, especially if you take care to reserve veto power. Kids who feel they have some role in choosing their home are much more likely to handle the move with only a reasonable number of nightmares and tantrums.

As you take turns listing desired features, keep in mind that *a home is not just a house or apartment*. In fact, the physical space itself (except for the number of bathrooms) will quite likely rank lower on your quality-of-life scale for the next several years than other important features, like neighbors who have kids too; good schools, including preschool or daycare; proximity to a playground, emergency room, and all-night pharmacy; a safe backyard; an easy commute so you're not too crabby after work to have fun with the kids; and the availability of slimy things to catch and keep in jars. (Visit www.ourfamilyplace.com/homebuyer for various useful lists and tips, keeping in mind that the site tends to focus more on concerns like first-floor powder rooms and mortgage rates than the local slug population.)

Step Two: Reality-Check It Twice

While still sitting at your kitchen table, lists in hand, grab the real-estate ads, listings from your realtor, print-outs from the Internet, and descriptions from in-the-know friends, and be *ruthless* about selecting to visit *only* places that sound *really* promising—that is, places that sound promising *after* you have completely revised your "Must-Have List" now that you realize that you cannot afford a four-bedroom, three-bath house in a nice neighborhood. Trust me (because even though I lie a lot in this chapter, I'm not lying now), looking at lots of unsuitable houses gets old in a *hurry,* even if you're childless, which you aren't.

Step Three: Hire a Sitter

Wait a minute, you say—*I thought these were tips for house hunting with your kids!* See, I told you there was lots of lying in this chapter. But I'm also kind of telling the truth, because you will hunt with your child—later. If you can possibly afford it or bear to impose on your neighbors or mother-in-law again, get someone to watch your child while you head out and make the first cuts without the little guy. Take your video camera along and make short highlight tapes of the houses (and neighborhoods) you like best, and watch these with him afterwards. Remind him that the *stuff* doesn't come with the house; I remember a friend's kid who was bitterly disappointed when they moved in and he discovered that all the toys that had been there when they looked at the house were *gone!* Another option if you can't get a sitter (suggested by my wonderful editor and based on real-life experience), is to divide and conquer: have one parent remain with the kid and arm the other with a camera to go out and make the first cuts alone. This strategy will work best if you and your partner are in pretty close agreement about what you're looking for in a home.

Step Four: Plan B

Let's say your sitter, Grandma, and all the neighbors coincidentally have to wash their hair the day you've chosen to go house hunting, you're not sure you trust your spouse's taste, and you're stuck bringing your child with you. Or you're down to the final contenders and you're bringing him along to look at those. Prevent disaster by limiting your looking to three houses at a time, max. Promise him a fun outing, like getting more pizza, for afterwards.

Prepare your child for the experience. Let him know what *he* can expect (i.e., it will be really boring) and what behavior *you* expect (no wiping boogers on other people's kitchen tables; whining limited to ten minutes total, no exceptions; and no playing with toys in the houses you visit). Make a picture scavenger list, including a mixture of easy-to-find items (like, say, a kitchen, a bathroom) and rarer things (like elevators and roller coasters). Give him a reward, maybe gummy bears or stickers, for each item he finds.

Go potty first. Although if you forget this tip, you'll get a chance to check out the plumbing under real working conditions…

If you like your real-estate lady, take your own car. Or at least don't bring any snacks involving peanut butter.

Step Five: Hire a Sitter Again

Do not make the mistake of thinking you can make a major decision (like which house to buy) with a child in tow. Go back when you can look at the house and neighborhood carefully and actually do all the stuff on those checklists, like seeing if all the appliances work (because even—or perhaps especially—if your child already "checked" them, they may not work anymore).

Living a Lie

✳ ✳ ✳

Helping Your Child Cope When Your House Is on the Market

Here are tips from friends with preschoolers who were completely crazy and moved instead of remodeling—and not only lived to tell about it, *they sold their houses*! For something reasonably close to the market price! And their children aren't in therapy!

Purge and Store

When real-estate agents tell you that houses sell more quickly and for more money when they look "lived in," they do not mean lived in pre-schooler-style. The mere presence of primary-colored plastic in your home probably drops the price of your house ten grand. So you'll need to fork out bucks for a storage unit or prevail upon friends with extra space in their attics, then pack up lots of toys and other clutter, and hide it out of sight.

This will distress your child, but you can minimize the sting. Reassure your child that it's only temporary; she'll get all her stuff back after you move. (See? The lying thing's rubbing off on you too.) Be sure to save out some of her favorite toys. Set a number (and size) limit, and encourage your kid to choose classic toys with multiple uses, like blocks, dolls or figures, and balls.

Pack up toys for storage (or tossing) when your kid's in bed or visiting a buddy. *Out of sight, out of mind* still works for many preschoolers. Buy attractive storage containers (preferably with lids) to hold and hide the toys you keep out. Put anything you throw away in opaque garbage bags or card-board boxes and seal tightly. Put these out for the garbage at the last minute, or better yet, stick them in with the neighbor's garbage. Seize the opportunity before you move to divest yourself of any stored toys your child seems to have forgotten.

Remember, if you do accidentally throw away a beloved toy, your child will get over it someday. For example, I hardly hate my mom at all anymore for tossing my Elly Elephant when we moved when I was ten.

Crown Your Child the "Quick-Clean Queen"

Assuming you haven't decided you no longer need to move now that your house is so uncluttered and attractive, devise a plan that gets your house tidy enough for prospective visitors in fifteen minutes or less. Well, actually more. Place a tiara on your kid's head and put on some appropriate work music. I like the theme from "Mission Impossible."

Get a laundry basket for each level of your house. Just before a visit, assign your child to scoot each basket around, filling it with anything out of place. Store the baskets in your car if possible.

Then hand each family member a baby wipe or two. They can use them to surface-clean the bathroom, kitchen, and even floors. Things won't be antiseptic, but they'll look good—well, better than they did. You can even put socks on your kid's hands and feet and let her "skate" along hardwood floors, poking her toes into dusty corners and dusting surfaces with her sock-hands.

Be Prepared for Escape

Do not stay in your house when people come to look at it! It makes people uncomfortable (and therefore less likely to buy your place)—and it will completely freak your kid out to see and hear strangers evaluating his home. Be prepared for the resulting last-minute exiles by storing a plastic bin in your car with snacks, toys, a change of clothes, and a list of possible *fun* activities, like going to the library, a fast food place with an indoor playground, or a park, pool, or museum. (Just remember to save room in the trunk for your laundry baskets of clutter.) While you're out, feel free to run an errand or two—but always follow with something fun before you go home. You want your child to have positive associations with these outings; otherwise, the whining will increase exponentially every time you have to vacate the premises.

Can't afford trips to restaurants or major destinations each time? Get an easy chapter book (the kind where each chapter is a complete story, but the chapters also hang together) from the library. Good choices include books by Johanna Hurwitz, like the RUSSELL AND ELISA series, and Ruth Stiles Gannett, like the MY FATHER'S DRAGON series. Go to a quiet, comfortable spot near your home (a park, the library, or even an attractive parking lot) and read aloud to your kids. (Mine liked to play with Silly Putty or doodle while I read.)

Because desperate times call for desperate measures, I, the anti-electronic-media maven, will even give you full permission to indulge in evil plug-in drugs, especially if takes more than six weeks to sell your home. Buy, rent, or borrow an in-car DVD player, Game Boy, or whatever other mesmerizing, beeping thing your child covets. Get earphones for them (or earplugs for you). Drive to a shady parking space out of sight of your house, and let your kid veg while you read your book in peace. A snack and a cup of juice or decaf make this a downright pleasant interlude. Increase the magic by limiting other electronic opportunities during the day. (Opt for an indoor activity instead if the weather's too hot or cold.)

Stress Bust

No matter how decluttered your house is, and no matter how flexible and cooperative everyone is, having your house on the market will boost everyone's stress hormones. Budget time daily for one or two easy relaxing activities, like these:

✳ *Run around the house.* Preferably outside, and preferably fast. Or find some other way to get in fifteen to twenty minutes of vigorous exercise to work out the box-packing kinks and emotions.

✳ *Making a mess.* Well, a clean, controlled one. Time for shaving-cream finger painting in the bathtub or scribble therapy using washable markers to cover the old yucky shower curtain you've just replaced.

✳ *The cinnamon treatment.* Let your child help you bake something that will leave tummies happy and your house smelling wonderfully inviting to prospective buyers. And make it easy on yourself by using semi-prepared foods like Rhodes Frozen Cinnamon Rolls or those buns that come in a tube that you get to whack against the counter edge.

✳ *Dust your child.* Before you tidy the house, gently stroke your child head to toe with a clean feather duster. Then have her do you.

Your Child Can Help Pack!

✳ ✳ ✳

How to Fit Six Stuffed Animals, Fifteen Mismatched Holey Socks, Last Month's Newspaper, a Bag of Stale Cheerios, and a Live Goldfish into Thirty-seven Boxes and Other Useful Tips for "Painless" Packing

These ideas may keep your kid out from underfoot while *you* pack up and give him the occasional genuinely helpful thing to do. But maybe you like surprises, in which case, feel free to ignore the child-labor laws and make your kid pack.

First, Clear the Room!

This is my favorite packing tip with young kids. Choose one room (preferably carpeted, and preferably not his room) and empty it out *completely* to use as a playground. Try parachute play with an old sheet, pillow-and-cushion obstacle courses, and beachball games. Let him spread out a waterproof tarp and picnic in there. If the weather's good and you have a safe yard, set up a tent in your backyard and give your kid a flashlight and a few other appealing supplies for imaginary camping. That will keep most preschoolers happy for days, though you'll probably attract the whole neighborhood too.

Box the Kid Up

There are still few toys as delightful to a child as an empty box. So, assemble (or buy) a few extra cardboard boxes, including at least one big one. Add features like doors and windows, giant eyeballs and nostrils, or portholes and gangplanks. Then your kid can decorate the boxes and play to his heart's content while you work your butt off. And, if you're desperate for an extra box at the last minute (and who isn't), you can use some duct tape to patch up his play box and voilà!

Pack Kid-Smart

Which means pack boring grown-up stuff first (like your good china, books with no pictures, and tax documents). Last, pack up crucial kid stuff, like his special dishes, room things, toys, and the box of mostly-used-up markers. Also pack and bring a bag or box of must-haves, like a night-light, a special "stuffy," and your kid's favorite pink sippy cup, so the first night won't be a disaster even if the moving van gets lost and ends up in Pough-keepsie with all your stuff. (Bonus tip: :Number the boxes as you pack them starting with one—then unpack in the reverse order. Label the contents, too.)

Put Your Kid to Work

Here are useful things your child can do, packing-wise:

✳ *Color code boxes for you.* Assign each room in your new home a color, making a chart as you do so. When you arrive at your destination, you can label each room with a color sign, so movers know which boxes go in which rooms. And who better to do the color-coding than your kid! Let him decorate boxes with markers, bingo-dot markers, single-color stickers, crayons, rubber stamps, and even tempera paint (if he can work outside). Just take care to dole out only one color at a time.

✳ *Gamble.* Have pools for things like how many boxes it will take to pack all your stuff, who will be crabbiest on moving day, how many moving guys (and gals) will show up, or whatever else you can think of. Payoff doesn't have to be money—I myself am partial to kitchen clean-up excuses.

✳ *Pack his own fun bag.* Before you load up his toys and stuff, give him a bag and tell him to fill it with fun things he'll want en route or for the first day or two. Tell him the rule is that everything that goes in the bag has to be his—otherwise you won't be able to find your drill—and it all has to fit. Plus it shouldn't be breakable or likely to die or rot. You can have a discussion about smart strategies, but let him make the final decisions without hovering. (But pack up a few tried-and-true toys yourself, in case of boredom emergencies.)

* *Pack a first-night party box.* Let your child box up all your left-over birthday-party crap, like streamers, Ninja Turtle paper plates, birthday candles, stray favors, and party hats, and then open it for your first meal in your new home. When he's not looking, sneak in a small wrapped gift as a New House favor for him or for the whole family—preferably something to keep people happy during the unpacking phase. Also a book of matches to light the birthday candles, because you'll never find the box that has them.

The Long Good-bye

* * *

Helping Your Child Say Farewell to Everyone from Her Best Friend to Her Favorite Toilet

Saying good-byes can be so painful that many parents are tempted to skip them altogether, instead ushering the kids away quietly with a promise to visit soon and often. But that approach usually backfires in the end. Here are some ideas that don't require scrapbooking classes, big bucks, or gobs of time, but still let your kid say a proper good-bye and cart some memories along—and maybe leave her mark on her old home too.

Parting Gifts

Nothing softens good-bye pain like a goody bag. Grab your leftover party bags and have your child fill each one with things like a picture of your kid or family, a stamped postcard or envelope addressed with your new address, a writing utensil, and, of course, candy to commemorate "how sweet it's been." (Give your kid some candy too.) You could even be completely wacko-crazy and throw yourselves a good-bye party with take-out pizza and games for the adults like Scrub the Toilet and Carry Boxes to the Garage.

Souvenirs I: Good-bye Potty, Good-bye Sink

Before you start packing, grab your video camera and walk through your house as your child says good-bye to each room and tells a little about it. Also take the camera along on last visits with friends and final outings to special places. Be sure to take one good photograph of your child's room (in its natural state is fine, even preferable). Get it enlarged and framed, so she can gaze at it and pretend she's there when she's missing her old room the first few weeks.

Souvenirs II: The Scrap Collection

Encourage your child to start collecting mementos of some of her favorite things, like a leaf from her favorite tree, a pebble from the playground, and a hunk of grass from your lawn. If the new people are going to be redecorating (check first!), peel off some wallpaper or snip out a section of carpet. She can even collect a little of the air from her old home in a small food storage container (making sure to label it as "Old House Air" so you don't accidentally store the leftover spaghetti in it).

Souvenirs III: Life Goes On

Take cuttings or divisions from shrubs or perennials (or dig up a plant if you're confident it won't cause your real-estate deal to collapse at the last second)—and take them with you to plant at your new home.

Kilroy Was Here

Leaving your mark to prove that you were there makes departures less wrenching. Let your child secretly leave a little of herself in one or more of these ways:

✳ *Leave hidden evidence.* Have her write her name, stamp her handprint or draw a picture in some spot that's unlikely to be noticed, like the underside of a storage shelf, the back of the plumbing access panel, the ceiling of a dark closet.

✳ *Leave a record.* Help her write a welcome letter to the new tenants. Include stories about funny moments in your home. Learning some of the history of previous occupants has always cemented my bond to my homes. (My favorite story was about a kid who'd lived in one of my childhood homes who jumped down the laundry chute—from the second floor to the basement, where fortunately his family of six had a major pile of dirty clothes to soften his landing.) You might also include useful tips, like where to find the best ice cream or which neighbor child is most likely to share action figures.

✳ *Hide a time capsule.* Collect things like a current newspaper, a few small toys or recently minted coins, and place everything in something "archival" (i.e., plastic and thus bound to last forever) like a two-liter pop bottle, seal it with duct tape, and stick it up under the eaves in the attic or another not-likely-to-be-noticed-for-a-long-time spot.

✳ *Plan a nice time-delayed prank…*like planting a small patch of bright red tulips that will bloom next spring—in the middle of the front lawn.

Sanity for Moving-Day Madness

✳ ✳ ✳

Helpful Tips and Reassurances

Oh geez, I've been lying again! There is no sanity on moving day, unless you're lucky or rich enough to go stay in a five-star hotel while skilled, careful movers come in, pack everything up, move it to your destination, and unpack for you. But these tips can make things slightly less crazy—for your kids at least.

Forewarn

Even if you read tons of books and played moving with little figures and dollhouses a few weeks ago, expect your kid to be pretty close to clueless about the reality of moving day. Prevent ugly scenes (like the one where a friend's kid kicked and swore at the moving guy for taking his bed apart and "stealing" it) by talking through everything that will happen and how it will all work out. Make sure your kid understands that it will take time—more than a few days, even!—to get everything sorted out on the other end. Many kids do better if you predict their emotions for them, too. Try saying something like "At first you'll feel excited and a little bit sad. Then we'll probably all be tired and crabby. Mommy and Daddy may even say some bad words, but you should just cover your ears when we do. Luckily, soon we'll all be happy in our new home."

Maintain a Semblance of Routine

If your child has still been attending school or daycare, see if you can send him there for at least part of the day. Try to serve meals at something close to your usual schedule, remembering that this is the perfect time for those ridiculously expensive packaged meals like Lunchables that are completely lacking in nutrition but contain a tasty candy bar. Finally, don't forget your party box and the number for pizza delivery for your first dinner in your new home (or last one in your emptied-out old one).

Kick 'Em Out

Some kids *think* they want to hang around and watch all the excitement as the movers wedge the sofa in the doorway, drop the box containing your great-grandmother's china, and make fun of your taste in artwork. But they really don't. So recruit Grandma or a buddy to get your child out of the house during most of the commotion. One thing that can be fun for your child to do is to go visit the empty new home and do things that will be impossible once it's all filled up with stuff, like ride his Big Wheel from room to room or play Shout and Echo.

Plan B

If you don't have anyone to watch your child on moving day, you'll have to find other ways to keep him busy and out of harm's way.

Load the TV (and the DVD player) last. Rent videos, buy some snacks, and have a mega movie festival. Just be sure to pop in frequently for some kiss-and-tickle breaks plus lots of jumping around or you'll pay for the all-day zombie fest at bedtime. And don't forget to return any borrowed or rental videos before you take off.

Use a baby gate to keep your child trapped in one room or area (but still able to watch what's happening). Let him signal you for assistance by ringing a bell, or use your old baby monitor—just don't pack it up by accident.

First-Night Soothers

Help your child dump his jumpy jitters and relax for a good sleep with some of these ideas:

❊ *Run around the new block.* Or choose some other vigorous exercise an hour or more before you start your usual bedtime routine to help wind everyone down.

❊ *Have a first night party.* Serve your dinner by candlelight (or dimmed lights) while playing quiet music.

❊ *Bless the house.* Have a whole house blessing, or at least bless your kid's room. Make up a prayer or solemnly chant something sappy like "Peace be in our home and in our hearts. Let us be warm, safe, and happy here." Light (and relight) a special candle (an extra birthday candle will do fine) and let each family member blow it out. Or wave a little incense about, or spritz the air with "magic potion."

❊ *Test out the tub.* Make your housewarming gift to your child a packet of plastic glow-in-the-dark toys or stars from the dollar store, and make the occasion especially magical. Charge the glow stuff well (by holding it up to a light for several minutes), drop it in the tub with your child, and turn out the lights. Give him a plastic cup with holes punched in it to scoop up the stars. A waterproof flashlight is fun too. Just go easy on the scrubbing and hair washing—you can do those things tomorrow.

❊ *Keep his room the same.* Make up your kid's bed with the dirty sheets you took off that morning. That way his bed will at least *smell* familiar. If at all possible, load your kid's bedroom stuff on the truck *last*; that way it will be unloaded first, and you can be setting it up so that your child's bedroom will be all ready by bedtime.

❊ *Have a slumber party.* Let siblings share a room and have the comfort of company for a few nights.

❊ *Light the way…*to all the important places. Use night-lights, or even better, glow sticks to mark the way from your child's room to the bathroom and your room.

As If Anyone Needed to Make Moving with Children More Difficult

✳ ✳ ✳

Surviving under Tough Circumstances

Moving from one home to a bigger one in the same town is pretty darned hard on young kids. But it could be worse! For example, you could move to a country where you don't speak the language. Or you could have to juggle the selling, moving, and child rearing while your spouse relaxes in a four-star hotel with room service. Or move into a house plagued with scorpions and fire ants. Or… Okay, I'll stop terrifying you. Just try these suggestions if you find your family in one of these really bad scenarios. (And if you find yourself in an even worse case one, because of losing your home or a severe family crisis, please see the tips in Chapter Eight on pages 278–286.)

One Parent Moves First

Whether you're stuck behind to deal with kids and real-estate ladies and movers all on your own, or forging bravely ahead in a new place where you can't find a decent grocery store, let alone an affordable preschool and a gynecologist who doesn't creep you out, feeling put out is inevitable. Discuss this likelihood *in advance* with your spouse, and come up with ideas to ease your stress (like agreeing to splurge on a sitter weekly so you can go out with your buddies). Also eat plenty of ice cream and get regular exercise to combat the extra calories, as well as the pressure. Your little guys will be grateful for your efforts, whether they realize it or not.

Help your child stay in touch with her absent parent through regular phone calls, e-mail, letters, and so on. And keep reminding her that you will all be reunited before long.

You Have to Serve Time in a Temporary Home

Even a few weeks seems like a long time to a young child, so you'll need to settle in more than you probably would if you were on your own. You can add a few touches to make your temporary abode seem more personal and familiar. For example, replace impersonal wall art with your own pictures or some lovely masterpieces by your child and scatter photographs on various surfaces. Put your child's own comforter on her bed.

Even more importantly, let her form attachments. Many adults are reluctant to invest in relationships they know won't last, but your child's perspective is different. Encourage her to bring a flower to the newsstand lady each morning, to exchange high fives with the desk clerk, or to find a buddy to play with daily at the park.

You can even get some bonus mileage from the experience if you play up the camping-out, adventure, or luxury aspects. For example, when my family lived in a large hotel for six weeks, my sisters and I delighted in dancing in the empty ballrooms in the afternoons. Plus, we had maid service and didn't have to make our own beds as usual (which were Murphy beds that folded up into the wall by day, and how cool was that!)

Serial Moves

I've known military families that were so good at these that I'm embarrassed to pretend to offer advice—so I'll pass on theirs! First, streamline moving routines by paring stuff to a minimum and keeping notes from each move about what works and what doesn't. Make a checklist of activities to do upon arrival in a new home, like getting library cards and checking out museums.

Once you arrive in your new home, quickly involve your child in discovering the great stuff about your temporary location. This will be easier if you adopt a tourist attitude; buy guides for each new locale and keep a journal to help your child remember and value his adventures.

Keep in mind that friends are key for everyone, and the one advantage of frequent moves is having friends everywhere! Make an effort to form real relationships in each location, and help everyone keep in touch with former friends, especially during the transition phases.

Culture-Shock Moves

Moving to a different country or even to a different *region* of the country may require some extra adjustments. These will go more easily if before you move, you help your child learn as much as possible about the differences—and similarities—she'll notice in her new home and neighborhood. Adopt a positive attitude yourself toward your new culture, paying attention to the benefits, like how much better the ice cream is.

Finally, aim to assimilate, not isolate. Your child will adapt quickly—and drag you along if you give her a chance. If possible, send her to a local school, or at least take her out to play in the local park. (Keep in mind that, although young children generally acquire second languages more easily than adults, it still takes work and time for them to adjust, and involves much frustration.)

Moving Following a Crisis

If at all possible, avoid moving for at least six months to a year following a significant family crisis. A move at that time will just multiply stress for all family members.

Once you've relocated, help everyone count their blessings. A weekly ritual of listing all the things that make you happy will foster an optimistic attitude.

Maintain consistency in as many areas of your child's life as possible. Especially make sure your child continues to see her friends on a regular basis.

Moving In and Moving On

✳ ✳ ✳

Managing Unpacking and the Transition Period

Expect the worst. Then maybe you'll be pleasantly surprised! But probably not. Moving involves so many transitions and stressors that most preschoolers take weeks or months to adjust. In the meantime, expect them to regress, sucking their thumbs again, peeing their pants once more, or clinging to yours (with luck after they've changed out of the peed ones). But go ahead and try these ideas to speed up the adjustment period, or at least reduce the number of times they pee their pants.

Children First

A good rule for loading lifeboats, and a good rule for unpacking. After you've set up your kid's room, get the parts of the kitchen that matter to him arranged (i.e., the peanut-butter-and-snack cupboard, the cookie jar, and the plastic dishes), and then move on to a play area or two.

If your child is getting underfoot while you unpack, let him decorate the *inside* of an already unpacked box while you work. Play music for him to draw to. Or reseal boxes for him to use as giant "blocks." Another option is to let your child draw on low windows or glass doors with dry erase markers while you work. (Just protect his clothes and your floors in case he drops them.)

Create Islands of Sameness

Anything you do to make life feel the same as before will smooth your child's adjustment. Pay attention to little easy things, like hanging the same pictures next to your child's bed or following the same bedtime routine. If you've moved within reasonable driving distance, try to keep the same pediatrician and dentist for at least six months; the continuity will prevent stress overload in those already trying situations.

Many children have a honeymoon period right after the move where they seem to be coping beautifully. Then a few weeks later, they may suddenly fall apart. Give them extra attention, talk through concerns, and reduce demands for a while.

Make New Friends

Here are some ways for your child (and you) to make new friends.

✳ *Stroll about the neighborhood daily.* Not only will you probably spot potential (and, more importantly, convenient) buddies, the neighborhood will begin to feel familiar and comfortable.

✳ *Go to library story time.* It's free! The nearest playground and neighborhood pool are also good bets for spotting potential playmates.

✳ *Find a group activity.* Join a little-guy sports team; dance, music, or art class; or Sunday school. Or, *you* can join an adult exercise class, book club, or something else just for you—and ask people about their kids.

    ✳ *Sell lemonade.* And chocolate-chip cookies. Lots of kids will stop and if you have some toys or bubble stuff handy, maybe they'll stick around to play.

    ✳ *Throw a party for yourselves.* Invite neighborhood families with children (including some that look to be babysitter age). Make it easy by serving take-out pizza or only dessert. And have a notebook and pen handy for guests to leave you their contact information.

Keep Old Friends

    Sing the old Girl Scout friendship song: "Make new friends, but keep the old. / One is silver and the other's gold." Then help your child remember his former buds, relatives, and caregivers by visiting them (best of all if you can manage it), having them visit your new home, calling them on the phone, or writing to them (or even e-mailing them). Good ways to encourage conversation instead of tongue-tied shyness from little guys:

    ✳ *A picture is worth a thousand words.* Let him hold a photograph of the person he's talking to. Snapshots and other objects can also serve as conversation prompters for phone calls.

    ✳ *Write kid-friendly letters.* Have him dictate his answers to a fill-in-the-blanks letter that you devise. Or take snaps of your child in his new surroundings, and ask him to dictate two sentences to go with the picture: one about something he likes in his new home, and one about how much he misses his old friend.

    ✳ *Humor is a good icebreaker.* Pre-teach him a joke to tell his friend or think up some silly questions to ask her.

Make Fun the Rule

    Even though you'll be crazy busy for a while, commit to taking a fifteen-minute break every hour to focus on your child and do something fun. And devote at least a half-day every weekend to a fun family activity, like exploring a new museum, meeting the local fauna in a nearby woods, comparing ice cream parlors, or playing putt-putt.

It's New! It's Improved!

✳ ✳ ✳

Ways to Sell Your Child on a Different or Redecorated Bedroom

Recently I talked my twenty-year-old into taking down the giraffe quilt that had hung on his wall since he was one-and-a-half years old. My sixteen-year-old's ceiling, though, is still festooned with the faded, lopsided construction paper stars she cut out when she was four. She's incensed that I would even consider removing them. Do these examples give you an idea of how your child will likely view your generous offer to redecorate her room? That's right, with suspicion or outright hostility.

Unless you enjoy redecorating every couple of years, pause to think the almost unthinkable—about how your child will look (*much* bigger) in five or six years, and about how much her tastes will change. That may make you hesitate before you invest too much time or money in a princess-themed room. Especially if she's resisting that look now. I promise you she won't like it better as a preteen (though she may nonetheless refuse to let you change it—she'll just ridicule you in front of her friends for having once indulged that impulse.)

But if you're determined to get rid of the ducky wallpaper, especially if you want to replace it with something that doesn't involve cartoon characters, or if you want to transfer her into the bigger bedroom down the hall, you may have to break out your best Madison Avenue tactics. So paste on that toothy smile, and…

Play Remodeling

Get out the dollhouse or action-figure clubhouse and involve your child in repainting it, rearranging the furnishings, and buying or making some new stuff. Let her do some of the work even though you're tempted to take over. Be enthusiastic about the new look even if it looks like it was painted by a four-year-old. Which it was.

Offer Choices

Two choices. As in, "Would you like me to paint your room blue or green?" Your child will feel involved and thus more likely to buy in to the idea, and you'll be less likely to end up with a black room. If you're moving your child into a different bedroom, give her choices about where she wants her furnishings.

Grab Your Camera

Plan to take before, during, and after pictures. That way if your kid hates her new room, at least she can look longingly at the photo of the old room and sob, "Wasn't that the best?" Another way to preserve the old room for your child is to collect souvenirs of her old stuff. My kids still have scraps of the worn upholstery from the nasty foldout chair they were loath to throw away and pieces of the kitchen wallpaper we stripped despite their objections.

In with the New

…and still in with the old. For kids who are resistant to change, the more you preserve some things the way they used to be, the easier it will be for them to tolerate newness. So if you buy new furniture or shift your child's room, preserve the layout and/or the bedding. Or buy a new comforter but use the old sheets (which no one can see when the bed's made—so you both win, sort of). Some kids can tolerate gradual change—start by painting the walls, then a few months later buy new furniture, then rearrange the floor plan a while after that, etc.

Incorporate at Least One Dream Feature

Something extra-cool may entice a change-resister to take the plunge—or at least dip her toes in the pool. A few ideas: a chalkboard wall (using special paint), weird mirrors (available in places like IKEA and the automotive department at K-Mart), a sheer canopy thing for over her bed (widely available and fairly inexpensive these days), a swing or rope ladder (that you are careful to anchor in a joist for safety), a platform bed with a slide down to the ground, imagination-stimulating features like a steering wheel anchored to the wall by her bed or—and I've always wanted this myself—a closet door disguised as a bookcase. Just aim for features that are inexpensive or easily changed when your kid outgrows them. (But I'm sure she'll never outgrow the false bookcase. I mean, who would?)

Hand Her a Brush

Helping with the work will make your child feel proud of her room. If you can't bear to watch her wield a paint roller on the walls (which she really can do for a few minutes until she gets bored, so long as there are drop cloths *everywhere*, you load the brush yourself, and an adult paints the second coat), at least let her help paint the closet. Then let her sign her work, perhaps with a handprint and the date. Many kids also appreciate the opportunity to draw on the wall with pencil or chalk before you paint or wallpaper.

Finally, Remember It's Your Kid's Room

Not yours. And what's so terrible after all about letting her sleep every night under the watchful eyes of the teddy bears from her baby nursery? If her friends tease her, she'll either change her mind about redecorating or become a tough-minded, independent kid who isn't swayed by peer pressure.

Introducing Major Chaos and General Disorder

✳ ✳ ✳

A Strategic Approach to Helping Your Child Face the Front Lines of a Major Home Remodel

In my experience, remodeling is even worse for the adults than the kids, especially if it involves more addition than change to what's already there. But reducing your child's stress will reduce your own too and make the construction period easier to survive.

Foresee the Future

And then tell your child all about it. Young children often have no idea of the construction process; they may imagine that the changes will take place quickly and almost magically—I know I did, and I was thirty-three when we did our big remodel. You have to warn them about the destruction, the mess, the noise, the inconvenience, and the strangers in their house. They also need you to discuss the reasons for the remodel, and how things will be different afterwards. Give them a sense of how long the project takes (i.e., however long the contractor says, times two or three). Talk up what a wonderful and interesting adventure it will be...

Put Safety First

Layers of precautions like these will help keep your child safe during construction:

✳ *Review safety rules with your child frequently.* One good blanket rule is that he must *never* enter the construction area unless he is accompanied by one of his parents. Another is that he cannot touch *any* construction tools or materials without both your permission and your presence.

✳ *Have your child make and post "signs" to indicate off limits areas.* Or put crime scene tape across entrances to the construction area when workers aren't there.

✳ *Get out your baby monitor again.* And put the broadcast part in the construction area. Out-of-sight children may be irresistibly drawn to power tools or second-floor framed-only walls; you need to keep extra close tabs on little guys.

✳ *Remind your contractor (frequently) that you have small children.* And you need him to take extra safety precautions, like blocking off areas securely.

Dust from construction can pose significant health risks. Make sure your contractor checks for harmful substances like lead or asbestos that may be disturbed during construction and takes appropriate precautions to protect your family. Minimize allergic reactions by covering your child's bed with a plastic cloth during the day, keeping doors closed, using plastic dust barriers, and giving your child a rinse-off bath or shower nightly.

✳ *Vacate the premises.* As often as possible. If you possibly can, move out at least for the most disruptive periods of the construction.

Enjoy the Adventure Together

Construction is inherently interesting to preschoolers, so you might as well take advantage of their curiosity about the process. Try these ideas:

✳ *Take a nightly inspection stroll.* Note how things have changed from the day before and examine any cool construction equipment *together.* Take photographs regularly during these inspections to help chart the "during" phase of the work.

✳ *Learn all about building.* What a great chance to educate everyone about the materials and processes of construction, as well as to boost general skills in pattern recognition, sequencing, and other cognitive abilities that will serve your child well in school and life! Collect the different kinds of nails and screws, and help your child learn to tell the difference between framing nails, carpet tacks, and Phillips-head screws. Get out books or look at diagrams on the Internet to discover how electricity moves from the pole on the street to the outlet you'll use for his night-light. Talk about why the carpenter holds the hammer at the bottom of the handle and not near the head—then let him experiment himself. The possibilities for learning are nearly as endless as the project itself.

✳ *Let your kid do some construction in parallel.* Get out all your blocks, Legos, Lincoln Logs, and Tinkertoys. Other good toys include supplies for building forts (like old sheets, cushions, and appliance boxes), and children's tool sets. And what kid could resist the opportunity to use real hand-woodworking tools? With supervision, most preschoolers can hammer nails (that you start for them), help screw in a wood screw (especially if it's been screwed once and then restarted in the same hole—and coated with soap to make it move more easily), and operate an eggbeater-style drill. Even just using a level or measuring tape (without any real ability to measure) is fun. If you're handy, help your child to make an actual project. THE FATHER'S ALMANAC by S. Adams Sullivan has great tips for doing woodworking with preschoolers, as well as directions for easy (but often really cool) projects to make.

⁎ *Let him do some real construction.* If you're doing the work yourself, it will be relatively easy to give your child an opportunity to lay a couple of tiles or help prime the wood trim before you nail it up. But even if you're using a contractor, most will be happy to share their craft with your child and let him participate, as long as you stay to supervise, agree to be content with his imperfect efforts, and keep the help session brief. Making the effort to involve your child is likely to pay off in his greater sense of ownership of the new space, greater tolerance of the inevitable crankiness that will infect the whole family at times during remodeling, and, with luck, an enduring sense of pride and competence.

⁎ *Let him make a good impression…*in any wet cement, that is. Try a handprint, and writing his name and age in the wet cement. Press in a leaf or two to make your own fossils. Also, let your kid draw on the bare studs or the sheetrock before it's painted.

⁎ *Celebrate completion by christening the new space with a party.* Family-only is fine; just be sure to have hats, noisemakers, candles, bubbly drinks, and party bags. Give the new space a name—what you'll call the space (like *family room*), plus a pet name (like *Fred*).

CHAPTER SEVEN

"That's a Tough One"

✳ ✳ ✳

Dealing with Concerns about Sex, Death, Religion, Race, Money, and More

The themes that screenwriters milk for crime shows—sex, death, religion, and money—fascinate preschoolers too. In fact, one of the main differences between Hollywood writers and preschoolers is creativity; screenwriters repackage the same tired plot lines over and over, but young children are endlessly inventive in finding new angles of these topics to explore.

Which is why you need to stay on your toes. You should spend some time thinking about the answers to difficult questions like, "When God goes poop, where does He go?"—an actual question I once overheard a tot asking his father at McDonald's. I was as anxious to hear his response as the kid was, but disappointingly for both of us, the dad just muttered something about having to look it up later. (I wonder where the heck you look that up. I'm pretty sure there's nothing in the Bible about it. I tried Googling it and got nothing useful, though I did find an ad for a Jesus toilet you can buy in case the Second Coming happens when you're indisposed.)

You'll also want to plan for how to handle awkward moments, like when your kid boasts to the mailman that your breasts are really big, much bigger than the lady's in the movie you and Daddy watched the other night, or when he loudly points out that Mrs. Snodgrass has a mustache just like Uncle Frank's. And you'll also need to be ready for the moments that tug at your heart, such as when his pet spider Leggy dies and he cries and can't eat his chicken nuggets because he's just too sad. Or you overhear a kid in the sandbox asking him why he has those funny-shaped eyes instead of proper round ones.

The main guideline for most of these situations is to think of yourself as an educator. A calm educator who's not stammering or hushing or scolding too much. During most of these difficult moments, kids need you to satisfy their curiosity, teach them a lesson in etiquette, and explain or affirm your values. Figuring out which task to do first can be pretty tricky in the heat of the moment, although in general, if someone's feelings are injured or at risk, I'd opt for the etiquette lesson first, followed by the educational and moral value ones later in private.

More important than saying the exact right things, though, is communicating to your child your willingness to answer hard questions and respond to his mistakes in ways that feel respectful and supportive. Because, for example, in less than ten years you'll want him to feel comfortable talking to you about his friends who are having oral sex. (You may be thinking, *No I won't!* but sadly you probably will; oral sex is very popular these days among young teens, and at a minimum, you'll want to make sure your kid knows where your family stands on the subject and what to do if the opportunity arises. Hey, doesn't this make you appreciate the fact that right now you only have to answer questions about things like why mommies have big boobies and daddies don't except for Brian's daddy who kind of does?)

Anyway, take a deep breath, practice your poker face, and read on.

Answers to "Why Is Your 'Bagina' Fuzzy?"

* * *

Everything Your Preschooler Wants to Know about Sex and Isn't Afraid to Ask in a Loud Voice in Public

Preschoolers are sexual beings and enormously curious about everything. If you doubt this, I challenge you to spend ten minutes with a three-year-old in a restroom stall along the Pennsylvania Turnpike, as I did on one memorable occasion. My daughter asked me every question about genitalia and reproduction she had ever considered. And her voice was so loud and penetrating (despite my shushing) that not only was every woman in the restroom sniggering when we emerged, but my waiting husband and sons were giggling outside the door, and I swear half the Burger King clientele was in stitches. I can't help prevent the giggles in bystanders, but here are some reasonable answers to frequently asked questions so at least you'll know what to whisper in reply.

Is This My Richard?

Most sex educators and psychologists urge parents to call genitalia by their proper names: penis, scrotum, vulva, clitoris, vagina, urethra, anus, etc. Oh, and boobies—wait, I mean *breasts*. Their reasoning is that having pet names for these body parts as opposed to other parts gives children a sense of shame about them and makes it hard for them to communicate with health-care workers in the event of a problem. Me, I'm not worried that you'll screw up your son if you call his penis a *willy* or label your daughter's vulva her *privates*. The reality is that our society *does* treat these body parts differently. We keep them covered up, we urge people (except for professional athletes and rock stars) not to rub them in public, and we don't sing about them when we do the Hokey Pokey. In addition, the cute names for genitalia are (mostly) so well known that not only is your child *not* going to bewilder the doctor when she talks about her "down there," she's not going to fool Great-aunt Bertha either. Probably the best strategy is to teach your child *all* the different words she's likely to hear.

Can I Play with Your Torpedoes?

This was a question one of my kids asked in front of company as he dumped a pile of unwrapped tampons onto the coffee table. "No, those are Mommy's and they're expensive," was my answer (after a period of dead silence). Another friend told me her son waltzed into a room full of relatives gathered for a seder wearing her diaphragm as a miniature yarmulke. While I encourage you to discuss issues like menstruation or birth control when these sorts of "teachable moments" arise (because believe me it's much harder to raise these topics for the first time when your children are on the threshold of adolescence), you won't harm your child if you offer to discuss her questions *after* the company leaves. Also, keep sex toys and birth-control methods locked up and your tampons in a high cupboard, at least when you're having elderly guests.

How Come I'm So Plain and You're So Fancy?

Preschoolers, with their budding observational skills, are bound to notice during these years that not only are you bigger than they are, but your equipment is a little more interesting too. Many preschoolers become fascinated by breasts and may pat and stroke women's chests, even rubbing their nipples. Other kids will be curious about pubic hair, the size of a grown man's penis and scrotum, or the need for adults to shave. Many will ask to touch your genitalia—or will just go ahead and do it. Most of the time, kids are just seeking reassurance that their own body parts are normal, and they may be wondering whether or how their bodies will change as they get older. As with most of these questions, giving calm, matter-of-fact answers is the best approach. You can say something like "Daddy's penis is big and he has hair around it because he's grown-up. Later when you're a teenager, your penis will get bigger and you'll grow hair there too." Or whatever reassuring answer is right for the question. You can also tell a child to stop if she rubs your breasts or touches your scrotum; after all, you want her to be able to tell people to stop touching her if it makes her uncomfortable.

Why Did You Cut the Baby's Penis Off?
Can I Have a Penis Like Mike's?

Here we get to deal with two of Freud's favorite topics: castration anxiety and penis envy. Freud believed that boys who saw naked females (especially their mothers) became terrified of losing their penises, since someone (Daddy?) had already maimed Mom. Similarly, he was convinced that girls who'd seen naked guys had a desperate longing for penises. Nothing in my years of working with young children has supported these theories, though I have heard lots of children wonder why girls don't have penises. *When kids ask these kinds of questions they are not asking for a detailed description of intercourse.* Most of the time, the question underlying this is "What's normal?" and that's the question you should answer by saying something like "The baby doesn't have a penis because she's a girl. Girls have a vulva instead of a penis." Girls may have a little penis envy when they want to pee in the woods or write their names in the snow, but otherwise, most are satisfied when you reassure them that their bodies are normal and wonderful just as they are.

And While We're on the Topic, Why Is Joey's Penis So Weird?

This is one of the topics that just didn't come up thirty years ago in the U.S. and Canada because circumcision was nearly universal. Today, though, some parents choose to have their sons circumcised and some don't, so there's a good chance that your son will encounter a penis that looks different from his in the bathroom at preschool, the locker room at the pool, or even at home. Or your daughter may see one that looks different from Daddy's or her brother's. No one really knows how many boys are or aren't circumcised these days, because no one keeps records on it—an omission that astounds me in a society where the grocery store tracks exactly how many pounds of M&Ms I've bought in the last year. But one thing seems fairly clear: circumcision rates vary greatly by region, with circumcision most common in the Midwest and least common on the West Coast.

Okay, so what do you say when your kid asks you about the opposite style of penis? You give him a calm, matter-of-fact, *nonjudgmental* answer, of course. Something like "Joey was circumcised, so his penis doesn't have a foreskin like yours does. But it doesn't matter. Both of you have very nice penises that work just fine." Or the other way around. I say this, because the question of circumcision generates the same kind of sanctimonious fervor among Perfect Parents as discussions of abortion, breastfeeding, or letting children watch Cartoon Network. But no matter what your views are on the issue, you don't get to tell your kid things like "Joey's parents decided to maim him and cut off part of his penis" or "Joey's parents didn't care whether he gets penile cancer or has horrible infections so they didn't remove his foreskin as they should have."

Can Girls Marry Girls?

As I write this, the factually correct answer in the U.S. would be "depends where you live." But, before you launch into a tirade against homosexuality or a lecture on tolerance and acceptance, or freak out that your child is or isn't homosexual, take a moment to find out what your child is really asking. When kids ask questions like these, usually they're just wondering if they can both be mommies in their game of house or stage a pretend girls-only wedding—and the answer is *sure.*

Mommy, Will You Marry Me When I Grow Up?

Again, stop to think what this question is really about. Usually kids are seeking reassurance that you will always love and protect them, and always let them be near you. Or they may be asking about how your relationship might change over the years. A good answer is something like "Mommies can't marry their children. But I will always love you, and you can live right near me if you want to." And write down this moment so you can remember it when he's fourteen and won't be seen in public with you.

The Bare Facts about Prudes and Nudes

✳ ✳ ✳

A Butt-Nekkid Discussion

The bottom line for preschool nakedness (at home, at least) is that it's up to you to decide how much to allow. You won't harm a child this age by letting him prance around the backyard *au naturel* or by exposing him to casual nudity. The only caveat is that you should start teaching public modesty standards around three because it takes most kids a while to grasp the rules about when, where, and how much bareness is okay. I remember feeling quite anxious as kindergarten approached and my oldest still didn't seem to have gotten the concept of leaving his pants UP until he was safely in the bathroom, much less the one about closing the bathroom door. Fortunately, I never got any phone calls from the principal, so I guess he never mooned the class. *Phew!*

Bathing Beauties

Is it okay for opposite-sex pre-schoolers to bathe together? How about showering with a parent? The rule of thumb is that it's okay as long as all the individuals involved feel comfortable—and many parents (and kids) start feeling less comfortable sometime during the preschool years. If you're both okay with it, though, shared bathing (or using the bathroom together) provides teachable moments for young kids. It may even satisfy their curiosity about other people's body parts enough to prevent surreptitious games of Doctor with the neighbor's kid. Just not comfortable but still want to let sibs or pals bathe together? Have them wear bathing suits.

Pint-Size Prudes

Occasionally a parent will talk to me about a child who is modest to an extreme degree—maybe he won't change his underwear or get in the bath because he can't stand to be completely naked, or maybe the kid is excessively giggly and silly when he has to visit the doctor or an adult tries to help with toileting. Most of the time, mega-modesty is nothing but another example of normal preschooler quirkiness, and it tends to fade before long. Many overly modest kids have hypersensitive skin or are overgeneralizing the lessons they've learned about modesty. Now and then, though, excessive modesty results from sexual abuse or overstimulation; it won't hurt to ask your child some gentle questions or to seek help from your pediatrician if you're concerned.

LITERATURE LINKS

Despite our culture's push for openness, there are surprisingly few books truly aimed at preschoolers that name and show all the body parts or answer questions about sex in straightforward ways. Here are a couple to try: THE BARE NAKED BOOK by Kathy Stinson and Heather Collins, and IT'S SO AMAZING: A BOOK ABOUT EGGS, SPERM, BIRTH, BABIES AND FAMILIES by Robie Harris (better for slightly older kids).

Handling Wardrobe-Malfunction Moments

Let's say your kid wants to check out the latest and greatest soccer balls online. DO NOT, I REPEAT, DO *NOT*, GO TO www.dicks.com. I have made this mistake (and others) with kids perched on my lap, and let me tell you, fodder for discussion popcorns up faster than you can close windows. (Tip: turn off the monitor and shoo everyone out of the room; then you can gawk in private as you try to get everything off the screen.) No matter how much you try to shield your children, there is a good chance that he'll encounter some disturbing naked images on the Internet or TV, in books or magazines, or even while strolling through the park. While the temptation is to ignore the incident, you're better off discussing what your child has seen and helping him put it in perspective, as well as communicating your values. I usually start by asking kids what they saw and what they thought about it—a good idea since they may not have even noticed what you did. For example, I watched the Janet Jackson Super Bowl show in a room full of kids and adults, *and I was the only one who noticed anything amiss!* My husband says this indicates something about my mind and morals, but I think I'm just more observant. Right?

(Incidentally, the site you want is www.dickssportinggoods.com.)

Lessons in Modesty

These are some of the general lessons your preschooler needs to learn about modesty. Teach the specifics (like the rule about waiting until you are in the bathroom to pull down your pants) as they arise.

✳ *There are different rules for different places.* Use phrases like, "In our family, we ____" or "Around your grandparents, you should _____."

✳ *In public places, we keep our clothes on.* There may be some exceptions to this rule for young children, but it's a good general rule.

✳ *Closed doors mean privacy.* Preschoolers can start learning about knocking, though expect to teach this lesson many, many times.

✳ *People feel uncomfortable if you stare at their bodies or make comments about how they look different.* This is a useful rule because it covers many potentially awkward situations.

✳ *You can ask me any questions you have about bodies.* Let kids know that they don't have to sneak to find out information they want.

It's Passé to Say, "You'll Grow Hair on Your Palms"

✳ ✳ ✳

Modern Responses to Masturbation

Instead you should show your child the video where Barney teaches kids that their dingdong will fall off and never grow back if they play with it. *Just kidding!* (But *for real* I saw a discussion-board post suggesting that masturbation would be less common if someone got Barney or Sesame Street to do a video like this!) Many parents worry about childhood "masturbation." A child's genital touching, though, is not the same as adult masturbation. Here are ways to respond appropriately to your young child's normal interest and pleasure in her body.

What's Normal

Genital touching is completely normal, and begins even before birth. (The first time I saw one of my sons playing with his penis was during a sonogram.) Most young children periodically "hold themselves" or rub their genitals with their hands or against objects (like pillows). Some children do it frequently or with vigor—a process some kids call "getting sweaty" for obvious reasons. Although it may make you feel uncomfortable to see your child doing this, *it does not mean she is perverted, hypersexual, immoral, or anything else bad.*

So why *do* kids touch and rub their genitals? Sometimes it's a sign that a child needs to go to the bathroom. Other kids do it as a self-stimulating comfort behavior, much like sucking their thumbs or twirling their hair. It often increases in response to stressful situations like a new baby or starting school. Mostly, though, kids do it just because they've noticed it feels good—like jumping on the bed or spinning in circles—and they don't know instinctively that it's considered impolite to do it in front of others.

They may even call everyone's attention to their amazing discovery! Finally, not touching genitals is also normal; some kids seem to do it rarely, and don't grow up to be repressed or frigid.

Occasionally, masturbating is a sign of abuse or overstimulation (e.g., witnessing sexual behavior), irritation or infection, or a developmental or mood disorder. Talk to your pediatrician if your child is scratching rather than rubbing, seems unhappy or excessively anxious while masturbating, insists on vaginal penetration with her fingers or objects, or seems unable to inhibit the behavior in public. Probably nothing is wrong, but it won't hurt to check it out.

What to Do When Your Son Tugs His Penis in Front of Grandma

First, *calmly* ask him whether he needs to go to the bathroom. Often kids are not aware either of their bladder sensations *or* that they're touching their privates. If he doesn't, distract him, preferably with an activity that will keep his hands busy or provide a more acceptable public outlet for his tension. Later, remind him that touching genitals is a private behavior, and discuss places in your home where he can have privacy (e.g., the bathroom or his bedroom). You should agree that it feels good—it does—and go ahead and talk about what marvels our bodies are. The vast majority of pediatricians, psychologists, teachers, and other child-development experts recommend allowing young kids to touch their genitals, but teaching them to do so in private. Even many religious leaders now advise a relaxed attitude. Ironically, getting angry or shaming kids frequently increases the behavior.

That's All Well and Good, but You're Just Not Comfortable

Or your spouse gets freaked out or your religion forbids it. Or your kid seems to be doing it all the time and you'd like to see her doing other things. What can you do? These strategies may not eliminate genital touching, but they will probably make it less frequent or public, especially if you stay calm and matter-of-fact:

✳ *Make her wash her hands.* Most kids resent the bother—plus it's a good idea anyhow, since she could get fecal matter on her hands if she's sliding them inside her underwear.

✳ *Avoid triggering situations.* For example, if your child likes to rub her vulva while she watches TV, limit TV time or invite her do something like assemble a puzzle while she watches.

✳ *Keep her hands busy.* Offer your child Silly Putty to stretch and squeeze, finger puppets to wiggle about, board games to play, bowls of buttons or dried beans to sift, and extra time to play in the sandbox or bathtub. These techniques can have short-term effects—by providing an alternative behavior—and long-term ones—by soothing stress. Vigorous exercise seems to reduce tension as well, and thereby may reduce touching.

✳ *Have a private signal.* Agree on a hand gesture or magic word to remind your child to stop if you notice her touching her genitals in front of other people.

Flower Boys and Lumber-Jills

✳ ✳ ✳

Cross-Dressing and Other Gender-Role Issues

Sex-role issues invariably crop up in this age group (and big time again during the early teen years). For example, as a modern woman who bought my sons baby dolls and showed them how to care for them, I confess I was appalled to see the boys drag their babies about the yard caveman-style—and even worse, use dolly's head as a hammer to pound golf tees into the dirt. Other parents fret about boys who love tulle or girls who don't. So here's some reassurance—and some tips for coping in case that's not enough to make you relax.

Girls Who Would Be Boys

…and vice versa. By the age of three, most kids know whether they are boys or girls—but most are five to seven before they are convinced that their gender won't change. This is an important fact to keep in mind when your four-year-old daughter tells you she wants to be a daddy and a linebacker for the Steelers when she grows up. Correct any misperceptions about changing her gender, but go ahead and support future career choices, whatever they might be. (If preschoolers didn't invariably change their minds, our society would be overrun with police officers, superheroes, and fairy princesses, and there would be absolutely no lawyers or accountants.) If your child persists in believing she is the wrong gender, consult your pediatrician to rule out a medical basis for her impression.

Boys in Tights

If your daughter trots into the kitchen in your best lingerie and Estée Lauder makeup, chances are you'll scold her for getting into your things without asking. And that's *exactly* the same reaction you should have if your son comes into the kitchen similarly attired. Dressing in women's clothing is *not* a sign that your preschooler is gay or a pervert! Boys are attracted to women's clothing and adornments for the same reasons girls are. Let's face it, women's clothes and accoutrements are intriguing and sensually appealing—bright colors, soft fabrics, nice smells. Nonetheless, if it bothers you when your son wants to wear pantyhose or put on blush, or your daughter wants to shave her face, try these gender-neutral dress-up activities that satisfy similar urges:

✳ *Let him wear tights.* For example, as part of a Peter Pan or Robin Hood costume. Stock up on varied or unisex dress-up clothes for kids of both genders, like hats, capes, scarves, and jackets, sports gear, a variety of shoes, and animal ears and tails.

✳ *Show her how to shave or apply makeup.* Children of both genders like "shaving" with shaving cream and a Popsicle stick, or applying face paint or Halloween makeup—just watch for skin sensitivities. Temporary tattoos are fun too, and most kids like having their faces gently stroked with a makeup brush or paintbrush (with water or nothing on it).

✳ *Give kids a fabric collection.* They can use an assortment of scarves, towels, old sheets, and different kinds of fabric remnants for making forts, creating costumes, or just stroking to satisfy tactile needs.

✳ *Help kids play-act.* Taking on different roles—animals, good guys and bad guys, as well as people of different genders—helps kids learn about how other folks feel or see the world, and that is a good thing!

Girls Have to Be Nurses

A typical preschooler goes through a phase of being stereotyped and rigid in his sex-role attitudes. (I'm not sure where today's kids pick up these messages, since kids' books have been all but purged of female nurses and old people who wear glasses.) And although insistence on same-gender play doesn't peak until the early school years, some preschoolers exclude playmates of the "wrong" gender. Others will tease kids who seem to be breaking gender rules, such as boys who like the color pink. Calmly correct misinformation—but if your son still wants to be a doctor and your daughter insists on being his gaggingly subservient nurse complete with white feather boa, *chill.* I promise you most kids change their minds completely about these issues within a few years.

> **LITERATURE LINKS**
>
> Some good picture books for talking about these issues with your child include the classic WILLIAM'S DOLL by Charlotte Zolotow and OLIVER BUTTON IS A SISSY by Tomie dePaola.

One More Thing

Many parents discourage any behaviors considered atypical for their child's gender. You should know, though, that there is no evidence that early childhood behavior determines adult sexual orientation—it's probably determined before birth. In addition, cross-gender play typically teaches children skills and attitudes that *all* people need, such as nurturing and assertiveness. Finally, all young children—and older ones and adults too—deserve to be loved and accepted by family and peers for who they are.

Oops! Part I

✳ ✳ ✳

What to Do When You Catch Them in the Act

Playing Doctor is such a common activity among young children that I'm sure I don't even have to tell you what this euphemism means. Others go for the more straightforward You Show Me Yours and I'll Show You Mine. Or they may be creative, like my friend's daughter who played Zoo with her buddy, which, they explained to her mother, they had to play in the nude because animals don't wear clothes. These games are typically motivated more by curiosity than eroticism, and rarely signal a worrisome situation.

What to Say and Do

Calmly say something like "In our house we play with our clothes on. Why don't you two get dressed and come in the other room with me?" Then you can talk to the kids about feeling curious, tell them that it's normal and okay, and remind them that nakedness is for private times. You can reassure them that there are other ways to learn about bodies, like reading books and talking to grown-ups, though I would avoid teaching a friend's child without permission. Then I would distract them with another activity—and let the other parent know what occurred. Wouldn't you want to know?

Prevention Tactics

Supervise preschoolers and limit opportunities to play out of sight of the rest of the household. I discouraged my kids from playing alone in their rooms because the inevitable mess overwhelmed all of us—but it also discouraged sex play and amateur haircuts. Even if your household has casual attitudes about family nudity, enforce rules about being dressed when anyone has visitors over.

Need-to-Know Basics

The best prevention tactic is to provide alternatives for kids to learn about genitals without having to resort to playing doctor. You can always do what generations of American parents have done—leave copies of *National Geographic* lying around—or you can respond to questions your child asks during bath or toileting times, have her assist you in diapering or bathing a baby, or look at "complete" body-part books for preschoolers. You can get anatomically correct baby dolls. (The award-winning Gotz Aquini dolls come with a potty chair. They're available from www.absolutelydolls.com and other doll sites.) Finally, animal encounters can spark some interesting discussions too, as my family discovered during one memorable visit to the elephant exhibit at the zoo. (Okay, I was impressed too—you wouldn't believe how big an elephant erection is! Even more amazing than the size of their poop, and that's saying something.)

More Need-to-Know Stuff

You'll also want to reinforce lessons designed to protect your child from sexual abuse. *Your body belongs to you* is an important basic lesson for all kids, including the idea that they have the right to refuse hugs, kisses, or other unwanted touches, even from Aunt Tillie. (That guideline is especially important because children are most likely to be abused by people they know.) And remind them that the rule goes both ways: no hugging, kissing, or touching other kids without their permission. Finally, I recommend telling kids to do a "tummy check." If something someone asks them to do makes them feel uncomfortable or funny inside, they should tell you about it, even (especially) if the other person suggests keeping it a secret. This rule guarantees that you will know all your birthday presents in advance—but chances are the kid was going to break and tell you anyhow.

Occasionally childhood sex play isn't just kids' play. You should be concerned if one child is several years older than the other, there is oral-genital contact, pretend intercourse, or the use of fingers or objects for vaginal or anal penetration. I'd also be concerned if one child feels fearful or angry, or the kids won't stop even after being told to. Talk to the other kid's parents and seek advice from your pediatrician if you have a problem like this.

Oops! Part II

* * *

What to Do When They Catch You in the Act

Everybody remain calm!

I feel like a broken record, but that really is the best advice for most of the sex stuff—or other difficult situations—you'll face with kids. Having said that, you also have my permission to blush, grab for the covers, and silently curse the constant disruptions of your sex life.

Then you need to say something like "Sweetie, Daddy and I were having some private time. Go back to your room, and I'll be there in just a minute." You can grit your teeth while you say this, but try not to be too obvious about it. And no, you cannot just quickly finish up—you and/or your spouse need to grab some clothing and hustle in to talk to your traumatized child. (Bonus Tip: If you go by yourself, turn on all the lights and the TV on high volume so your honey stays awake until you get back.)

What to Say

Freud prophesied all kinds of doom and gloom for kids who came upon a "primal scene," and while I think he got a little carried away, many kids *are* confused or frightened by what they saw (and heard). Preschoolers tend to assume that one parent was hurting the other. Reassure your child that what he saw was just a way that grown-ups show love for each other—and that it's something that's only for grown-ups, like drinking beer or getting the last of the ice cream. (Oh, wait, some households don't have that good rule. Okay, like voting for president.) If your child expresses concern about noises, tell him that grown-ups sometimes like to make silly sounds when they're playing, just like kids do, and assure him that no one was getting hurt. Answer any other questions matter-of-factly, remind him that he needs to knock when your door is closed, give him a smooch, and go back to bed, keeping your fingers crossed that the lights and TV have done the trick. Also hope your kid doesn't return promptly to test the knock-on-the-door rule.

Experiences like this, awkward though they may be, are good teachable moments for values. Emphasize that sex is an adult behavior, one that occurs within the context of a loving relationship (or only in the context of marriage, if that's what you believe), and that people aren't allowed to hurt one another.

The Morning After

As long as your child seems relaxed and only normally crabby the next morning, you don't need to bring up the incident again. He may or may not even remember it, depending on how awake he was at the time. But if your child has more questions, answer them too. The vast majority of kids are unaffected by an *oops* experience, but occasionally kids will seem preoccupied by what they saw, and will act it out in their play. As long as the theme dies out in a few days, you don't need to be concerned.

Lock your door! Enough said.

Can Dead People Watch Cartoons?

✳ ✳ ✳

Q&A about Death (and Other Sad Endings)

Preschoolers encounter death in their everyday experiences—they come upon the houseplant you *meant* to water or they take their pet carpenter ant to school and some more observant child informs them that Anty is dead. That happened to my son in October one year, and he was so bruised by the sad event that when the kids were instructed on the last day of school to draw a picture of their most memorable kindergarten moment, he crayoned an illustration of Anty, his six legs stuck stiffly in the air, with the simple caption "The Day Anty Died." The picture hung in our kitchen for several years so we could all be reminded daily of the tragedy. While most preschoolers won't be as saddened by these small encounters with death, nearly all will have dozens of questions about the facts of death, which they will expect you to answer with all the expertise and conviction of an experienced funeral director or priest. Consider the following your cheat sheet, though you may have to tweak it here and there to fit your own religious beliefs. (If you need advice on supporting your child through funerals or the death of a close family member, please see pages 264–266 in the next chapter.)

Can Dead People Watch Cartoons? Eat Cookies? Go Poop?

These kinds of questions represent your preschooler's attempts to understand the physical state of death, a concept that's hard for most young children to grasp. Tell your child that when something dies, it can't breathe, eat, or go to the bathroom anymore. It can't see, hear, feel, think, or talk. It might look like it's asleep, but it can't even sleep anymore. The more your description is concrete and specific—e.g., that the squirrel can't eat acorns or run away from dogs anymore—the easier it will be for your child to start to build up a concept of what death is and isn't.

When Are We Going To Wake Up Spot?

Preschoolers don't understand figurative language. That's why it's so important to avoid using euphemisms for death around them. Telling your child that the vet put the dog to sleep or that Gramps is at rest may leave her terrified of bedtime or naps—or angry that her sleeping friend won't wake up and come back to play. In addition, if a child hears that someone died after an illness, she may become fearful the next time she has a cold or ear infection, so it's important to distinguish between serious illnesses and the minor ones from which people easily recover. Finally, most preschoolers see death as reversible, and you will probably need to remind them again and again that death is forever.

Aaah! Why Did You Kill My Tricycle?

Preschoolers have a hard time telling the difference between what is alive and what is not, especially since these days they may encounter many nonliving things that can move and talk and even seem to think. Thus if you run over their tricycle because they left it in the driveway right in front of your bumper *again*, it may seem to them that the toy died. Phrases like, "My car died" or "The vacuum cleaner kicked the bucket" reinforce this perception. Continue to point out the differences between living and non-living things—and go buy a new tricycle AND, get in the habit of walking all around the car before you drive off—it would be far worse to crush a little person parked in front of your vehicle.

When Are You Going to Die?

This is a particularly difficult question for parents, torn as they are between being truthful and protective. I recommend saying something like "I'm planning to live for a long, long time. Long enough to play with your kids some day, and maybe with their kids too." If your kid pushes, then you can add that no one knows when they'll die, but you are healthy and take good care of yourself, so you will probably live to be very old. Also reassure your child that someone would always take care of her, even if you weren't there.

Many kids ask questions about when other people are going to die, including themselves. The same kinds of matter-of-fact but optimistic answers will usually do, unless your child has had a recent experience with death or if the person she's asking about is in fact very ill or dying. In the first situation, you may need to provide more specific reassurances, like "Bobby's grandpa had a very bad illness that made his body stop working. Your grandfather is healthy and probably won't die for some time." In the latter situation, you need to find a balance between being honest and reasonably hopeful: "Grandpa's heart is very, very sick. The doctors are trying to fix it and make it better, but they might not be able to. And if they can't, Grandpa will die. We are glad that he has good doctors though, and we are hoping he will get healthy again."

Where Is Heaven? How About Dog Heaven?
Can We Go There for Vacation?

During the preschool years, kids tend to adopt a very concrete vision of the afterlife, which can be comforting to them at times and confusing at others. For example, they may wonder why they can't see a dead relative up in the clouds or why they can't make a short visit to heaven. Most try to construct a very clear picture in their heads, asking you to confirm or deny details. Few will be satisfied with vague responses about nobody knowing, and they may turn to images from the media, friends, or their own imaginations to help them "see" heaven. Don't fret if they end up constructing a concrete view or philosophy of the afterlife that differs from your own; kids struggle with these concepts for many years (as we all do), and what they believe ten years from now may bear no resemblance to what they profess now.

Does It Hurt to Die? What Happens to Bodies Afterwards?

If your child comes across a squished squirrel, she may be obsessed with the blood and condition of the body, especially since she is probably now sharp enough to put two and two together and realize that it may have hurt the squirrel to die, much as it hurts her when she scrapes her knee.

Kids who play Cops and Robbers with dramatic deaths, have sandbox funerals for extinct plastic dinosaurs, or play Angels in Heaven are not being excessively morbid; they're just using play to help figure out a difficult concept.

Answer questions honestly, but emphasize how quickly death often happens, minimizing suffering. (You might also want to add a gentle lesson about why it's a good idea for her to stay out of the street unless a grown-up is helping her.) Your child will need to know that the dead body can't feel pain anymore, just like it can't see or run. Finally, most kids are curious about what becomes of bodies. Take advantage of chances to observe how a dead animal, insect, or plant changes over time. Some kids want to stage funerals, too, like my tenderhearted daughter who liked to bury even drowned worms with full rites.

Flush with Dignity

✳ ✳ ✳

Some Serious Tips for Handling the Death of a Pet

A preschooler who seemed indifferent to the death of a distant grandparent may be devastated by the death of his pet cricket. Young children typically grieve in relation to the amount their everyday lives are affected, so it's not surprising that the loss of the pet he kissed daily might upset him more than the loss of someone he saw a few times a year. In addition, most young children identify with animals, which after all may be small and helpless like them. And a preschooler may feel responsible for the death, even if he wasn't because *you* always fed the critter when he forgot. Ultimately, the death of a pet, whether household vermin or a beloved dog or cat, represents an ideal opportunity for you to teach your child about grieving, remembering, and moving on.

To Replace or Not to Replace

When my son's white mouse Robin died, like parents everywhere I was tempted to rush out and get a new one before he noticed. But as a trained psychologist, I knew better. Plus I couldn't face several more years of cleaning out its smelly cage. Okay, so that was the real reason I didn't. But *you* shouldn't replace a pet either. Remember, this is a good rehearsal for other more significant losses your child will face. Plus, some kids are very good at recognizing distinguishing details and will discover your charade.

If you do opt to get a new pet, be sure to give your child time to grieve first. The idea that no one is replaceable is an essential life lesson. I also recommend getting a new pet that looks significantly different from the old one to emphasize this message.

Dying and the Postmortem

If you notice that a pet is seriously ill or dying, call your child's attention to the problem. This will give him a chance to do some anticipatory grieving, by working through his questions and feelings before the actual death. Let your child see your sadness, but remain calm for his sake.

If you decide to euthanize your pet, talk to your child about it. Tell him that his pet is very ill, cannot get better, and is suffering, so the vet will give it medicine that will make it feel peaceful and then die. *Do not use the phrase "put to sleep"*—it only confuses young children. Most vets recommend against letting preschoolers be present while the pet is euthanized, although many will let children view their pets' bodies afterward. Good ones will talk through what has happened. If the pet's eyes are open, some children may have a hard time accepting that death has occurred; conversely, others may insist that a pet with closed eyes is only sleeping. It won't hurt your child to touch the body (but make sure he washes his hands well afterward). Many children alarm their parents by seeming detached or clinical in their reactions; others are prostrated with sadness. Both reactions—and everything in between—are perfectly normal.

Most kids will have questions about the death, why it occurred, was it their fault, etc., and these you should answer as honestly and calmly as you can. Praise your child for giving his pet a good life and for being a good friend. If the pet was a small animal, help your child wrap the body in a rag or paper towels (or toilet paper in the event of a burial at sea, aka the toilet). Some families place the body in a "coffin" (like a shoebox). If necessary, reopen the box later to show your child that the pet is indeed still dead. If you choose to have a larger pet cremated, invite your child to join in making decisions about what to do with the ashes.

The Pet Funeral

Ask your child if he would like to hold a funeral for his pet, explaining that a funeral is a time to remember the "person" who has died and bury the body. To give you ideas for a good pet ceremony, I'll describe the funeral we held for Piggy, the guinea pig formerly known as Hamster. After Piggy died, his owner made a picture of a happy time they'd spent together and placed it in the shoebox with his pet. We also included a carrot, Piggy's favorite treat, but talked about how she couldn't really eat it. Then we placed everything in a heavy-duty freezer bag to await a thaw, since the January soil was rock hard, and I hid the package deep in the freezer so it wouldn't creep me out every time I needed more ice cream. As soon as there was a day above freezing, my husband chipped out a crater in the garden, only destroying several dozen prized flower bulbs in the process, and the whole family gathered for a simple service. We sang a song Piggy had seemed to like, and then each person took a turn to say what he'd liked best about Piggy. Then everyone tossed a spadeful of dirt on the coffin. We were all teary, even my husband, though he insisted he just got some frozen dirt in his eye. Afterward, we each placed a stone on the grave, which is a Jewish custom one of my kids had learned about at school. Then for the next several nights we lit a candle at dinner for Piggy, and we framed a photograph to hang in the family room as soon as Piggy's owner felt ready to face it. Finally, in the spring we planted a bleeding heart perennial to mark Piggy's grave (and to replace the mangled bulbs). Each step of the memorial process gave us a chance to talk some more about death and loss and incorporating the best of Piggy's spirit in our daily lives.

Peeing the Bed and Other Expressions of Grief

Young children do not grieve in the same way as adults. For example, your child may not cry. Often, their intense feelings come out in annoying behaviors, like wetting the bed or refusing to separate from you at school. Be understanding, and continue to talk and answer questions. It may reassure your kid if you draw the connection between his behavior and his feelings, saying things like "I think your body is telling you that you still miss Piggy and wish she hadn't died." Provide other outlets for feelings, like art supplies and water play, as well as pretending opportunities.

Time, the Great Healer

Over time, your child's grief will lessen, and as it does, it will become easier for him to remember the happy occasions with his pet. Kids lack this perspective about the course of grief, so they may need you to remind them that they will feel better after a while.

LITERATURE LINKS

Every few years a new good book on pet death comes out, and the classics continue to be reprinted. My absolute favorite is THE TENTH GOOD THING ABOUT BARNEY by Judith Viorst. I also like I'LL ALWAYS LOVE YOU by Hans Wilhelm, GOODBYE MOUSIE by Robie H. Harris, and Mr. Rogers' classic photo-essay, WHEN A PET DIES.

Oh God!

✳ ✳ ✳

Responding to Your Child's Spiritual Concerns

Young children, who possess faith strong enough to believe the friend who tells them that boogers are brain seeds (and a sense of wonder flexible enough to detect beauty in those "seeds"), are a spiritual delight. At this age, most will readily accept the values and beliefs you share with them, though they may need many repeated lessons and might be slow to apply what they know. This is the perfect age to introduce your child to some of the formal practices of your religion and to start encouraging her to express her faith.

Even if you do not practice a formal religion, your child's budding conscience means the preschool years are an important time to teach moral values, as well as to introduce her to the natural delights of our world. Here are some of the spiritual issues that preschoolers struggle to grasp or reconcile, along with some activities that promote faith and values.

A Child's Vision of God

Preschoolers typically imagine God as a real person, and may even be convinced they've seen Him on the subway or sitting in a pew where they worship. They talk easily to God through prayers or artwork. Some confuse the concept of God with religious leaders, Santa Claus, or even their house of worship. Or they may imagine that leaders of all sorts have godlike abilities to see what they're up to. Nearly all view good and bad as black-and-white issues, and you may be surprised at their Old Testament view of divine justice. Continue to talk about these issues while recognizing that it will be several years before most can let go of concrete, rigid beliefs.

Mixed Blessings

Children whose parents practice different religions or who express their faith differently may be confused during these years. More than one child has worried about a parent who appears to be heading in the wrong direction (if you know what I mean) according to the beliefs of the other parent's faith. In addition, many kids are concerned about friends who seem to them to have the wrong beliefs. You'll need to work through issues with your partner so that you can provide a united front and reassurance to your child.

Junior Missionaries and Converts

Slightly older kids are more prone to trying to convert nonbelievers, but many preschoolers engage in some outright proselytizing among their friends and neighbors. Some kids decide to convert. Many parents get worked up about these incidents, but usually their concern is wasted. The vast majority of kids will readopt their parents' beliefs (or nonbeliefs), as long as no one turns the issue into a battle. Even preschoolers have the right to question and explore their faith or lack thereof; in the long run, this process will make their views stronger. Finally, I encourage you to teach your children to be respectful of other's beliefs.

Playing God: Activities that Promote Faith and Values

There are many things you can do to encourage a child this age to embrace her faith or adopt your moral attitudes, including:

✳ *Tell or read stories of faith and optimism.* And help your child act them out in her play. For example, give her toy animals and the garden hose to play Noah's Ark, or puppets to act out the story of David and Goliath. Or plant seeds after reading Ruth Krauss's classic story of faith THE CARROT SEED. Activities like these help kids grasp the details as well as the bigger picture of the tales.

✳ *Love thy neighbor.* Have your child join you in performing small acts of kindness for those near you. Shovel a neighbor's walk, take cookies to newcomers, or throw a block party.

✳ *Teach your child to pray or express gratitude and hope.* A simple prayer repeated at mealtime, a practice of thanking others or "the world" for good things at bedtime, or tossing an extra penny in the fountain to make a wish for someone else can help young children feel appreciation for others. Made-up prayers also provide a way for your child to talk to a higher power whenever she needs to, not just during church time.

✳ *Sing and dance your joy.* Religion doesn't have to be somber. Encourage children to express their feelings through music with spiritual or moral themes, as well as making up their own songs or dances to celebrate what they believe.

✳ *Share traditions from your family and faith.* Talk to your children about what your traditions mean, while encouraging active participation. Emphasize the spiritual aspects or positive values inherent in holidays.

✳ *Appreciate the natural world.* Looking at the stars together, admiring the silver flash of minnows in a stream, or collecting different kinds of leaves gives children glimpses of the miracle of our universe and inspires awe.

Beyond Shushing and Blushing

✳ ✳ ✳

Handling Insensitive or Prejudiced Behavior

One thing that's great about preschoolers is their rapidly improving ability to notice details and discern small differences. It's also one of the terrible things about them. Your child may comment loudly on how amazingly fat the lady waiting for the bus is or wonder why his friend doesn't wash her dark skin and get it clean like his. Or he may be scared of Grandma's friend in the wheelchair. You can't avoid these moments entirely—a preschooler's creativity guarantees there will be situations you could never foresee—but a proactive approach can reduce the number of times you wish the ground would swallow the two of you up. I also have practical tips for handling some of these awkward situations, which are useful given the rarity of earthquakes.

A Laundry List of Issues to Anticipate

These are *some* of the characteristics that young children tend to notice and wonder about. Talk about as many as possible, using books, TV shows or videos, and museums or ethnic institutions. Always let kids know they

can ask you questions, but that *they should wait until you're alone to do so.*
Children often want to know how or why a condition occurred and whether
it might happen to them. They may also need reassurance that people who
seem different aren't necessarily bad or threatening.

✳ *Mobility issues.* Preschoolers are curious about people in wheel-
chairs or who use crutches, canes, walkers, or other assistance to get
about. They also want to know about people who move in ways that
surprise them, like limping, shuffling, or walking stiffly or jerkily.

✳ *Extreme size.* Expect your child to comment on people who
are unusually tall or short, or who are exceptionally fat or thin.

✳ *Disfigurements.* Amputations, prostheses, burns, scars, tumors,
and limbs that look twisted, wasted, or otherwise atypical will attract
your child's attention. Your child may also perceive tattoos, piercings,
and other body art as the result of injury, drawing his stares and loud
comments.

✳ *Skin color and hair.* Children want to know about anyone who
has skin that looks significantly different from their skin or that of the
people around them. In addition to racial differences, they may wonder about things like moles, freckles, acne, birthmarks, or wrinkles.
Youngsters may also be curious about hair or facial hair that's different from what they're used to (e.g., baldness, different texture or
color, beards, or facial hair on women).

✳ *Funny ways of talking.* People who speak a foreign language, or
have an accent, stutter, or other speech impediments intrigue
preschoolers.

✳ *Hygiene problems.* Expect your child to criticize people who
smell bad (or wear too much perfume or cologne), have poor or
missing teeth, have dirty hair or clothing, or otherwise seem unap-
pealing to them.

✳ *Inappropriate behavior.* Even very young children may be surprisingly observant of people whose behavior seems off, such as
someone who's drunk or high, mentally ill people who talk to themselves or don't respect boundaries, or homeless people sleeping on the
sidewalk.

✳ *Unusual clothing.* Young children may wonder about women in burqas or headscarves, men wearing turbans or cassocks, young people in creative outfits, costumed characters, anyone dressed provocatively, people wearing unusual jewelry or accessories, or folks wearing uniforms, costumes, or masks.

Etiquette Lessons

During the preschool years, children can start learning that it makes people uncomfortable to be stared at or commented on; however, it will be years before you can count on your child to remember the rule in the heat of the moment. If you know you'll be someplace where he'll encounter people who look different (for example, if you're going to visit a relative in a nursing home), prepare him for what he might see, answer questions in advance, and remind him of the rules for being polite.

Secret Signals

Agree on a signal (like a hand squeeze) to remind your child to wait to comment or ask about someone. You'll also want him to signal you when he notices something he'd like to ask you about later.

Empathy Lessons

Even more important than learning to be polite is learning to be tolerant, accepting, and respectful of others. To do this, your child will need experiences that let him walk in another's shoes—or ride in her wheelchair.

Many children's museums include exhibits where children can try out equipment used by people with disabilities. You can also create challenges for your child at home, like trying to navigate from the family room to the kitchen with his eyes closed, build a block tower using only one hand, or communicate while wearing earplugs.

Talk openly about prejudice and discrimination and how they hurt people. Use examples that your child can understand, like asking what would happen if people who had eyes the color of his weren't allowed to use the playground with other children? Emphasize the ways that people are mostly similar, even if they have some features that seem different.

Learn about other cultures in a hands-on way. Try ethnic foods, attend family-friendly cultural festivals, incorporate holiday traditions from other cultures, and make friends who come from different backgrounds.

Finally, keep in mind that empathy develops slowly.

Remove Your Child's Foot from His Mouth without Putting It in Yours

Once when my young brother and I were waiting for our father at his office in a hospital clinic, he pointed out a woman who had several large tumors on her face and announced loudly, "That woman in the blue coat is *ugly*. I think she's a witch." As a teenager, I didn't have a clue what I should do; I just scooped my brother up and moved to another waiting area. And in truth, sometimes there isn't much you can do to repair the situation. General strategies:

* *Apologize.* Say something like "I'm sorry if my child hurt your feelings. He's just learning about other people and sometimes he makes mistakes."

* *Provide corrective information.* Quietly validate your child's perception. I'm not suggesting you say, "Yes, she is ugly," but you could say, "Everyone looks different. It's not how people look but how they act that makes them good or bad." *Later* explain in a matter-of-fact way any additional information he needs about the person's appearance.

* *Demonstrate your own acceptance of the other person.* If you can do so without compounding the other person's discomfort, smile and chat with her. This will show your child that you believe the other person has worth.

* *Debrief your child in private.* Remind your child how remarks can hurt people's feelings and review what he can do if he has questions for you. Enlarge on your earlier comments and explanations if necessary.

Tease Proofing and Pride Promoting

✳ ✳ ✳

Helping Kids Who Are Starting to Notice Their Differences

What's even worse than hearing your child make an insensitive remark is hearing someone make one to *her.* If your child has a condition or situation that makes her stand out from her peers (e.g., minority ethnicity or ethnicity different from yours, noticeable disability or hyper-ability, unusual appearance), it's important to start teaching her now how to handle insensitive comments or outright rejection, and to build up her sense of herself as a worthwhile person.

By the preschool years, children who feel different may already be starting to suffer from poor self-esteem. Their low self-image can create a vicious cycle in which they avoid opportunities to learn skills, have fun, or play with others—and then feel even worse. These activities or strategies may give a needed boost for keeping your child feeling connected, competent, and content.

Head 'Em Off at the Pass

Kids who are open about their differences and can answer questions about them (or even better, volunteer information) tend to fare better socially (and emotionally) than those who try to ignore or deny their differences or special needs. Often this technique is effective in *preventing* teasing from ever occurring. (Keep in mind that most teasing by young children happens out of ignorance, not a desire to be cruel.) At this age, your child needs you to teach her what to say or do to educate others—and she may even need you to do it for her while she watches and learns. Practice by playing What If? or acting out situations with dolls or puppets.

Block and Tackle—and Cheer from the Sidelines

A preschooler still needs you to be her protector and advocate. Go talk to her teachers and classmates at daycare, educate friends and relatives about how best to support her, and keep her away from people who can't stop being unkind, *but* help your child by respecting her growing strength and ability to fend for herself. Be especially careful not to rush in too frequently with siblings and peers.

May I Validate That for You?

Teach your child feelings words so she can tell you what she experiences. (Read the book FEELINGS by Aliki to help your child learn to identify and begin to understand her own and others' emotions.) *Just labeling feelings will make your child feel more in control.* Words like *frustrated* and *embarrassed* are especially useful for older preschoolers as they start to experience more complex emotions. Using a calm, matter-of-fact voice will help your child feel understood without fueling strong feelings.

Give your child chances to let off steam and express powerful emotions in positive ways, (like vigorous exercise, art, music, and pretend play). Be accepting of whatever she feels while still insisting on appropriate behavior (e.g., persisting in trying even when she feels discouraged, trying to problem-solve to change a rotten situation, being assertive rather than aggressive when angry or hurt).

Disarmament Techniques

Teach your child that ignoring someone who teases, surprising your tormentor by reacting in an unexpected way such as laughing or agreeing, avoiding the kids who are unkind to you and playing with others, and even simply being cheerful and persistent can all work to diffuse or end teasing over time, if not the first time. A reputation as a tattletale will only add to your child's social woes, so teach her to seek protection from an adult *only* when she is being hurt *and* can't protect herself.

Strength Training

Encourage your child to develop skills, habits, or attitudes that distract others from the way that she's different. Having athletic prowess, having good play ideas, being the class expert on something, and just being a thoughtful and enthusiastic playmate are all attributes that attract other preschoolers—and qualities you may be able to teach or encourage in her.

Come Into the Light

To avoid the risk that she'll get hurt, you may be tempted to keep your child out of preschool or other public situations. DON'T DO THIS! Hiding her just gives your child the message that there is something shameful about her—and puts her farther behind her peers.

Goal Models

Search out role models in your community or the greater world who have succeeded despite (or even because of) the difference they share with your child. (The Internet and public library are great places to start your search.) If you can't find anyone with your child's particular challenge, then make a habit of reading and talking about people who have faced other kinds of adversity and succeeded regardless.

Help Her Change the World

Help your child set preschool-level goals for making the world a better place. Volunteering with you, helping out around the home or neighborhood, or becoming an ambassador for people who face similar challenges (even in an informal capacity) can make your child feel powerful—and that feeling can spread to other situations.

Walk Tall

Play games that teach your child how to move in a confident, controlled way, like pretending to be different animals or types of people. Urge her to strut like a peacock, glide like an eagle, or parade like a powerful princess. Dance classes, horseback riding, martial-arts training, tot swimming classes, skating lessons, and other physical activity can also give your child body confidence. Many are available with adaptations for children with special needs. As a bonus, these classes provide opportunities for making friends.

A World of Snowflakes

The child who feels singled out for being different may be comforted by knowing that like snowflakes, no two people are alike—and that's wonderful. She may also like learning that people are more similar than different—and that's wonderful too. Make a wall in your house with one half devoted to celebrating ways friends and family members are unique and special, and the other half showing activities, skills, or characteristics they share.

Someone Just Like Me

Having even one friend who shares her difference can have profound benefits, easing loneliness, encouraging risk taking, and relieving anxieties. Even if you can only provide a once-a-year camp or other activity for your child to be with others like her, the trouble will be well worth it. It will also give *you* a chance to meet parents who understand the challenges you face and who may be able to share strategies for supporting your children.

Dollars and Sense

* * *

Allowance, Greed, Philanthropy, and Other Money Issues

Toddlers like to play with money; preschoolers like to spend it. As kids begin to understand what money can buy—from candy and the latest toy they've seen on TV to trips to Disney World—they start pestering you to fork it out. Most have a sense that money (especially in the form of credit cards or checks) is limitless. Thus you need to start teaching about money during the preschool years, from personal-finance concepts like budgeting, saving, giving, and the work-money connection to a quick lesson on how the banking system works. It's a big task—but one kids will love to participate in, especially if you pay them to do so.

Allowance for Children Who Don't Know the Value of a Dollar

Should kids this age get allowance? That's up to you, but most experts recommend a small allowance once kids start asking you to buy things for them. How much money should you allot? Again, that's up to you and your bank account, taking into account what you want your kids to pay for themselves. Some families link allowance to chores, but many experts say kids need at least some guaranteed income to learn money management. We gave our little guys a quarter per year of age each week. That meant the three-year-olds had a quarter to spend on a bouncy ball or gum, a quarter to put in the Salvation Army kettle, and a quarter for their piggy banks. Fours could do all of the above, plus save money to buy their own gifts for family members (from the dollar store). And fives had an extra quarter to distribute into whichever of those categories they chose—and *oooh*, that choosing could be hard.

Choice Morsels

Get in the habit of using the phrase "We choose not to spend our money on that" rather than "We can't afford that." And from the time your child can talk, start involving him in making choices about how your family uses its money. Teach him about needs versus wants. Talk about what might happen if you didn't buy various items. If you don't buy food, the family will be hungry and eventually they'll die. If you don't buy the latest Transformer, your child may be bored or feel left out with his friends or just be sad and mopey, but he won't die.

Involve him in spending your entertainment budget. Does he want to have dinner at McDonald's or for the same amount of money, cook burgers at home, rent a video, and eat ice cream for dessert? (It's good for kids to regret some decisions.)

Let him help decide how to distribute charity money. My kids often pool their money to give to charity and my husband and I match it. I offer lists of possible kid-friendly recipients, like the Smile Train (which trains doctors to provide cleft palate surgery in developing countries), child sponsorship, and the local no-kill animal shelter. We discuss pros and cons and then vote.

Find ways to steer your child to good choices. Make a family "store" where he can spend his allowance so you can limit his choices. Or allow him to pick between just two or three items you designate at the store. My parents refused to buy us any toy advertised on TV, so we kids avoided watching TV so we could always claim we'd never seen what we wanted in an ad. Hey…was that a trick?

Lessons from the Rip-Off Machine

My oldest was fascinated with those machines where you manipulate a claw-thingy to try to catch a biggish prize. I kept explaining that the game was rigged so that even adults would rarely get a prize. But he was determined, so finally I agreed to let him try with his own money. It took three tries (consuming about three months' worth of his savings) and three failures to finally grasp that it was indeed a "rip-off machine." Why did I let my child squander his money like that? Because the lessons he learned were worth *way* more than three dollars. That's why you should let your child occasionally spend his own money on stuff you know is crap; sometimes the most powerful lessons are learned the hard way.

Some Money Games Worth the Trouble

As with so many things, play is the most effective avenue for teaching young kids basic concepts they need to know. These activities require some supplies and support from you, but are simple and appealing enough to bear the repetition that small fry need and crave.

✳ *Lemonade stands.* Selling things teaches kids about the work-money connection, and might teach them concepts like making change or the value of good marketing.

✳ *Store, Bank, and Restaurant.* Give your child props to play pretending games involving the exchange of money. Gradually introduce concepts like credit cards, loans, checking accounts, debit cards, and staying within a budget. Your kid won't really get them, but the background knowledge will make it easier to grasp these concepts as he grows older.

✳ *Making commercials.* Get out the video camera and let your child pitch various products and services. You'll get the best material for discussion if you give him things that are hard to sell like broken toys, moldy potatoes, or last week's newspaper.

Inoculate Against Affluenza

Having too much money and stuff is as bad for kids as having too little— just bad in different ways. That's why you need to resist the urge to buy your child everything you wanted as a child, even if you can afford it easily. That's why you *never* buy everything (or even close to it) on his birthday list, and why you give some gifts that cost nothing, like a coupon book of piggyback rides. That's why you make him save and scrimp for months to buy a toy he wants instead of just getting it for him, and why you insist that he contribute some of his own money toward family purchases or vacations. People value what they pay for and what they have to work to earn, and children are never too young to learn that lesson. It's also a good idea to start exposing your child to poverty (in small doses—you don't want to depress him). Notice homeless people when you go shopping downtown, discuss inadequate housing when you pass through neighborhoods that are crowded or rundown, and draw your child's attention to some images in the media (avoiding ones that are likely to be too disturbing). Imagine with him what it might be like to have so much less. Then let your child do his part to help out. For example, before gift-getting occasions, urge your child to pick at least one toy to donate to charity to make room for new things; let him stack boxes with you at the local food pantry or choose to go without his weekly gumball to give the money to a local shelter instead.

When the World Intrudes

✳ ✳ ✳

Ways to Un-scare Your Child During Disturbing Times

September 11th. The war in Iraq. The subprime-mortgage crisis. The threat of bankruptcy at Toys Я Us. What should you tell your young child?

What can you do so that fear doesn't rule her life? Try these tips to keep the media from controlling your child's emotions.

Provide Age-Appropriate Information

Inquiring minds need to know—and who has a more inquiring mind than a preschooler? Respond to questions about the news by asking your child what she's heard. You may be surprised to discover how much she has picked up. Correct any misperceptions and fill in the blanks in words she can understand. Reassure your child that you and others are working hard to keep her safe. Talking about fears is a good way to reduce them; however, if your child doesn't want to discuss an issue, respect that need.

Turn the News Off

Graphic images on TV and in photographs are particularly disturbing to young children. So turn off CNN and the Today Show (Darn! There goes my invitation to be a guest someday!) and even NPR when sensitive or scary topics are featured. Store newspapers and news magazines with frightening photos out of your child's reach, and censor what you say to others (for example, on the phone or at the dinner table) if your child might be listening.

And Put on Your Listening Ears

Listen to your child's concerns and questions, no matter how silly or trivial they seem. Remember that children communicate through their behavior and play as well as their words. Be alert especially for aggressive and scary themes in their pretending play and artwork. Redirect hurtful or dangerous play. And remember it's okay—and often powerful—to respond to their concerns through joining in their play.

Look for the Helpers—And the Good News

Mister Rogers said that his mother taught him to look for the helpers in times of crisis—and that's still good advice today. Discuss the different kinds of people who help us—and provide props for your child to play

Helpers too. Point out good things in the news, your family, and your community so your child will see the world as basically a good place. Emphasize the ability of people to bounce back after difficulties.

Help Your Child Become a Helper, Too

Even very young children feel more in control when they do something kind or useful in a time of crisis. For example, young children can send drawings, help assemble care packages, or sell lemonade to raise money for a good cause.

What serviceman or servicewoman wouldn't love to get a care package with a beautiful drawing by a preschooler? Organizations such as Military Moms at www.militarymoms.net can forward care items and letters to military personnel. (You can't send things to "Any Service Member" since 9/11.)

Be creative! For example, after 9/11, my dog-crazy daughter and her buddy raised money for the rescue dogs by selling Milk-Bones and poop-disposal bags at a stand targeted at neighborhood dog walkers.

Model Calmness and Courage

Kids take their cues about how to respond during a crisis from you. This means that you can't rely on beer and fudge ripple to calm your own fears. Darn it. Try going-down-the-twirly-slide-without-barfing contests; kid-and-parent yoga, meditation, or silence contests; telling diarrhea jokes; and okay, a *little* ice cream. Hey, it has calcium and protein, and those things are nutritious. Even if you do not feel calm and courageous, simply acting that way will help your child feel safe—and may even lead you to start feeling that way!

Be Alert to Signs Your Child is Overwhelmed

It's rare that even very scary news derails young children. However, some sensitive children or those at risk because of previous experiences with loss or disasters may become overwhelmed by exposure to bad news, even if it doesn't touch their lives directly. Watch out for sad or anxious moods; difficulty sleeping, eating, or playing; and regression, like loss of toilet-training skills. If these changes persist for more than a couple weeks, seek help from your pediatrician or a mental-health worker.

Raise a Future Peacemaker

Our kids are probably our best hope for world peace, so teach them well. Model empathy, kindness, and tolerance, and talk through the reasons for your behavior. Encourage children to express anger in ways that don't hurt others or damage objects. Remind your child to use her words, not her body, and to avoid words that wound. Teach her to share and take turns, as well as to resolve disagreements in fair ways, like compromising or using impartial "choosers" (such as counting-out rhymes like eeny, meeny, miny, moe or flipping a coin).

CHAPTER EIGHT

Family Crisis!

* * *

A Catalog of Coping and Hoping

"You can't keep the birds of misery from flying overhead, but you can stop them from pooping in your hair." —Variation on an old saying

Remember this saying. It will be useful someday for aggravating your teenager when she whines about how unfair it is that she has homework *and* chores or complains that her heart is broken because that cute boy in her physics class promised to call and he hasn't. But these words of wisdom can also be useful for aggravating yourself—wait, I mean "for helping you mobilize your resources"—if your family is facing a difficult time, like divorce, remarriage, death, illness, or the aftermath of a natural or financial disaster.

Because here's the sad truth: even if you're a parent with young kids, and even if you're a good parent and a good person, you don't automatically get a free pass on Terrible Things. Heck, most of the time, you're not even entitled to preferential parking spaces (though I personally think anyone stuck hustling an overtired four-year-old through the supermarket at dinnertime deserves a spot right out front).

If you're reading this, I'm assuming you and your child have already discovered that there are some things neither Band-Aids nor Elmer's Glue-All can repair (as miraculous as those substances are) and some things neither birthday wishes nor bedtime prayers can change (as powerful as those things are). This chapter is thus not about keeping the birds of misery away, but how to quickly put up your umbrella, duck beneath an awning, or clap a wide-brimmed hat on your kid's head as soon as you notice those buzzards circling.

If you're a parent with young kids and the birds of misery are flocking about, right away you have to cope and find hope, whether you want to or not, and you have to show your kid how to do those things too. No pity parties, no moping around all day in your old bathrobe eating double-fudge-ripple ice cream, watching soap-opera marathons, and crying about how the world is coming to an end. Well, okay, you can do that for a day or two as long as you share the fudge ripple with your kid and substitute Winnie the Pooh videos for the soap operas. *Then* you have to get up off your fanny and take care of your child because little kids lack the knowledge, experience, and wisdom to take care of themselves when something bad happens. This chapter will help you figure out how to do all that taking care, especially if you feel a little short in the knowledge, experience, and wisdom departments yourself, what with all the poop dropping around you.

You may notice that I'm not exactly taking a properly sober attitude about all of this. It's not because I want to minimize the pain you're feeling—I've seen enough sad things to have a very clear idea of how much families can hurt. But I want to remind you that a light touch helps everyone when the skies are dark.

Have courage. You can do this. You are not alone. I'll be right here with you.

Ten Best All-Purpose Coping Strategies

✳ ✳ ✳

For Your Child—and You

These approaches to stress management can help your child and family, no matter what challenges you face.

Embrace Routines and Rituals

Routines—whether they're small things like overfeeding the goldfish every morning or bigger things like going to preschool or daycare—give children a sense of predictability, security, and hope. Family rituals, such as "toasting" at dinner, reassure your child of your support and availability. Finally, involving children in formal rituals, like funerals or divorce ceremonies, can help them heal much in the same ways that these customs help adults.

Play Pain Away

Kids need vigorous, running-around types of play to diffuse the effects of stress hormones and improve sleep and appetite. They also need time to play with buddies, both as a distraction and as a reminder of normalcy. Finally, pretending gives children a way to explore and express complicated feelings, and gives you a window to see how they're coping.

Take the Talking Cure

Make sure you talk and talk and talk to your child about what's going on during hard times. In particular, kids need details about what will happen in their daily lives: who will care for them, where they'll sleep, what's for snack, etc. They also need reassuring answers to the questions they're afraid to ask, like was the divorce their fault, or will you die too. And most need to hear those things—plus "I love you forever"—over and over.

Try Different Strokes

A caregiver's touch is such a fundamental comfort that a child in distress will choose it over food, even if he's ravenously hungry. Touches don't have to be all gentle, poor-little-thing pats and strokes; roughhousing, knee bouncing, bear hugs, "circus tricks" like flipping kids or swinging them about, and other vigorous ways of touching soothe psyches too.

Provide a Sound Track

Adjust the mood in your household by playing the right tunes at the right time. Try peaceful music at bedtime, rousing marches in the morning, and boppy, silly songs to boost energy when folks feel down. Children are also more compliant when you sing requests; adapt versatile songs like "Here We Go Round the Mulberry Bush" or "The Wheels on the Bus" to direct your child's behavior as desired.

Phone a Friend

For each of you. Your child needs *you* to have a supportive friend so you're less stressed (and less tempted to use him to unburden your feelings), and he needs a friend too, especially someone who's been through what he's experiencing to help normalize the situation and make him feel less different or alone. Don't know anyone who's been in the same position? Talk to a counselor or a member of the clergy, or search on the Internet to locate nearby support groups.

Giggle and Guffaw

Laughing—even if he's forcing it or faking it all together—improves the functioning of your child's immune system and gives his cardiovascular system a workout. But laughter can be hard to come by when you're facing a life-changing emergency. If your child can't think up any good diarrhea jokes, prime the pump for giggles with silly books like DIARY OF A WORM by Doreen Cronin or THE STINKY CHEESE MAN AND OTHER FAIRLY STUPID TALES by Jon Scieszka. Or plop underpants on your head and serve an April Fool's dinner even if it's August. See http://familyfun.go.com for menu suggestions and ideas for silly pranks too.

Create!

Mobilizing the energy to create something together can distract your child, promote resourcefulness, and erase hopeless feelings. Read the Caldecott award–winning JOSEPH HAD A LITTLE OVERCOAT by Simms Taback, and then craft a project from materials on hand (like window hangings made by ironing crayon shavings between sheets of waxed paper). Other arts-and-crafts activities, as well as making music or dancing, give kids a chance to express feelings while they gain pleasure from using their hands and souls.

Escape from Misery

If you don't already have a hidey hole for your child, clean out a closet or large cupboard, make it over so no one can get hurt or locked inside, and help him decorate it with cozy comforts like pillows and blankets and a few favorite toys. Or throw a sheet over a card table or cut doors in a big box—just make sure your child has a place to be alone (but near you) when he needs to be.

Book 'Em

Books can help kids understand and resolve problems or give them hope and inspiration. Ask your librarian for appropriate nonfiction picture books and leave them handy for frequent rereadings. And don't forget fiction books that speak to your child's heart about resilience or the power of relationships. Some of my favorites include classics like Virginia Lee Burton's MIKE MULLIGAN AND HIS STEAM SHOVEL and THE LITTLE HOUSE, Watty Piper's THE LITTLE ENGINE THAT COULD, and Margaret Wise Brown's THE RUNAWAY BUNNY and THE IMPORTANT BOOK (which you can expound upon with a discussion about the important things about your child, you, his family, etc.).

Fun and Games When Life's Not Fun and Games

✳ ✳ ✳

Play Therapy for Amateurs

Seriously troubled children may need the help of a well-trained play therapist, but if your kid is suffering from garden-variety misery during a difficult situation, you can help her tackle tough issues through games and pretending. These basic therapist techniques can boost the impact of your play sessions:

✳ *Label and reflect feelings.* Kids often lack the vocabulary or self-awareness to express their feelings in words, and everyone likes to feel understood. So, for example, if your child keeps smashing the little dinosaur into the big one as it tries to leave to go live in a different cave, you might say something like, "The little dino is angry and sad. She wishes the Daddy wasn't going away."

✳ *Ask questions.* Check in about motivation, desires, and feelings, ask about alternative approaches or endings, and confirm that you understand the action.

✳ *Empathize and normalize.* This can be done in the context of the play, with your character expressing compassion, or as a comment about the play.

✳ *Offer hope.* Remind the characters that things will get better, notice a character's strengths and support, or suggest happier endings.

The following activities give you openings to relieve your child's stress or even intervene to help her cope better.

Play-gression

The urge to hurt someone else when you're in pain yourself is instinctive. Obviously, you don't want your child to harm anyone for real. However, aggressive pretending games like Doctor with Syringe or Bad Guys give hurting children acceptable ways to retaliate for pretend. Talk to your child while playing; say things like "Ow! That shot really hurt me. I know you're just trying to keep me from getting sick but it still makes me mad!" Be patient if she insists on the same theme repeatedly, but seek professional help if she seems unable to move on after a while.

Break the Rules with Impunity

Kids in crisis situations generally have to play by other people's rules. Perhaps that's why unhappy preschoolers cheat even more than usual—and jump at the chance to make their own rules. Offer to let your kid change the rules to a game like Chutes and Ladders any way she wants to (like letting herself have two spins for every one of yours). While playing, talk about issues like feeling frustrated when rules seem unfair, what it feels like to play by different rules at different times (good topic for shared-custody situations), and the difference between wishing for something to happen and causing it to happen (a hard distinction for preschoolers).

House

Family play is often an obsession for children in stressful home situations. Give your child many pretending options: props for dramatic play, families of dolls or stuffed animals, miniature animal families, puppets of all sorts (make your own from tongue depressors or paper bags), and dollhouses with furnishings. Many kids also like to play Baby, which gives them a chance to get some extra attention and holding. *Bad* Baby may be even more fun.

Leverage and Pull

Boost your kid's sense of control with science activities that showcase her power. My kids loved to demonstrate to friends how they could lift our family-room sofa—using a lever. (You'll need a broomstick or a hardwood dowel about four feet in length and one inch in diameter, which you can pick up from the hardware store. Have your child slide one end of the stick a foot or so under the end of the sofa and lift up on the other end of the stick.) Scooting boxes of heavy books around the house, banging nails into a slightly rotten tree stump, and other power-demonstrating activities give preschoolers a chance to feel like superheroes. And don't forget how much grown-up activities like cooking or even cleaning can make kids feel competent and in control. Need more ideas? Consult THE FATHER'S ALMANAC by S. Adams Sullivan (which taught us the lever trick) or, for sillier ideas, the Klutz Press book KIDS' SHENANIGANS.

Smash, Pillage, Squash, and Scribble

Research has shown that activities like smacking a punching bag when you're mad may actually *increase* aggression, not drain it. Nonetheless, I'm including some destructo-play here because I have seen it help many kids— especially if the kid plays to the point of exhausting the urge. Try shredding newspaper, knocking down targets (e.g., toppling over empty plastic bottles with Nerf guns, playground balls, or a jet from the hose), and popping balloons or water balloons in a variety of ways. (Remember that balloons can be a choking hazard, so supervise carefully.) Jumping onto old mattresses or beanbag chairs, stomping a sheet of bubble wrap, and scribbling frantically all over a large sheet of paper (buy it by the roll) also deplete adrenaline stores.

Re-Creation

This is a great game for kids who are experiencing changes in their households. Give a child a pile of blocks, a bunch of Legos, or a lump of Play-Doh and challenge her to build something like a fort, a dream house, or a face. Then *take away from* or add to her materials as appropriate, and challenge her to rebuild it differently using the supplies she now has. The message that things can change, but still be good, is powerful.

I'm Gonna Getcha

And similar games like hide-and-seek provide reassurance at the unconscious level that you won't abandon your children, no matter what— not even if they run away, not even if you or they seem angry. Pretending to eat kids up, even though it doesn't make sense on an adult level, also seems satisfying to most little guys. Maybe they like the idea of becoming a part of you.

Let Him Sleep on Your Face

✳ ✳ ✳

Comforts When a Parent Is Absent from Home

Military deployment. Business trips. Kid-free vacations. Whatever the reason, lengthy absences from their parents are hard on preschoolers. These techniques help your child understand the scope of a parent's absence and make him feel connected despite time and distance.

Make a Memory

Before a separation, assemble memory boxes for each of you with items and photos to remind you of happy times together, or exchange love tokens like stuffed animals covered with enough kisses to last until your return, lockets with pictures inside, or a special object to protect—but not anything too special or fragile. Take a moment to make mental memories, noticing and talking about how the person you each love looks, sounds, smells, and feels.

Map out Your Absence

Show your child where you'll be on a map or globe (not that preschoolers really understand scale) and play riding on an airplane and sleeping in a hotel (or tent or whatever) to give him some sense of what you'll be up to. Count out M&Ms (or other small treats) to equal the number of days you'll be gone and let him nibble one daily. (Just keep them out of reach or he might try to speed up your return "magically.") If possible, link your return to an event (like "after three school days" or "pretty soon after Mommy's birthday").

Battle the Departure Blues

It's normal for spouses to have a big fight before an expected separation—and it's equally normal to squabble with your kids. Just knowing this can ease *everyone's* tension. Be sure to remind your child that you *are* coming back, which is not always obvious to young kids. Talk to him about why you're leaving too, reassuring him that the separation is not his fault. And absolutely, positively, no matter what, *do say good-bye*, even if it's painful.

Let Her Sleep on Your Face

Find ways to be with your child at bedtime. Get a photograph transferred onto a pillowcase (most copy stores can do this), so you can sleep cheek to cheek, or hang a photograph or collage next to the head of the bed where he can gaze into your eyes as he gets dozy. Even better, make your child recordings of yourself reading him bedtime stories. United Through

Reading sponsors programs to help deployed military personnel, distant grandparents, and families facing physical separation for various reasons build bonds through sharing books on DVDs. (Learn more about the organization at www.unitedthroughreading.org.)

Keep Talking

Remember that phone calls to young kids rarely go smoothly; they usually get completely tongue-tied the moment the phone goes up to their ears. E-mail—or instant messaging or video chat sites like Skype (www.skype.com)—may be easier ways to talk on a frequent basis. Children can dictate notes and send drawings made with computer software or scanned from paper and attached as a file. If you don't have a webcam, your public library or military base may have one that you can use for occasional chances to see each other again. Good conversation topics with young kids include pets, friends, preschool or childcare, what they ate during the day (which often sparks more topics), and how to make milk come out of your nose—or something else silly.

Package Your Care and Send It Off

For longer separations, help young children assemble items for care packages, including crafts they've made themselves. One idea is to send a paper hug. Have your child lie down on a roll of paper (or multiple sheets taped together) and trace his arms and hands and head. Cut out the big hug and have your child decorate it with a drawing of his face, lipstick kisses, Xs and Os, hearts, and a message. (For more craft ideas, check sites like www.familyfun.go.com or www.enchantedlearning.com.) Departing parents can also hide a small wrapped gift for the child before they leave. Then they can send directions for a treasure hunt to find it.

Take It Ease-y on Return

The return of the absent parent may be as hard as his absence. Prepare for a happy reunion, but steel yourself for surprising reactions. Young children often act standoffish initially, even if they've been coached to give a warm greeting. Get down at eye level, smile, ask questions, engage your child with a toy or book, and only gradually get physical. It also takes time and effort to adjust roles and routines. Limit-testing, regression, and signs of stress are all normal during this period. Routines, extra hugs and kisses, and reassurance will usually help your child return to an even keel.

Parental Etiquette for Separation and Divorce

✳ ✳ ✳

What to Say, Do, and Even Wear during the Transition

Handling this difficult change well can help your child adjust a little more quickly and easily. Just remember that it is normal for a child to be *very* upset, and that everyone needs *lots* of time to adapt to significant life changes like this one.

How and When to Tell Your Child about an Impending Separation or Divorce

Ideally, once the separation is certain and one parent is moving out within a few days, you and your spouse should tell your child about the planned change *together.* Don't do this, however, if you cannot be calm and civilized in each other's presence. Your child does not need the added stress of open conflict.

First warn your child that you have some upsetting news. Explain what *separation* or *divorce* means (i.e., parents won't be living together anymore, either short-term while they're working out problems, or never again because they won't be married anymore).

Provide logistical details: where everyone (including pets) will live, how often and where she will see the departing parent, how her routines will or won't change, what's for dinner tonight, etc. It can help if your child can see a picture (and soon visit) the departing parent's new home and her space in it.

Don't detail the adult reasons for the divorce. A preschooler only needs to know that the split is because of problems the adults have and that it has nothing to do with anything she's done or said.

Finally, reassure your child that both of you will always love her, and that parents don't divorce their children.

More Things to Say—Repeatedly

It will take time and lots of repetition for your child to absorb all the ideas that come with a major change in her family. These are some of the messages you want to make sure she understands.

✳ *"It's not your fault."* Preschoolers, more than kids of any other age, are prone to magical thinking and tend to feel guilty that something they've done (or not done) has caused the divorce. Watch out for kids who are "too good" as they may be harboring fantasies about causing the separation or getting you back together.

✳ *"You can always love both of us."* Make sure she has readily available photographs and mementos of the absent parent, as well as opportunities to call or have other casual contact between visits.

✳ *"Nothing you say, do, or wish can make Mommy or Daddy get together again. Wishes can't make good things—or bad things—happen."* Don't give your child conflicting messages.

✳ *"It's okay to be [sad, mad, confused, scared, worried, etc.]."* Be sure to provide art supplies for expressing feelings and "whisper buddies" (like stuffed animals or worry dolls) for thoughts too scary to say aloud. Friends who've also been through a parents' divorce can share experiences and be a big comfort.

✳ *"It's okay that you peed your pants. Lots of kids have accidents when their families change, but you'll get used to things soon. I'll help you clean up."* Reassure your child that regression is temporary and normal under the circumstances—and that she still has your love *and* support.

What Not to Say

These are things better expressed to your best friend or your lawyer.

✳ "Your *mother*" or "your *father*." Continue to call your ex *Mom* or *Dad* or whatever your child calls the other parent. Adding *your* is not just placing distance between you and your former spouse, but also between you and your child.

✳ *"He's such a jerk!"* Or anything else negative about your ex-spouse. Badmouthing him in your child's hearing damages your child, no matter how true. Remember, your child is biologically half you and half that person, so when you call your ex a jerk, you're telling your child that half of her is a jerk too.

✳ *"Who do you want to live with?"* You and your ex-spouse need to work out custody and visitation details on your own. Consider mediation rather the traditional court system to work out custody issues if you can't do it on your own.

What to Do

Reread the coping strategies and play ideas on pages 235–238. And try these other suggestions:

✳ *Share the news.* The other important people in your child's life—teachers, grandparents, the mom who drives car pool, and even the chatty neighbors who might make insensitive comments—need to know what's up so they can be supportive.

✳ *Avoid other changes in your child's life.* Try to delay moving or making changes in childcare arrangements or daily schedules. If possible, wait to divide up furnishings.

✳ *Show your love with ordinary words and actions, not your MasterCard.* It's normal to feel guilty and to want to soothe your child's pain, *but,* everyone needs *time* to adjust and nothing you buy can change that fact—and in the long run it will do your child additional harm if he begins to equate love with stuff.

✳ *Affirm your child's ability to cope.* In large part, you do this by maintaining your usual standards and expectations. Make small allowances for normal regression, but continue enforcing normal limits and avoid excessive babying. For example, if your child previously slept in her own bed, expect her to keep doing so—but you could offer ten minutes of extra cuddle time if she wants it, provide a night-light if she's scared of the dark, or help her devise a plan to combat nightmares, like turning her pillow over or hanging up a dream catcher.

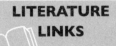

LITERATURE LINKS

Some of my favorite non-fiction titles about divorce are DINOSAURS DIVORCE by Laurene Krasny Brown and Marc Brown (of ARTHUR fame) and LET'S TALK ABOUT IT: DIVORCE by Fred Rogers. Fictional picture books that address divorce include LOON SUMMER by Barbara Santucci and RAINY DAY by Emma Haughton.

✳ *Act like a grown-up.* Find mature, healthy ways to assuage your own pain. Excessive drinking, poor eating habits, rebound dating, etc., will hurt your child (and you). Avoid the temptation to retaliate against your ex in childish ways, like sabotaging visits. Finally, communicate with your ex directly or through his lawyer; young children should never be in the position of relaying messages or acting as spies.

✳ *Consider having a divorce ceremony.* Many groups, including the Unitarian Universalist Association, the United Methodist Church, and some Jewish synagogues, now perform ceremonies to mark the end of a marriage *and the ongoing commitment of both parents to their children.* Some couples also choose to melt down their wedding rings and use the metal to make new jewelry that symbolizes their mutual and unending love for their children. These formal markers can help kids accept the finality of the divorce and give you chances to offer reassurance.

✳ *Police friends and family.* Insist that others behave appropriately around your child—no criticizing your ex, rejecting your child, or spoiling her on your behalf.

What to Wear

For the swimsuit competition, one-piece suits without artificial padding are required.

Okay, just kidding about this one—sort of. I do recommend that around your child you wear comfy, come-hug-me clothes that can stand up to some rough-and-tumble play. When I was working as a therapist, I often had parents who came to my office in dressy clothes, and I was struck by how their outfits put a barrier between them and their needy (but grubby) tots. Distressed kids are *hard* on their parents' clothes—tugging, kicking, spilling, and more. So get out your sweats and jeans and save the "evening wear" for later.

Visitation Excitation

✳ ✳ ✳

Smoothing out the Highs and Lows of Shared Custody and Visitation

When visitation or shared custody goes smoothly, it helps children adjust to divorce. If necessary, seek help from a neutral third party—preferably a mediator or therapist rather than the courts. Remember that arrangements can (and should) be adjusted as your child grows and situations change. Try these tips to make visitation an asset in your child's life.

Some Logical Logistics

In general, young children do better with frequent, short visits (e.g., one full day and an overnight visit every week, plus briefer contacts, like car pool or chatting on the phone). Children also benefit from annual longer vacations with noncustodial parents, sharing some holidays and other special occasions, and spending time with their extended families. Finally, visitation tends to be more regular and successful when parents live within twenty minutes of each other and when visits generally follow a consistent schedule.

Shift Changes

The transition from one parent to another tends to be stressful for all involved. Don't read too much into a child's balking or eagerness to leave one parent for the other; both reactions are normal and expected.

Make it easier for your child to say good-bye to you by having him ready to go on time, telling him you hope he has fun, and having a short good-bye ritual like the one you use for other partings.

Be timely when you fetch (and return) your child. Greet him with open arms. Get down on his level and give him your full attention for a few minutes. Let him know you're delighted that he had a good time. Some families find it easier (and possibly more civilized) to make the switch at a neutral site like a fast-food restaurant. Being on time is critical for this arrangement to work.

Many preschoolers benefit from having "transitional objects"—something of theirs to leave behind with you as a placeholder and something of yours to take with them as a reminder of you. Photographs, stuffed animals, or inexpensive jewelry are appropriate items.

Never ask your child to be a go-between. Deliver all messages to your ex yourself or through a third party.

Parent in Parallel

Especially in the first few months, preschoolers gain security from continuing the routines and rules they've always followed—so aim to be consistent, even if you disagree with your ex-spouse. Ideally, you'll agree on house rules and a schedule for meals and sleep. Avoid the urge to become a Disneyland parent; ordinary fun activities like picnics at the park, playing board games, doing projects, and even sharing chores actually give you the best shot at creating a good, lasting relationship with your child.

Make a Home for Your Bunny

Children need a dedicated space in both homes. Create a sense of consistency between his rooms with the same bedding, similar furniture arrangements, and matching stashes of favorite books and toys. Duplicate as many necessities as possible (e.g., medications, clothing, and toiletries) to minimize the amount of stuff that has to be transferred each time. Make sure both homes are childproofed and child-friendly.

Decorating matters too. Hang a family collage in your child's room. This small gesture means a great deal to children struggling to understand their changed relationships. Obtain photographs of *all* family members, including extended family and pets. And while you're at it, explicitly remind him that he has your permission to love *all* his family members. Finally, display the macaroni-and-packing-peanut mobile your child made for you and scatter photographs from his babyhood and your times together so he can see he still has an everyday presence in your heart.

Live the Golden Rule

Regardless of how much of a shmuck your ex is, be courteous and generous, especially within your child's hearing. Keep your criticisms and resentments tightly zipped behind your lips, and resist the temptation to compete in the Santa Parent Sweepstakes. I know this can be very, very, very difficult (which is why I keep repeating it) but in the long run, *being mature and cordial will cement your child's bond with you!* Over and over, I've seen how much kids come to despise divorced parents who can't stop sniping and squabbling, and how grateful they are to a parent who takes the high road. If you must whine (and it sure can feel good), find a friend or therapist who will let you do it in private.

Preschoolers and the Dating Scene

* * *

Q&A for Single Parents and Their Kids

Q: Are you saying my preschooler should date? She seems awfully young.

A: Yes! She should date *you*! All kids need time alone with a parent who focuses on them—and kids of divorce or single parents need it doubly. You don't have to spend any money, or even go anywhere; all you need to do is *schedule* a regular time to be alone with your child, and give her your undivided attention. If you stay home, turn on the answering machine and hang a do-not-disturb sign on the door.

Q: All right, but what about me? Is it okay for me to go on dates with other grown-ups?

A: Yes again! At a minimum, adults need adult friendship, so even if your "dates" are just lunch with a buddy, they'll benefit your child by giving him a happier, less-stressed parent. As for romantic dates, keep the following recommendations in mind:

Wait several months after your separation or the death of your spouse (at least) to reenter the dating scene, even if your ex is serial-dating every aerobics instructor at the gym or your sister has found the perfect guy for you. Both your preschooler and you will benefit from taking it slow. It's hard to nurture a sound relationship on the heels of any major life change, and the last thing your child needs is a parent struggling with the distractions and woes of the dating scene.

If possible, schedule your dates for when your child is away from you anyhow (e.g., with your ex, at the grandparents', or at childcare). If you do go out on your kid's time, use a familiar, consistent sitter. And balance your adult-date time with kid-date time.

Don't introduce dates to your child until your relationship is serious. But do tell your dates *from the start* that you have kids and that you're a package deal.

Q: Can I have my date for a "sleepover"?

A: Better not to, at least not until your relationship is extra serious. Even if you plan to usher your date out of the house before your child wakes up, there's a good chance you'll have a little visitor during the night. If you ignore this advice, *lock your bedroom door.*

Q: My relationship is serious, and I brought the guy home to meet my kid—and she screamed, "I hate you!" and kicked him in the shins. What do I do now?

A: First you apologize to your date for your child. Then you calmly but firmly remind your child to use her words, not her body, and to treat adults with respect. And *then* you sigh, remembering that it's completely normal for a preschooler to feel distressed about your dating, as it crushes her fantasies of reuniting her family, takes your attention away from her, and disrupts her schedule. Next time, you'll prep your child by describing the behavior you expect from her, remind her that you'll always love her, and tell her that you'll make it easier for her by meeting in a setting like a playground where your child can come and go. Empathize with her that it's hard to meet new people or to think about your lives changing more, but be matter-of-fact about continuing to date and enforce rules about good behavior. You'll both be relieved to remember that it takes time for people to learn to like each other.

Q: Ever since that incident, my boyfriend keeps saying he has to wash his hair when I suggest a date. What should I do?

A: I'd say good riddance. Anyone who dates a parent (and especially anyone who enters a stepfamily relationship) has to be tolerant of normal, obnoxious kid behavior—*and* have a double dose of patience for coping with the extra testing a stressed child will do. But there's no harm in reminding your shy guy that things will likely smooth out over time and letting him know you've traded your child's steel-toed boots for soft sneakers. If he's willing to give it another try, great.

Q: My kid loves the woman I'm dating. And she loves my daughter too. Only now I'm not sure I like her anymore. Will it kill my kid if I dump my girlfriend?

A: It probably won't *kill* her, but yes, it will be painful. In the short run, expect your child to be sad and angry and perhaps to have behavioral problems similar to those at the time of your divorce, like difficulty sleeping, wetting herself, and being fearful. The longer your girlfriend has been in your life and the bigger the role she's played in your child's, the harder the loss is likely to be, especially in the short run. On the other hand, if you really don't like the woman, the longer you let the relationship continue, the harder it will be for everyone when it *does* end eventually. Finally, before you enter another serious relationship, consider getting therapy.

Q: Just as I'm putting on my panty hose before a date, my kid gets a tummy ache. Sometimes she even throws up. And then I have to cancel. Does she need to see a doctor? Should I quit dating? Or just stop wearing panty hose?

A: I know *I'd* give up the panty hose. And you should take your kid to the pediatrician, just to rule out a physical basis for her tummy aches. But more than likely, her aches and pains are caused by emotional stress (which doesn't make them any less real or legitimate). You don't have to give up dating, but you do need to help your child manage her stress. Most kids worry about being abandoned again when a parent goes out. Give your child a clear sense of how long you'll be gone (e.g., "I'll be home soon after you and Grandma finish watching *Monsters vs. Aliens* and you have your bath"). Make sure you keep your promise. At first, keep your dates short and return while your child is still awake. *Yes,* I know that's murder on your social life, but it's only temporary. Do your best to get the same well-liked sitter each time, and plan fun activities for your child to do in your absence. In the short run, you can soothe her sore belly with a heating pad on low heat and a little ginger ale. Over time, her tummy should hurt less.

Q: My boyfriend has kids too. Should he bring them when he meets my child?

A: In general, it's better to split up the two events. First let your child meet your boyfriend, and mention that he has children. He could show her pictures of them, talk about them a little, etc. And you should go meet his kids alone too. *Then* get the kids together *on neutral territory* like a fast-food restaurant or play area. Avoid overpromising (e.g., "You'll love his daughter!"), and don't get too worked up if the kids don't seem to get along at first.

Weddings, Honeymoons, and Marriage— for Three!

❊ ❊ ❊

Helping Your Child with the Transition to Remarriage

If you thought planning your first wedding and honeymoon was complicated, wait until you try it with kids and ex-spouses involved! Plus, as before, remember that the wedding is actually the easy part! It's *marriage* that's tough. But here are some ways to smooth out wrinkles when you roll out the white carpet for your new lives together.

We Have an Announcement to Make

Tell your child together, prefacing it with, "We have something important to tell you about our family."

First, spell out how and when the change will affect him: when the wedding will take place, where everyone will live, and how his status will change (i.e., becoming a stepchild and/or stepsibling). Let him know whether his other parent knows about the plans (and it's a good idea to give your former partner a heads-up). Be sure to include the usual reminders, especially that he'll still be loved and part of your family and that his other parent isn't being replaced. Finally, treat the occasion as a happy, optimistic one; you might open some ginger ale or sparkling cider to toast your new family.

Plan to keep the announcement brief, and let your child have some time alone with you immediately afterwards. Go for a walk or play with clay while you talk through any questions or worries he has.

Expect to talk about the change on many occasions. When he seems to feel insecure, try this to put his mind at ease. Get some small toys and a large sock. Show your child how you can fit in as many toys as there were members of your old family. Then add another toy and show him how the sock can expand to fit everything. Talk about how people's hearts are like socks; the more people you have to love, the bigger your heart gets.

Cope with Reactions

Preschoolers may be excited, angry, confused, disappointed, worried, or sad—or, more likely, all of the above. Remarriage typically dashes hopes for parental reunion, stirs jealousies, and creates new anxieties. You may see different reactions on different days. Expect your child to regress again, even if he seems delighted, because even welcomed change stresses his body and emotions. Many kids also test limits, especially with the newcomer(s). Just continue to provide the usual structure and limits, and keep answering questions and offering reassurance.

The Name Game

Not surprisingly, many families struggle with how to handle name changes when one parent remarries, because names are symbolic of ties, loyalties, and power. There are no easy answers, either for surnames or for what your child should call his stepparent. Some issues and options:

✳ *Surnames.* When one child's last name differs from the others' in his home, he may feel different or rejected. Giving up his father's name, though, may not be legally possible without Dad's permission, and even if agreed to, tends in practice to dilute the strength of the father-child relationship. Some other options include taking the new family name as a middle name, hyphenating the two names, using different names in different situations (check first to see whether this option is legal in your state), or having everyone in the family use different last names (e.g., you revert to or continue to use your maiden name, etc.) In this last case, you may want to adopt a common family middle name.

✳ *Step-names.* If your child still has an active relationship with her nonresidential parent, it will confuse her to duplicate *Mom* or *Dad.* On the other hand, when a young kid calls his stepparent by her first name, it can undermine her authority in her parental role. Other options include: combining first name and a parent name (e.g., *Daddy Jack*) or using a grandparent-style name (e.g., *Mimi* instead of *Mommy*).

Be Bound by Ceremony

The wedding ceremony has survived many centuries and repeated societal upheavals with its core elements intact for one reason: it *works* in helping everyone celebrate (or at least recognize) the changes in family structure. Try these tweaks to adapt the occasion for the special needs of a child in a changing family.

✳ *Involve your child in the wedding planning.* (As usual, letting your child pick between two choices that are acceptable to you is the safest way to get his input.) Also make plans for him at the reception to minimize stress without making him feel pushed out. Consider letting him invite a friend or two to play with; appointing another much-loved adult to keep an eye on him; pacing favorite activities (like cutting the cake) to suit his schedule; letting him change into more casual clothes; and planning a dance for him with the bride and groom.

✳ *Make a role for him in the ceremony.* Many parents now include either a unity candle ceremony or a family medallion ceremony as part of their vows. In both cases, parents pledge their shared commitment to their existing children. They mark this commitment either by lighting a candle together or giving the children a medallion to symbolize the bond. I also like the idea of having the whole family (including the nonresidential members if possible) hold hands and step up to mark their promise to go forward together—and to help forge and acknowledge relationships between all the branches of the family.

✳ *Give your child a wedding gift too.* Good choices include a book, wedding party dolls to reenact the ceremony (and act out new family relationships), something to entertain him during the event, or a piece of jewelry or other talisman.

✳ *Document his role in the festivities.* Remember your child when you take photographs! Try to capture him in both formal portraits and casual snaps.

Planning a Not-So-Sticky Honeymoon

Although you may be tempted to dash off for a childless week in the Bahamas, many stepfamilies with young children opt for alternate arrangements. Weddings and big family changes stress a preschooler to the max; separation from his parent may push him over the edge.

Consider taking a mini honeymoon (just the wedding night or weekend) to affirm and strengthen your couple relationship (which helps your child in the long run) while your child stays with grandparents, cousins, or her other parent. Or go on a family vacation instead. This gives everyone a chance to settle into new roles on neutral turf. You can even divide the trip into a mixture of family trip and honeymoon.

Another possibility is to postpone your honeymoon for several weeks or months until everyone is more comfortable in their new family roles.

Stepping In—And Up

✳ ✳ ✳

Some Stepparenting Strategies That Work

Biology is *not* destiny. Over time, step relationships *can* acquire much of the strength and warmth of biological ones. Initially, though, stepparents have to assume an awkward, poorly defined role and be patient with uncomfortable feelings and difficult behavior (often from the adults as well as the kids). Below are some tips that other stepfamilies have found helpful in the slow process of creating a new and workable family.

There are lots of great sites where you can get (or share) advice about stepparenting. Try www.cyberparent.com/step, www.stepfamilies.info, and www.foreverfamilies.net. Also, if you can't find a local stepparent support group, you can get help locating or starting a group at www.stepfam.org.

Learn What's Normal

...and then chill! All members need to educate themselves (often repeatedly) about the normal feelings and stages that stepfamilies go through. For example, in the early weeks, there *may* be a honeymoon period in which all family members are on their best behavior (and the whole thing seems like an easy adjustment). This stage is often followed by the horror-movie phase, in which everyone morphs into a jealous, rampaging Godzilla, Dracula, or a werewolf. Fortunately, that stage *can* be followed by another in which people settle into their new roles. Just keep repeating, "Love takes time," and "Give change a chance." Finally, all adults should educate themselves about normal child development, so they can tease out what's normal kid stuff from what's a problem needing professional help.

Start at the Bottom

It's tempting for a new stepparent to jump in as family CEO and start setting new policies and meting out discipline (especially when the family looks poorly managed). But don't do it, unless you'd also like to be outsourced promptly. It's better for stepparents to assume a role akin to a newly hired junior assistant or friendly aunt or uncle (i.e., polite and helpful, but deferential, especially about disciplinary matters). The biological parent should keep this role in mind too, and not engage in kid dumping, especially not on a new spouse who hasn't had kids before. Both parents should also be respectful to the competition (i.e., the other biological parent), even if she's an ignorant slut or he's a controlling you-know-what.

Then Take Baby Steps up the Ladder

A problem I often encountered working with stepfamilies was a stepparent who failed to take on more responsibilities over time. Although in many stepfamilies, the stepparent never becomes a full parent (and that's fine), after several years, she should approximate at least a Vice-Parent. Both the stepparent and biological parent will have to work at making this role happen, and many families need the help of counselors or support groups while they work on their evolving relationships.

Post Family Rules

…and the consequences for breaking them. This simple act provides a neutral way for a stepparent to exercise authority in a consistent way. Posted rules also help biological parents control urges to be excessively permissive out of guilt or overly strict out of frustration.

Cement Your Marriage

Your healthy marriage provides your child with stability, happier care-givers, and a model of a good relationship to copy. Thus, you *must* give your marital relationship enough priority to help it last, without leaving any children feeling pushed out or neglected. This tricky balancing act requires frequent small corrections, like a tightrope walker makes. One of the hardest areas to reach this balance with young children tends to be with sleeping arrangements. Under stress, many preschoolers develop habits of sleeping with their parents—and many new stepparents understandably resent this arrangement. Gradually shift your child into a bed of her own well before the wedding.

Tackle Cinderella's Wicked Stepmother

…instead of just ignoring her. Although many stepfamilies try to ban stories of wicked stepmothers, I think they're making a mistake. For one thing, they rarely succeed; the myths are too embedded in our culture and Disney offerings. For another, the stories contain grains of truth, at least about feelings that are fairly common in stepfamilies. Sharing these stories gives families a chance to discuss the issues openly. With luck, you'll agree on a different, happier ending to your own story. Having a sense of humor about the stereotypes may even make them a valuable addition to your family culture; an in-joke about being the Wicked Queen can diffuse a tense moment.

Toughen Your Hide

When your stepchild screams, "I hate you!" do you a) burst into tears, b) scream, "I hate you too!" right back, or c) (hint, this is the right answer) shrug and say, "I'm sorry you're so angry right now." Two important things to keep in mind during emotional moments with your stepchild (or spouse): 1) many preschoolers say things they don't really mean, and 2) strong feelings of anger, resentment, jealousy, frustration, etc., are common and normal in *all* newly formed families, whether or not there are stepkids involved. Don't let your buttons get pushed unnecessarily, and learn to address the big issues that bother you directly with your spouse.

Combine Your Brady Bunch

If both of you have kids from previous marriages, some things will be easier; others will be *way* more complicated and difficult. The good thing is that both of you will have parenting skills, and both will understand the intensity of parent-child love. But issues are bound to arise about where to live and how to divide up space, what to do about family names, how to handle differences in the kids' relationships with their other parents, and how to handle discipline disagreements. The important thing is to keep talking. Schedule weekly parent meetings as well as regular whole family meetings; preschoolers are not too young to participate. And do things that help everyone feel nurtured and loved, like these activities:

✳ *Secret Santa.* Around the holidays (or another time, if that's better for your family), have everyone choose a secret pal within the family to do small, kind things for daily. Preschoolers need help coming up with ideas and implementing them.

✳ *Family-fun time.* Designate a family-fun time, like a regular evening when you eat dessert first or watch a video together.

✳ *New traditions.* For each holiday, make up at least one tradition that's new to both families.

✳ *Mix and match.* For outings or activities, mix and match parents and kids, dividing up by gender, interests, or by names chosen from a hat, as well as occasionally by family of origin.

✳ *Make memories.* Start a new family album with everyone in it. Make a point of photographing new sibs together.

✳ *Play together.* Play parents-versus-kids games, like family freeze tag (where kids get a safe base and adults don't).

✳ *Welcome new members.* If you have a child together, take extra care to involve the children from previous relationships in baby preparations and new-baby care. Emphasize the similarities between all the children—maybe post them on a big chart that can be added to over time.

How to Love a "Used" Child

A strong attachment and even true love between stepparents and stepchildren can be built *over time.* (In the meantime, settle for respect.)

LITERATURE LINKS

Many children's books about stepfamilies seem to be a bit preachy or stiff. A few I recommend: Fred Rogers's LET'S TALK ABOUT IT: STEPFAMILIES, the award-winning BOUNDLESS GRACE by Mary Hoffman (which features the African-American heroine of the excellent picture book AMAZING GRACE), CHARLIE ANDERSON by Barbara Abercrombie, and WHEN I AM A SISTER by Robin Ballard.

These strategies can help create tender feelings for a child who doesn't initially feel like yours—and help her develop a soft spot for you too.

✳ *Touch her.* Make a point of holding and touching your stepchild. Cuddling and rocking while reading stories is especially effective. If she pulls away, try roughhousing, tousling hair, kissing her after she's asleep, or playing gentle tickle games. Notice how soft her skin is and talk to yourself about how appealing she is.

✳ *Sniff her.* It sounds sort of gross or kinky, but on a primitive level, we're drawn to things with a familiar smell. Smelling a child's head seems to be a common parental behavior and probably promotes bonding.

✳ *Care for and comfort her.* Gradually take on some caregiving routines, like help with bathing, feeding, and getting ready for school. Wipe her runny nose. Stepparents should also make efforts to soothe hurt or ill children (which may require biological parents to back off at times). Not sure of your nurturing skills? Read parenting books, take a course, and talk to other parents.

✳ *Spend fun time together…alone.* Introduce your stepchild to your own passions, family, and friends. Do what she likes, too. At first, keep sessions short, and build them up gradually over time. Take photographs of the two of you together.

✳ *Practice small acts of commitment.* Attend school functions, athletic events, and recitals. Develop your own rituals for greeting or saying good-bye. Put her picture in your wallet and on your desk at work. Frame and display her artwork. Hug and kiss her in public and hold her hand crossing the street. Come along to the pediatrician and the dentist. Create new family traditions like having cocoa and animal crackers the first time it snows. Small acts like these build a foundation of shared experiences and caring—the necessary basis for lasting family relationships, however they're formed.

Life After Death

✳ ✳ ✳

Coping with a Preschooler's Grief and Needs

Young children do not grieve in the same way that adults do, but they do grieve. If your preschooler loses a parent, sibling, close grandparent, friend, teacher, or other important person in his life, he'll need support to get through the first days as well as the ensuing weeks and months until his life adjusts and assumes a new normal. These tips (in addition to others I've recommended in this chapter and on pages 207–210) can help him cope during this difficult period.

Explain What Happened

Start your discussion by saying something like "I have something very sad to tell you." Then tell your child about the accident, illness, etc., and tell him that because of what happened, the person died. Make sure you use words like *died* and *death*, because euphemisms like *at rest* or *with God* are only likely to confuse and upset concrete-thinking preschoolers.) Ask him if he knows what *died* means. Listen to his definition and then agree, correct misperceptions, or elaborate. He needs to know that someone who dies is no longer with us physically, not around to talk to or play with, and that her body no longer works and will either be buried in the ground or cremated. You'll need to talk about how that doesn't hurt her, because dead people can't feel pain, breathe, eat, sleep, talk, watch TV, or feel lonely.

Emphasize that death is permanent and irreversible and that your child did nothing to cause it—but that he will of course continue to remember and think about the person who died and can love her forever.

Predict for him some of the feelings he and others around him are likely to have, like surprise, sadness, anger, confusion or fear. Reassure him that it is okay to feel all those ways, and that he can talk to you about his feelings. Let him know very specifically how his life will be affected. ("So Sandy won't be at school tomorrow to take care of you. She won't be there any days at all anymore, but another nice teacher will play with you and care for you.") Answer any questions he has, and wrap up by doing something ordinary, like reading a book, playing a game, or having a snack. Young children have a strong need to see that life continues and that adults are there for them.

Most young kids will forget much of what you've told them or will come back with more questions. You will need to repeat information many times.

Accept Normal Reactions

Few preschoolers really understand the concept of death. Thus it is normal for them to act like nothing has happened! It is also normal for preschoolers to be scared—of losing someone else, of dying themselves, or of seemingly unrelated things, like suddenly being afraid of the dark or monsters. Some preschoolers are angry at the person who died, at the doctors, at God, at the person who told them, or even at themselves. Others just seem bewildered, asking the same questions repeatedly or seeming to forget about the death. Some kids will act sad, but will attribute their sadness to some other disappointment. Regression, tantrums, acting out, clinging, stomachaches and headaches, and being generally irritable are all likely expressions of a young child's grief. Some children may have vivid upsetting memories (especially if they witnessed something disturbing) or nightmares. Be patient and accepting and provide extra cuddling, reassurance, and nurturing.

How your child reacts to death will be influenced by many factors, including the nature of his relationship with the person who died, whether the death was sudden or anticipated, his previous experiences with death or other losses, whether the death was complicated by being a suicide or part of a public tragedy, and most importantly, by how the adults around him react.

Find Comfort in Faith—Carefully

Preschoolers are often comforted by the concepts of God and heaven, and by the ideas that the people they loved will be safe and happy. But many ideas that adults find reassuring only upset young children. Be extra cautious about sharing ideas like the following:

✳ *"God loved her so much, he took her to heaven."* Children may wonder why God doesn't love them as much, or feel guilty for not having loved the dead person enough. They may also be afraid of being loved by God, out of fear of being snatched away themselves!

✳ *"He's gone to a better place."* Again, young children may feel guilty about not providing a good enough place for the one they loved. In addition, some preschoolers have reportedly made suicide gestures in an attempt at reunion in that "better place."

✳ *"It was her time to go to God."* This is likely to cause unnecessary anxiety in preschoolers, who wonder when it will be time for others they love or for themselves to go.

The idea that we cannot understand why people died when they did is one that preschoolers can eventually accept. Preschoolers can also understand that we are sad because we miss someone, even if we feel they are in a good place, as long as that is explained directly. Be clear that the death was not anyone's punishment for anything. Preschoolers need to hear this last message repeatedly, whether or not they ask. You might need to hear it too.

Help Him Tolerate Others' Distress Too

Young children feel anxious when they see grown-ups crying or being upset. Explain that it's normal and okay for adults to be sad for a while and that in time they'll feel better. And give your child specific things he can do to comfort you (or other sad people), like patting you, giving you a kiss, asking for a snuggle, or distracting you with a game—whatever works for you.

Grief at Play

Preschoolers who are mourning may gravitate toward certain kinds of play. Encourage them to engage in activities like these:

✳ *Sandbox play.* It's soothing and undemanding, and it may give kids a chance to play out issues they have with burial. Similar play can happen with other materials like water, Play-Doh, and sand substitutes like rice or beans.

✳ *Baby.* Or Hurt Animal or other pretending themes that encourage playmates (adult or child) to take care of them. Other children will prefer the caregiver roles, and want to be a parent, doctor, vet, etc.—perhaps nice ones, perhaps cruel ones.

✳ *Good-bye games.* Younger preschoolers may enjoy even baby games like peekaboo. Hide-and-seek and pretend-play games like House (with family members leaving for work or the store) may help preschoolers work through the separation issues that are an inherent part of death and loss.

✳ *Cause-and-effect toys.* Electronic games, musical instruments, toddler pop-up or pounding toys—anything that gives kids a chance to feel in control and like their behavior matters. Similarly, some kids will gravitate toward playing characters like bosses, superheroes, or even God for the opportunity to make things work out the way they'd like it to.

✳ *Simple art activities.* Appealing because of their ease and the opportunity to express strong emotions indirectly. With kids who are distressed by mistakes, avoid messy materials or high-skill activities (like cutting with scissors) because spills, stains, and other "errors" may provoke excessive anxiety or frustration. Try washable markers, crayons, chalk, and even temporary materials like Magna Doodle.

✳ *Physical games.* Games with a buildup of tension followed by release, like Tag, sliding, jumping in the pool, or playing Crash with ride-on toys may also appeal to kids in mourning. Just supervise carefully, since stressed kids are prone to clumsiness and poor judgment.

Look for "Just Right"

Grief makes families lose their equilibrium. Finding a balance between being sad and relaxed and laughing often takes deliberate effort, so schedule fun activities into your day. If you can't turn off your despair for your child, make sure he gets out regularly (daily if possible) with friends or relatives who can help him preserve his light heart.

It is especially difficult for many families to regain a balance between being careful and being overprotective. Although it's normal to want to hold a little tighter to your child when a loss touches your life, doing so may strip your child of his sense of competence at a time when he most needs that resource. It will also make him feel unnecessarily vulnerable and anxious. Good strategies to avoid being overprotective include making sure he

---

LITERATURE LINKS

Picture books about death can help you explore the issue with your child. Try these classics: NANA UPSTAIRS AND NANA DOWNSTAIRS by Tomie dePaola; BADGER'S PARTING GIFTS by Susan Varley; THANK YOU, GRANDPA by Lynn Plourde; WHERE DO PEOPLE GO WHEN THEY DIE? by Mindy Avra Portnoy; LIFETIMES by Bryan Mellonie; and WHEN DINOSAURS DIE by Laurie Krasny Brown and Marc Brown. For helping children facing the death of another child, try Chris Raschka's THE PURPLE BALLOON. Finally, for kids (or adults) who seem stuck in grief, I recommend MICHAEL ROSEN'S SAD BOOK about his reactions to the death of his son.

gets regular opportunities to play with peers, posting a reminder list of "can-do skills" for your child's age, forcing yourself to use catchphrases like "You can do it!" and having a daily cuddle time when you can indulge your need to keep him close without undermining his growing independence.

Good Good-Byes and Memorable Memories

✱ ✱ ✱

Helping Your Preschooler Cope with Funerals, Memorials, and Anniversaries

Preschoolers can attend memorial and funeral services, and even visitations, provided their needs and abilities are taken into account and there is a caring adult available to them at all times. Here are some tips to make the experience a positive and healing one for a young child.

Prepare For Many Possibilities

Talk with your child about what will and won't happen at the service or visitation, making sure to include as many sensory details as possible. Also anticipate a preschooler's irrational ideas; for example, she may wonder whether the body or soul of the deceased will float up to heaven during the service. Talk to her about ways that other people may show their feelings, and what she can do if she's uncomfortable.

Always offer your child a choice of attending and let her change her mind even after arrival (which means you need to plan for a variety of arrangements). At a visitation, a child may or may not want to view the body or casket; respect her wishes. Assemble quiet toys like felt boards, stickers, pipe cleaners, or books, as well as a "silent snack" in case she becomes restless during the service. And if you're feeling needy yourself, make sure you have others available to support you and your child.

During the Service

Expect that your child will react like a young child. She may not appear sad; instead she may seem bored and squirmy. Talk quietly about what's going on and share the supplies you've brought to amuse her. Do your best to answer her questions matter-of-factly. Let her comfort you or others if she does so spontaneously, but don't be surprised if she's more self-centered even than normal.

The Children's Service

Funeral directors are increasingly helping families arrange separate services targeted at children, especially following the death of a child, teacher, or parent. These services contain some traditional features, such as music and lighting candles, but they also have features to meet the needs of children, such as brevity, trained clergy who directly address children's concerns about death, time for questions or for children to say something, opportunities to move about, and refreshments. Children may create artwork or be helped to write good-bye messages on paper stars. There may be rituals to symbolize letting go, such as releasing butterflies or blowing bubbles. Children may also be given a chance to offer a gift to the person who has died; tucking gifts in the casket can ease children's worries or allay irrational guilt.

Informal Memorials

If your child chooses not to attend a formal service (or you don't want her to), an informal ceremony at home or perhaps in a natural setting can provide closure. Consider incorporating elements of the children's service or designing your own rituals. For example, after a neighbor's grandmother died thousands of miles away and the family was unable to attend her service, they lit candles at dinner each night for a week, talking about happy memories of her while the candles burned. It was a simple act, but it eased my friend's grief and helped her children understand what had happened. Similarly, having reminders of the person who died available may comfort children. Have a place for photos and other reminders your child can look at when she wants to.

Introduce the concept of emotional Band-Aids in the weeks and months following a loss. Make a book or poster of things that help your child (and you) feel better, and direct her to choose one when she feels sad or anxious. Let her know that feelings heal much like bodies, and that although it may take a long time for a big hurt to feel all better, she will heal eventually.

Anniversaries

Preschoolers won't usually recall anniversaries or other special occasions (like birthdays) on their own, but may be sensitive to the emotional changes in you and the other adults around them. Talking with your children about the importance of the day helps them understand and cope with the tension. Preschoolers are also comforted by concrete remembering rituals, like preparing the person's favorite dinner, looking at pictures or artifacts, or recording happy thoughts and sending them on as wishes or by burning the slips of paper.

Cemetery Visits

Don't force your child to visit the cemetery if she balks, but keep in mind that young children may not yet have developed the fears or negative associations that older kids and adults often have. She may welcome a visit as a chance to be near the person she has lost. Help her bring a small gift, perhaps of hand-picked flowers (like dandelions), a picture she's made, a stone to place on the headstone, or a holiday decoration. She may enjoy scampering about the area or even having a picnic near the grave. Again, be accepting of a wide range of reactions and do your best to answer her questions about death and what happens to people after they die.

Stormy Weather and Other Scary Situations

* * *

On-the-Spot Crisis Management

Although different kinds of disasters (like floods, tornadoes, hurricanes, blizzards, storms, earthquakes, fires, accidents, riots, civil unrest, or violence, domestic or otherwise) require different specific responses, these general techniques will help you protect and soothe your little one in crises big and small.

Be Prepared

Being a parent means thinking ahead, especially if you're the parent who's the designated Keeper of the Anxieties. (The other is the self-appointed Fun Maker of the Keeper for Being Too Much of a Worrywart.)

Take a refresher first-aid class if you haven't had one since your scouting days, and make sure it includes lessons in performing CPR on young children. Equip your home with basic safety equipment, like smoke and carbon-monoxide detectors. Test them *monthly* (with your kids as helpers), and change the batteries twice a year when the time changes. Develop and rehearse a plan for getting out of your house in case of a fire or other emergency.

It's also wise to become knowledgeable about recommendations for the types of natural disasters that are most common where you live or travel. Talk with your children and read books about what to do in the event of one of these; familiarity makes it easier for everyone to be calm.

You don't have to go overboard like everyone did before Y2K (remember that?), but it's smart to stock an area of your home with enough basic emergency supplies to last three days. Store supplies like water, nonperishable food, flashlights *and* batteries, a couple of buckets, and assorted amusements. You can find lists of suggested supplies (and lots of information about potential disasters you hadn't even considered yet) at websites like the Federal Emergency Management Agency, found at www.fema.gov (which has checklists for what to do in specific types of disasters, as well as general preparedness tips) and the American Red Cross's www.prepare.org (which has good tips for families).

General Crisis Tips

In a crisis, your brain will turn off, so you need to have a well-rehearsed plan of what to do. Even kids can learn these tactics for dealing with crises large and small.

✳ *Stick with your buddy.* During a crisis, most preschoolers want to be held or even babied. If you can't remain with your child, give him a token like a piece of your clothing or at least a kiss to hold in his hand, let him know about when you'll be together again, and try to remain in frequent voice contact (e.g., via cell phone).

✳ *Stay calm, cool, and collected.* When you become a parent, you have to learn to fake all kinds of things, like admiration for artwork made from squished worms. And especially you need to learn to fake a calm voice and sense of competence in the face of bad times. *Faking it is good enough.* Take slow, deep breaths. Deliberately pitch your voice lower than normal, and say soothing things like "I know it's scary, but I'm right here." Tell your child in simple terms what's happening and what you're doing about it. "This is a big storm called a tornado. We're staying in the cellar where it's safer until it's over.") Who knows? Maybe you'll fake yourself out too!

✳ *If you can, get the heck out of there.* Move to a safe place, preferably far from the action, even if it seems overcautious. When you have kids involved, you *must* follow recommended evacuations before hurricanes or civil unrest, leave the house if there's a fire (even a small one), head for high ground when a flood threatens, hang out in the cellar if there's a tornado watch, and park yourselves in a doorway or under sturdy furniture during an earthquake. If you are evacuated to a shelter, make sure to take along child necessities, like security objects, favorite snacks, blankets and pillows, a much-loved book, and a flashlight or glow sticks.

✳ *Debrief after the danger has passed.* Talk to your child about what happened, focusing on the ways that things remain okay. Praise him for his courage and for following your directions. Let him know that his fear was normal and even helpful, since fear gives people energy to get to safety. Help his body calm down by holding him and breathing slowly in rhythm together. Try having him breathe like a train: first chugging along very fast, then slowing down, and ending with long exhales as it comes into the station and stops.

Shed Light on Power-Outage Fears

During a power outage, your child may be afraid of the dark, worried about the cause of the outage, and *bored* without access to his usual entertainment and routines. These tips can help:

✳ *Find an alternate light source.* Flashlights are best, but in a pinch, even the glow from a cell phone, handheld game, or light-up watch face may calm a child who's scared of the dark. Also consider using your car lights (briefly so you don't wear down the battery). Candles, fires, and camping lanterns are other sources to consider, but exercise extreme caution with young children and open flames. Or drive to a place that still has power for a light-and-potty break.

✳ *Reassure.* Preschoolers may assume that they have caused the problem or be worried that a monster has. Talk about more likely causes.

✳ *Distract.* Pretend it's the olden days or that you're camping. Sing songs related to light like "This Little Light of Mine" and "Mr. Sun, Sun, Mr. Golden Sun." Or play games that take advantage of the dark, like What Might This Object Be? (Hand your child a toy and see if he can guess what it is.)

Sound Advice for Scary Noises

Whether it's sirens, thunder, wind, or alarming newscasts, emergencies often involve noises that alarm youngsters. Quiet their fears these ways:

✳ *Normalize.* Explain what the noise is and why it exists. Some kids like to make up funny explanations for the sounds too.

✳ *Drown it out*…with happier sounds of your own. Sing, bang on pots and pans, and play instruments. Or stomp your feet and loudly chant rhymes like "Jelly in the Bowl," or sing songs about the noise, like "The wind in the storm goes *Wooo, wooo, wooo* (to the tune of "The Wheels on the Bus").

✳ *Muffle it.* Hold your child in your lap while keeping your hands over his ears. Have him wear a hat or earmuffs or put a pillow over his ears. Headphones to listen to music or audio books work too. Or whisper sweet nothings in his ear—concentrating on the soft sounds distracts from the loud ones.

✳ *Mute the TV.* Rely on the printed information that scrolls across the bottom of the screen to track the crisis.

Cooperation Tactics

During an emergency, it may be essential for your child to cooperate and follow your directions carefully. Young children, though, frequently fail to appreciate the seriousness of a crisis. Some ways to boost cooperation:

✳ *Look him in the eye.* Get down on your child's level and make eye contact. Tell him calmly but firmly that you need him to do *exactly* what you tell him to.

✳ *Invoke imagination.* Try saying something like "Let's pretend we're little mice and scurry down into the basement as fast as we can. We'll hide under the table and pretend it's our hole."

✳ *Tell him what to do.* Use the structure of a command game like Simon Says or Follow the Leader.

✳ *Praise him.* Offer frequent praise and expressions of gratitude for paying attention and obeying.

When the Boo-Boo Brigade Is Needed

Whether it's his own or someone else's, an injury may overwhelm an already frightened child. These steps calm and comfort.

✳ *Hide the blood.* Preschoolers tend to be inordinately scared of blood. Use bandages promptly, and hide wounds under towels, blankets, or clothing. Reassure your child that bodies have lots of blood and can make new blood too.

✳ *Soothe with touch.* Use firm pressure, like a hug, or soft stroking as your child prefers—just stay in contact.

✳ *Explain.* Simple explanations about what's wrong, what you're doing to help, and how the doctors will help (if necessary) reassure mightily.

✳ *Distract.* Songs are especially effective, as are stories with a refrain or movement component.

We're Not in Kansas Anymore

✳ ✳ ✳

Coping after Disasters

Most kids are distressed after a disaster. Expect them to be afraid of the disaster recurring and to be sad or even angry. They may want to be near you all the time (to the point of shadowing your every move), and many regress to outgrown behavior like wetting the bed. Their responses will be influenced by factors such as how you reacted, how close they were to the event, and how directly their everyday lives have been affected. Young children often seem disproportionately upset by the loss of playthings or other possessions. Time, of course, is the best healer of all for a freaked-out child. But in the interim you can help your child recover her equilibrium and minimize her upset in these ways.

Cling Together!

Although it might be tempting to pack kids off to friends or relatives while you deal with clean-up and insurance companies after a disaster, kids who stay near their parents actually fare better. When possible, let kids participate or at least watch repairs in progress. Try making a scrapbook to chart the steady return to normal.

Let Life Go On

…as much as possible. Reestablish routines, even if they have to be altered slightly from your previous ones. Make especially sure to join your child during mealtimes and bedtimes, and either continue usual rituals (like saying grace and reading stories) or add new ones. Point out to your child all the important things that have remained unchanged. And replace at least one or two possessions your child misses as quickly as possible.

Participate in Memorials

Even very young children benefit from being included in formal, community events to commemorate losses. If no appropriate formal opportunities are available, create your own ceremony to express sadness, say any good-byes (even just to a beloved swing set), and begin brainstorming together about how to move forward.

Challenge Irrational Beliefs

...and educate. Self-centered preschoolers need to hear repeatedly that the disaster was in no way their fault. They need you to explain about how the problem happened and what you're doing to keep everyone safe in the future. They need to know how likely the disaster is to recur, and what role bad guys, monsters, or the other usual suspects played in it.

Make Time for Play

First, turn off the TV! Especially if it's showing vivid images you don't want imprinted on your child's brain forever. Provide props for your child to enact themes of safety and security (e.g., playing superheroes, House, or Community Helpers), or even to replay the disaster if she wants to. Block play (especially involving knocking down and rebuilding), easy puzzles, and art projects remind kids of their competence and resilience. Don't forget to include lighthearted forms of play, including laughter and exercise. And participate in your child's imaginative play to emphasize themes of recovery and hope.

Discover Courage and Resilience

Praise your child for any ways she shows courage or a good attitude, and point out others who are coping well. Read or tell made-up stories about people who have faced similar problems and overcome them. Use catchphrases like "I think I can, I think I can!"

Teach Daytime Coping Skills

Help your child put together a "bag of tricks"—things that help her feel calmer or happier all on her own. Include a few favorite toys, a "lovey" for comfort, photographs of happy times, pictures of activities (like running on the playground) that relieve stress, and any other ideas she has. Encourage her to reach into her bag when she feels scared or acts up. Also teach "thought stopping." When she has a scary thought, she can say, "No!" or "Stop!" out loud (or clap her hands or stomp her feet) and then think about something happier. Help her come up with specific happy images, like petting a kitty or splashing in a pool. Some youngsters like to sing a silly song loudly to drown out scary thoughts. And continue to emphasize that thoughts and wishes can't make things happen.

Adopt Nighttime Coping Strategies

Nightlights, dream catchers, pictures of a guardian angel, or even signs warning scary dreams away can help keep an anxious child more content in her own bed. Develop a ritual for transforming her bed each night into a soft, safe nest or well-protected Bat Cave (or whatever image appeals to her as the safest thing she can think of). Kids who are troubled by nightmares may also be helped by a technique called lucid dreaming. Tell them they can become aware that they are just dreaming and then change the ending. Talk through ideas for how they'd prefer to have their dreams go. You can also post pictures suggestive of happy dreams, and offer kids a new pillow or pillowcase that's special for making good dreams.

LITERATURE LINKS

These books are good choices following certain kinds of disasters: ONE LUCKY GIRL by George Ella Lyon, a true story about a baby who survives being carried away by tornado; HURRICANE! by Jonathan London, which tells about a family's evacuation and recovery from a young boy's perspective; RIVER FRIENDLY, RIVER WILD by Jane Kurtz (about a flood); and SMOKY NIGHT by Eve Bunting (which deals with living through a riot).

Money Madness

* * *

Easing Family Stress During Tough Financial Times

If money is suddenly a problem, you're probably facing additional stresses too, like divorce, job loss, possible home foreclosure, or family illness. Add to that mix the demands of caring for an emotionally sensitive preschooler, who probably reacts to your tension by melting down at every opportunity, begging for things you can't give him, and generally being clingy and irritable, and you have the makings of your own volcano! These tips may tame the kid-related stresses enough to keep a lid on some of the eruptions.

Share Information

As always, preschoolers need the basic facts about what is happening in their family and how it will affect them. Families who attempt to hide a change in their financial situation (for example, by having a parent pretend to keep going to a job or by continuing to spend as usual) rarely fool even very young children for long, and only add to the tension in the household. Keep your message about your situation simple and general (remembering that your child is likely to share whatever information you tell him)—but offer concrete and specific information about the details that affect him (like whether he'll stay home with you instead of going to daycare). Also keep in mind that kids don't necessarily understand terms like *fired*, for example, so choose words carefully lest they fear you'll be set ablaze. Finally, emphasize hope, explaining that the situation is *temporary*. Talk about what you're doing to improve your family fortunes. And above all, keep teaching the message that what makes families rich is not money or stuff, but one another.

Band Together

Although you may be tempted to refuse your child's offers of help or see the issue as not his problem, a we're-all-in-this-together attitude is more likely to give your kid a sense of control and ease his anxieties. Make a list of things your child can do to help out while money is tight.

✳ *Have a good attitude.* He can make an effort not to whine for treats at the store. Instead, he can choose which game he'll play with you after shopping or have you record his desires on a wish list to save for the future.

✳ *Help out.* He could do a useful job for you while you shop, like matching up coupons with the right product or acting as cart navigator.

✳ *Make things last.* Your child can also take good care of his toys so they last longer. Help him do so by instituting twice daily clean-up sessions and labeling boxes from the supermarket with pictures of their contents to make tidying easier for him.

✳ *Be quiet.* He can think of ways to play quietly while you make phone calls, write resumes, or study.

✳ *Cheer you up.* Ask him to sing something like "Do Your Ears Hang Low?" with you every morning to help keep your spirits up.

Praise him for being a good family helper!

Cross Bridges When You Get to Them

Although you may already be worrying about major family changes, like selling your house, moving to a different city, or forgoing your usual summer trip to the beach, wait to tell your preschooler until a change is certain. *Maybe* is a tough concept for preschoolers to grasp, and you want to avoid unnecessary worry.

Forge New Routines

Chances are you'll need to readjust family routines and responsibilities. Make sure your routines carve out time for you to take care of your own needs, including exercise, adult time with your spouse, and opportunities to look for work or otherwise manage your finances.

Come up with a plan for your child to be occupied safely and happily while you do so. Trade childcare with a friend or neighbor, join a babysitting co-op, accept offers of help from extended family, have your child attend free programs at the public library (if your attendance isn't required), and gradually build your child's ability to play alone (or with siblings) for a stretch of time.

Beware the Telly Monster

Sorry, your plan cannot be to park your kid in front of the tube for more than an hour a day. All preschoolers should limit TV time, but during times of family stress, TV poses particular dangers. For one thing, watching commercial television tends to make kids want more stuff. For another, many kids become irritable after watching even an hour of TV—and the noise may get on your nerves too. In addition, TV watching tends to promote mindless eating. Finally, it's easy to get sucked into letting your kid watch more and more and more TV. Consider stopping cable or satellite TV services, both to save money and eliminate a time-eating temptation.

Discover Low-Cost Fun

Plan to do a small fun thing daily, and a big fun thing at least weekly. In bigger metropolitan areas, you can often find listings for activities that are free or nearly so in local weekly publications. For example, look for new parks to visit, free outdoor concerts, arts festivals (which often have free activities or entertainment for kids), fee-waived museum days, community celebrations, and events at churches, synagogues, and temples. Packing your own snacks and meals for outings saves money, and you can make from-home food inviting by packaging it in creative ways, such as putting small crackers in plastic Easter eggs. Most libraries have a wealth of free entertainment, from books and media to check out to programs for kids and families. Finally, start new no-cost traditions, like a family game night, going for a flashlight walk after dinner, or meeting up with friends at the playground instead of a fast-food restaurant.

Celebrate on a Shoestring

Many parents have told me that the one of the most painful aspects of tight finances is not being able to celebrate their child's birthday and other holidays the way they have in the past. The one bright spot is that there's a good chance that you feel the losses more than your young child does; preschoolers are usually satisfied with a handful of familiar rituals and fewer (and less expensive) gifts than adults think they need. Try these tips to pare down the costs of gifts, meals, decorations, and get-togethers.

✳ *Reset expectations.* Talk to your child if you'll be substantially changing the way you celebrate. Even little guys can understand the idea of staying within a budget and making choices. Shift the focus of holidays from *getting* to *doing* (which is wise even if you're wealthy). Traditions like a Birthday Poster (a poster showing all the special events of the past year), a gift hunt, or having breakfast in bed will be remembered long after your kid has forgotten what he received for his fourth birthday.

✳ *Be flexible and creative.* Hire inexpensive neighborhood pre-teens or trade a favor with a talented friend instead of using professional entertainers, comb sites like The Crafty Crow (www.belladia. typepad.com/crafty_crow) for ways to make appealing decorations from recycled materials, take one friend on an outing instead of having a large party—the possibilities are legion.

✳ *Go homemade and heartfelt.* This is a good idea even if you have plenty of money. A handful of cookies your child has helped bake, wrapped up in paper he decorated herself, will mean more to her teacher than yet another apple-themed knickknack. Even your own kid will likely appreciate something you craft for her more than an expensive store-bought item. One Christmas I made simple "snuggle quilts" for my kids from flannel remnants—the blankets took me one evening and cost less than $5 each—and all three kids still list them among their all-time favorite gifts (and still snuggle with them, tattered though they are).

✳ *Pare lists down.* Help your child go through his wish list and your checklist of usual activities and rank order the items. Which ones matter most to him (and you)?

✳ *Shop smart.* Watch for sales; use coupons; shop yard sales, eBay, and thrift shops—or just agree to exchange gifts of time and attention. Holiday decorations are often marked down a day or two before the big day; try adjusting your family tradition to decorating on the eve of the holiday instead of weeks in advance.

✳ *Accept help.* Many social organizations provide gifts and holiday meals for families in need at the holidays; it may hurt your pride, but plan to pay it forward when you're back on your feet.

Rough Housing

✳ ✳ ✳

Helping Kids Cope with Home Loss and Stressful Living Arrangements

If you've recently lost your home to foreclosure, a disaster, or some other unfortunate circumstance, then I don't have to tell you that for most families home loss is a triple-*S* crisis—Stressful, Sad, and Scary. Please, please, please, seek out solid practical and financial advice from professionals and wise family members and friends; the decisions you make now about your money and new housing arrangements may affect your family for years to come. Social service agencies, your state representative and congressman, and even your local librarian may be able to help you understand your rights and options, or at least put you in touch with reputable information sources and helpers. Meanwhile, there's much you can do protect your child's well-being and promote her resilience.

Okay, Now Cross that Bridge

When home loss is inevitable, you need to discuss it with your child and involve her in the process of moving and settling in anew. She doesn't need to know every detail, but it's fine to tell her that you're sad and wish things could be different. Answer her questions in simple kid-terms and anticipate those she's afraid to voice. ("Don't worry; we'll all still be together.") Read Chapter Six on moving for suggestions on how to say good-bye to your old home (and neighborhood) and greet the new one, as well as for tips on getting through the shifting. Once you've all had a chance to express your grief, it's time to trot out the usual platitudes:"No use crying over spilled milk," "Every cloud has a silver lining," "It's an ill wind…"—okay, that's just too barfy. But it is a fact that a we'll-get-through-this, let's-make-the-best-of-it attitude will serve everyone well. And let him know that your family is not alone; many others have been in the same situation and it has all worked out. This reassurance may help you too.

Surprise! You're Homeless!

Disasters, (natural or man-made), a landlord who fails to warn you about an impending foreclosure, or a domestic crisis could land you on the street without warning—and thus without a chance to prepare your child or make alternative arrangements. Panic is a completely normal reaction to this situation—but sorry, you still have to be the grown-up and pretend to be in control.

Your first priority is a safe place to sleep and eat. Social workers, police officers, and social agencies may be able to steer you to emergency short-term housing until you can make other arrangements. Many families in this situation stay briefly with relatives or friends (sometimes a series of them); if that's what you do, see the tips below on sharing someone's home. Other options include emergency shelters, hotels, and camping out. Other possibilities, like living secretively in your office or bunking down in your car are pretty tough with small kids in tow—but families have done it to avoid having to put their kids into the foster-care system.

Make a Home, Wherever You Are

Home means *security*. Although literal-minded preschoolers tend to link *house* and *home* (as do many older, less literal-minded sorts) *home is less about the place than about the relationships and experiences that occur there.* And those, luckily, you can largely duplicate wherever you lay your heads, although it may take some extra effort on your part.

First, when choosing your new living space, make a gigantic effort to stay in or near the neighborhood of your old home, even if it's hard for you to face that judgmental busybody down the street who makes snotty remarks—the more consistency your child has in her daily experiences, like playing with the same friends and attending the same school, the easier her adjustment will be. Similarly, neighborhood safety and easy access to recreation likely matter more to her than having her own bedroom.

Familiarity is a big piece of security. But if you're downsizing, dealing with temporary housing, or living in even more dire straits, you're likely choosing items to sell, give away, or store. Your child will sleep better if her bed and surroundings look and feel familiar, so your first priority should be to hang onto her bedding (which you can use even if you'll be staying in a motel or relative's home), her night-light, and a few familiar pictures or bedside decorations, as well as any lovey she's attached to (sorry—this isn't your opportunity to finally "lose" the pair of ratty panty hose she likes to stroke as she falls asleep). Family photos are reassuring, keep her connected to her past, and take up little room. And your kid will have a heartier appetite if she can eat off her favorite dishes and drink from her beloved Bob the Builder sippy cup.

For toys, narrow down the options and then let her help make the final decisions. You'll want to concentrate on toys that are compact, versatile, and *quiet*—nothing will drive a stressed adult off the deep end faster than incessant electronic beeping. You'll of course tweak my list to suit your child's interests, but in general, a set of construction toys and mini vehicles, some miniature dolls or animals with tiny props, simple art supplies (paper, crayons, markers, scissors, a glue stick, pipe cleaners, etc., all stored together in a bin or box), a deck of playing cards or set of dominos (or other beloved board game), and a few dress-up clothes or puppets give preschoolers a *wealth* of play opportunities. I'd pay particular attention to toys that let kids play House; you can make an excellent dollhouse with two or three shoe boxes and simple furnishings that your child helps you construct from cereal-box cardboard, softies like fabric scraps or paper towels, and tape and markers. The other important game for kids in this situation is Good Guys Versus Bad Guys, which is an easy theme to support with a couple of action figures or plastic animals/dinosaurs. Keep a few favorite picture books and then rely on the public library to provide variety. And don't be afraid to supplement purchased toys with temporary found playthings—a small box of sticks, pebbles, pinecones, and acorns that your child has gathered can provide hours of creative play.

The easiest way to make your child feel secure, though, is to give her a predictable structure to her day, laced liberally with affectionate rituals. Make up picture charts (sticking to the big, essential events) because it's easy to forget when you're distracted with worries, and visual reminders can be a big help. If your energy is low, which it may be if you're feeling depressed or discouraged, develop a few mantras you can repeat to yourself to urge yourself through the motions. ("Just do it," "DING—Do It Now, Girl!" "I can be a saint for now; I can do it for the kiddo" —whatever works for you.) Set a timer or alarm to remind you of the day's big events, like time for an outing to the park or reading time before bed. And don't forget that stressed kids have a particularly great fear of separation; make a point of helping your child know where you are even when you're apart, and be sure to touch base extra frequently.

Take the Squeeze out of Tight Quarters

One of the most likely results of home loss is that you'll end up in a smaller place, at least for a time. Less room inevitably leads to some tough compromises for the whole family; here are some ideas for coping with the issues most likely to get on everyone's nerves.

✳ *Sleep stuff.* Kids who are close in age usually adapt to sharing a room fairly easily (i.e., with only normal squabbling) and may even prefer it! If *you* have to share a room with your child, though, rig a screen with a sheet or something to give yourself the illusion of your own space, and get your hands on sleep masks for those who tuck in earliest. And if thin walls, anxiety, or other factors make it hard for your kid to settle down or stay asleep, try soothing white noise. If you can, run a fan or buy CDs or download mp3 files (some for free) of nature sounds, soft music, or peaceful noises like a dryer. Try sites like www.soundsleeping.com or www.partnersinrhyme.com. (By the way, if you're picking between affording a TV or a music player of some sort, opt for tunes; TV is both more expensive and more likely to increase jitters and irritability than music is—and developing strong listening skills will serve your child better than TV's zombie lessons. You'll also avoid the monthly cable bill, and you can get free or cheap entertainment for an MP3 or CD player, like audiobooks from the library and stories, podcasts, and other entertainment you can download free from sites like http://librivox.org.)

✳ *Lack of privacy.* Although your preschooler won't really crave privacy, *you* will, especially if you're like me and you get the heebie-jeebies from people crawling all over you and pestering you and getting into your stuff when you're already feeling cranky. The best way to teach your child to give you some space and privacy is to make a big deal out of forging some for *her.* Get her an opaque container with a lid, mark it with her name, and explain that it's for her to keep her special stuff in, and that *no one, not even you, can look in it without her permission.* (Though of course I would not look askance at a parent who peeked in when she was sure no one could see her, especially if it smelled suspiciously like rotting food or her best perfume.) Then use the same approach to designate stuff of yours as off-limits— "This is like your privacy box," you'll say, "so you can't touch it without my permission." Everyone in the family should also have a space that is hers and hers alone—it can be as simple as a corner marked off with tape or even just a special chair; others can come in only by invitation. Finally, do whatever you have to—trade babysitting, promise to care for your mother at home in her old age, sell your soul or major organs— to give yourself some time away, daily if possible, and weekly without fail. The break will be good for both of you.

✳ *Disorder. A place for everything* is a good policy with kids in any living situation, and it's *essential* if space is limited. Avoid a big toy chest, which just leads to dumping and breaking. Storage containers don't have to be fancy—think cardboard boxes, old backpacks, or dollar store dishpans—but they do have to be clearly labeled with a picture of the contents. Mark the parking spot for the container while you're at it, and if you have a place you'd like your child to use the contents (like art supplies at the table), then put a picture of that on the container too. It's also smart to have an extra container labeled "Work in Progress" that can be stored safely if your child has to interrupt a project or game. A good rule of thumb to limit mess is *no more than two containers out at a time.* Finally, designate two or three clean-up times a day—before dinner and before bed are key. Sing the clean-up song ("It's clean up, clean up / Everybody, everywhere! / It's clean up, clean up/ Everybody does his share!"), and then put on music to make the job fun and zippy.

✳ *Chaos and commotion.* Prevention is your best bet. Make sure your kids have daily outlets to exercise and be noisy. *Preschoolers need at least two hours a day of active play.* If possible, get outside, preferably during daylight hours. Walks—which should actually involve hopping, skipping, stomping like an elephant, or galloping—can combine transportation and play. If you're stuck indoors and have to worry about disturbing the neighbors, opt for songs with motions, like "The Hokey Pokey," "Shake Your Sillies Out," and "Head, Shoulders, Knees, and Toes." Play or sing quiet music when you need kids to settle down, and rely on nonverbal signals, like holding up two fingers or flicking the lights (rather than yelling) to tell them to dial down the volume.

Moving in with Relatives

Although no one seems to be gathering reliable statistics, anecdotal information suggests that this housing option is the most common arrangement for young families who have lost their homes. It has many benefits, including the chance for youngsters to cultivate special relationships with their relatives, but it can obviously lead to some difficult issues too. Here is some metaphorical Goo-Gone for those common sticky kid situations.

✳ *Courtesy and gratitude.* When you're a guest—even though it's your substitute home—you have to act like one. Even if you're just three and a half years old. All the adults should sit down and discuss house rules—which you will then convey to your child and enforce. For example, are there places off-limits for playing? Food they can't have without asking? Rules about how or when things are done? In addition, everyone will be happier if your family expresses its gratitude in both words and deeds. Help your child make cards, do small favors like fetching the mail and newspaper, and just generally show some sweetness in hugs, kisses, and sharing her experiences. These attitudes and habits will serve her well now and all her life.

✳ *Big Mother is watching.* And possibly itching to get in there and discipline your child her way. Or spoil the kid rotten. Or monopolize her—or be utterly hands-off when you desperately want her help. In my experience these issues are the ones most likely to lead to tension in combined households. There is no one-size-fits-all perfect solution, but talking often and mutually agreeing to respect certain boundaries make it easier to find a balance. Some general guidelines: The owner of the home gets to make reasonable rules about what does or doesn't happen in the house, the parent of the child gets to be the one to decide on consequences for misbehavior as well as to set reasonable limits on sweets and other indulgences (grandparents are allowed a little leeway in spoiling), and parents should mete out discipline when at home and available (while babysitters do it when parents are absent, following the guidelines set by the parents).

✻ *Babes in Adultland.* If you're moving into a formerly kid-free home, chances are the environment is not even a little bit kid-friendly. You may need to ask for adaptations to make the home both safe and supportive of your child's needs. But *ask* is the key word, keeping in mind that you are imposing. (The adult who is blood-related gets to be the asker, so that you're not making a prickly in-law situation even pricklier.)

✻ *Haves vs. have-nots.* If you're moving into a household with other kids and money is tight for you but not for them, your child's green-eyed monster is bound to rear its head. Sensitive hosts (adults and kids) will take care not to flaunt, but even if they don't, you have no right to ask them to stop giving their kid expensive toys or taking them on outings you can't afford. Instead, you'll let your child express her jealousy and frustration while showing both empathy and a that's life attitude; you'll gently encourage all the children to share and take turns—and you'll make sure your child gets a chance to escape regularly to situations where disparity isn't such a concern.

What about Fluffy and Fido?

Young children tend to see their pets—even if they're just friendly caterpillars or placid goldfish—as full family members, so giving up the family pet should be a last resort. Fortunately, many animal shelters and charitable organizations are stepping up to help families in tough situations hang onto their pets. Many organizations now have pet food banks or offer temporary foster homes to families forced into accommodations that bar pets, and disaster agencies increasingly have pet-friendly shelter options. You may also be able to make arrangements with friends or family members to help you out until you can support your pet again. Ideally, a pet placed in temporary housing will be near enough to allow for regular visits.

If you simply must give your pet away, discuss it openly with your child, offering explicit reassurance that you won't be giving her away too. Talk with your kid about the differences between people and animals, and how parents have to put the needs of people first, even though she probably won't really understand. Reassure her too that you'll find the pet a good and loving home; take it to a no-kill shelter if you can't find an adoptive family on your own. Read the information on helping your child cope with pet loss on pages 210–213; even though her pet is still alive, the loss of the relationship will prompt real grief. Expect your child to be sad, angry and perhaps scared, and give her opportunities to express all her complex feelings. Help her collect mementos for herself as well as assemble objects to send with her pet to its new home. Some kids may appreciate a chance to get updates and perhaps have visits later with a transferred pet if that's possible; others may prefer a clean break.

Moving On—and Up

I'll be honest with you. When I first started researching outcomes for families who have lost their homes, I felt discouraged. Certainly for many young children, losing their family home has launched or accompanied a tumbling snowball of bleak outcomes—frequent moves, poor nutrition, inadequate medical and dental care, behavior problems, poor school attendance and performance, and difficulties with relationships both short- and long-term.

But the shortcoming of most of those studies is that they've examined families who already had a multitude (and often multiple generations) of problems and risk factors, including inadequate schooling, domestic violence, drug and alcohol abuse, teen pregnancy, and so on; the outcomes for those kids were likely to be poor even without home loss. In contrast, many of the families losing their homes today are fundamentally different; often they were functioning extremely well until a natural or financial disaster beyond their control unraveled their housing situation. Although it will be years before outcome studies on this new group are completed, my guess is that kids from these families will prove much more resilient and successful. Many of these families have plenty of other resources, including social support, as well as the right attitudes and skills to support their children during tough times and to reverse their circumstances before long.

But what made me especially optimistic was talking with relatives and friends who grew up during the Great Depression. I was reminded that many people not only got through home loss then, but emerged strengthened by their experiences. And you can make sure your kids do too. The families who coped best then were those who remained positive about the future, were creative in making do with what they did have rather than bemoaning their losses, and who expected everyone to pitch in. These families took pleasure in their friendships and extended family relationships and offered help to others, even when they had little themselves. More than seventy years later, my mother still remembers helping her mom pull together a sandwich for every hobo who saw the cat (the symbol for a kind woman) chalked on their fence post and came to the door for food; they never turned anyone away hungry, no matter how tough times were for them. You too can provide your child with lessons in kindness and finding a way, no matter where you end up living.

Hospitalization Helper

✳ ✳ ✳

Easing the Pains of Procedures, Separation, and Fear

With luck, you'll get through everyone's childhoods without so much as a visit to the ER. I have not been so fortunate, and if you aren't either, try these ideas to make your child's experience of a hospital visit or stay less taxing for everyone.

Choose Your Medicine

Or at least your hospital. Get a second opinion and do your own research before you commit to elective hospital care for your child. I strongly recommend going to a children's hospital; not only will they have tot-sized equipment and doctors accustomed to working with tiny anatomies, but they're generally better at supporting your child and you.

Get Ready

Don't tell your child too far in advance. Once it's clear that something's up, talk about going to the hospital and exactly what will happen and why. Choose your vocabulary with care—words like *cut* and *remove* may freak little guys out disproportionately. Focus on the idea that the doctors and nurses will try to figure out what's not working the way it should and fix it. *Emphasize that your child has not done anything wrong and isn't being punished.* Your child will probably need you to repeat everything you say. Also, playing at what will happen makes it easier for him to ask questions and understand. Playmobil makes a very nice hospital set, and doctor's kits are still staples in most toy stores. Take advantage of hospital classes and brochures on how to explain the procedure.

Fast Tips for Fasting

If your child has to fast before surgery or another procedure, be sure to tell him in advance and, if possible, have a favorite food before he starts his fast. Lobby to be first in line in the morning so that he has as little time awake and hungry as possible. Line up distractions to keep his mind off food while waiting, and ask about allowed oral comforts, such as using ChapStick or wetting his lips with a lemon swab.

Stay with Your Child

For safety as well as your child's emotional comfort, a parent or other family member should be with your child at all times. Most hospitals now permit parents to remain with kids having surgery until they're sedated and to be with them promptly in the recovery room. They may also have rooms or foldout beds for parents remaining overnight.

If your child will be staying at the hospital and you can't be there every minute, make sure he has photos of you and other family members. This will comfort him and remind staff that he has a family who cares about him.

Normalize and Socialize

The more your child's world seems familiar and predictable, the less stressed he'll be and the more resources he'll have for coping with challenges. Make sure your child brings a lovey (with his name and address written on it somewhere) with him, as well as some not-too-precious (in case they get lost) toys from home. Many hospitals allow ailing kids to wear street clothes or at least their own pajamas. Although you'll probably be tempted to baby your sick puppy, it's better to encourage him to keep doing things for himself, like putting on his own clothes or feeding himself. If he's at the hospital for more than a day or two, help him settle into routines, even if they're somewhat different from his usual ones at home.

In many instances, hospitals allow siblings and even friends to visit. Bring some activities for him to do with visitors, so guests don't just sit around looking mournful or bored. Pediatric wards also usually have playrooms where children can interact with other patients. Playtime is more than distraction; it promotes healing and often provides rehabilitation. In addition, play can be emotionally therapeutic, enabling children to express feelings and ask scary questions.

Pain Management

Pain of varying degrees is a part of nearly every hospital experience. Fortunately, hospitals are getting much better at assessing and managing children's discomfort. Some things that help:

✳ *Provide explanations.* Knowing what to expect and *why* something's happening increases control and reduces pain. Insist that all providers talk to you and your child before doing anything. Always remind your child that he isn't being punished.

✳ *Acknowledge pain*…and let your child express it openly, any way he wants to. Let him know about how long the pain will last and what will be done to ease it. Finally, give him any control over the pain that you can. For example, let him count to three at his own rate before a shot is administered or choose which arm to use for the IV.

✳ *Assess pain.* There are many scales for young children to rate their pain. Some use frowny faces, numbers, colors, or other metaphors to help doctors and nurses understand what a child is experiencing. Make sure to check in frequently when a child is in pain as its status can change quickly.

✳ *Treat pain.* Discuss options for alleviating your child's discomfort. These may range from home remedies like ice packs or heating pads to medication or surgical procedures. Insist that your child's pain be adequately treated.

✳ *Be there.* Holding your child or at least staying near him reduces both fear and pain. Holding a favorite toy or blanket also comforts most children.

✳ *Distract.* Talking, singing, listening to music through headphones, playing with toys, and spending time with friends can help take kids' minds off discomfort.

✳ *Teach relaxation.* Have your child breathe deeply (by pretending to blow out birthday candles or float an imaginary feather), tense and relax his muscles, or close his eyes and visit a place that's fun or safe.

✳ *Reward courage.* Your frequent, sincere praise is best, but most kids also appreciate small gifts or special privileges when recovering from painful procedures.

When You Get Home

Kids generally need to keep talking and playing about their experiences for a while after they have recovered; some will need to do so for months and months. Make sure they have appropriate props to replay difficult experiences, and tension-reducing materials (like art supplies or musical instruments) to express lingering stress or feelings. Regression, like a return to bed-wetting, is so normal as to be an expected part of the recovery process; however, if a couple of months later your child has not largely returned to where he was before, you should consult your pediatrician.

CONCLUSION

A Fable

* * *

To Help You Solve All the Preschooler Problems
I Haven't Covered

I wanted to cover *all* the problems you might face with your pre-schooler, but my publisher refused to let me make this book the necessary 7,683 pages long. So I have to stop now, but in closing I thought I'd tell you a little fable that I hope will leave you wise enough to work through any other difficulties you might encounter with your young child. Fables have a couple of advantages over straightforward advice: first, stories speak to the heart, teaching principles in a deep and memorable way; second, characters disguised as foxes distract from any unflattering role I may have played in the incident.

The Fox, the Hammer, and the New Kitchen Table

One afternoon, Foxy Mama tucked her two youngest kits in for a nap and decided to relax for a bit with the mystery she was reading. But just as she settled into her comfy chair with a cup of tea and some chocolate eggs she'd swiped from the little one's Easter basket, the oldest kit (who at five had long ago given up napping) bounded up to her and said, "Let's play War!"

The vixen sighed. It had rained all week and she'd already played at least a gazillion hands of War. Plus, she'd finally reached the exciting point in her book.

"Perhaps there's a craft project you'd like to do instead," she offered. "Something you could do all by yourself, now that you're so big and clever."

The sly little fox thought for half a second. "I want to hammer nails," he said.

The vixen sighed again. Normally, hammering nails was an outdoor project, but the day was so cool and damp that she didn't feel like sitting at the wet picnic table to keep an eye on the kit while he hammered. Then she had an idea.

"You can hammer right here," she told the kit, "at the table."

Foxy Mama folded an old blanket and placed it on the new kitchen table to protect it. Then she set out a scrap piece of two-by-six lumber, a lightweight hammer that the kit had already been taught to use safely, and a handful of nails too short to go all the way through the lumber. She reminded the kit how to start a nail without banging his sweet little paws and explained about being careful with the new kitchen table.

Then she settled back into her chair with her book, which she held carefully in a position to hide the chocolate eggs she was sneaking into her mouth. Despite blinking like a deranged toad every time the kit's hammer connected with a nail, the vixen was utterly contented.

Riiiiinnnnggg, riiinnnggg. The phone interrupted the peaceful interlude. It was the vixen's best friend with some juicy gossip about the OTM (Over-the-Top Mom) who'd been threatening to join their playgroup.

BLAM! BLAM! BLAM! went the hammer. *Blink, blink, blink* went the vixen.

"Just a minute," said Foxy Mama into the receiver. She turned to her kit.

"Sweetie, I need to go in the other room for a moment. There is too much blamming and blinking in this one. Can you be very careful if I'm not right here?"

BLAM! BLAM! BLAM! "Of course I can," said the kit.

The vixen was gone for only 2.47 minutes, but when she returned, the kit quickly hunched over the piece of two-by-six, trying to hide it with his body. "Don't look!" he howled.

So Foxy Mama looked. But she saw nothing too alarming. No nails sticking out of the new table. No pools of blood. Nothing except…

"Sweetie," she asked, "didn't there used to be seven nails in your piece of wood? And aren't there only three now? And where did the blanket go?"

"It fell on the floor," the kit answered.

"And the nails? Where did the other nails go?"

"I had to start over," the kit explained and turned the two-by-six over. And sure enough, there were the other nails, sticking out here and there like jagged canines.

And there too in Foxy Mama's *brand new table* was a series of circular dents. Deep dents. Deep, deep, deep, no-sanding-those-suckers-out dents.

The vixen took a deep breath, grabbed the hammer from the kit's paws, said, "If you can't use your tools properly, you may not use them at all, ever again," and locked herself in the den's powder room until her own urge to use the hammer in an improper manner had passed.

When her husband, the fantastic Mr. Fox, returned to the den later, Foxy Mama gave him an earful about his son's transgression. Then, after grumbling through supper, she herded the two younger kits to bed while Mr. Fox stayed behind to have a chat with the oldest one.

While Foxy Mama sang "The Fox Went Out on a Chilly Night" to her little kits, she heard an odd sound.

"That *can't* be hammering," she thought. "Surely not."

The following Sunday was Mother's Day, and the kits tumbled into the vixen's room bright and early with breakfast and gifts. The oldest kit thrust a package into his mother's paws, along with a bouquet he'd fashioned from an entire box of Kleenex.

Inside was a fresh section of two-by-six with ten nails pounded into it. By holding it at leg's length and squinting, Foxy Mama could see that the nails formed a heart shape.

"I was trying to make something special for you for Mother's Day," the kit explained in a reproachful tone. "Because I love you."

Mr. Fox nudged him.

"And I'm sorry about the table," he muttered.

"I'm sorry too," Foxy Mama whispered, blowing her nose on one of the flowers. "Thank you."

The lump in her throat was so big she couldn't even choke down her scrambled eggs. Which was probably a good thing, because they were a bit burned and had some odd, greenish lumps in them.

The Morals of this Story

Aesop, who must have been an amateur, managed to distill only one moral per fable, but I, a trained professional, can pull *lots* of nuggets from a single fable. Plus, I am nice enough to explain my cryptic morals to make sure you really get my point, something I think it might have been helpful for Aesop to do from time to time.

The Main Moral of this Story: *A heart in your hand is worth a few dents in the table.*

Your ultimate job as a parent is to help your kid become a good person. Keep this in mind. Cross-stitch it and hang it on the fridge. Get it tattooed it on your forehead. (Oh wait, don't do that, or at least have it done in mirror writing, because otherwise you'll never be able to read what it says.) It's easy to get so bogged down in the minutiae and annoyances of daily life with young children—or to get so swept up by anxieties real and imagined—that you lose sight of what you're really trying to accomplish.

The heart of nails is the result of many, many things that Foxy Mama, the fantastic Mr. Fox, and the young kit are doing well. The dents, on the other hand, permanent and disfiguring though they are, represent only a couple of small lapses—ones that may even prove useful in developing the kit's character and Foxy Mama's parenting skills in the long run. Ultimately this story is one of success. Here are some of the characteristics the Fox parents have encouraged and the kit demonstrates with his project:

✳ *Healthy initiative.* Without a formal class, a prescribed routine, or even prompting—and with access to alternative passive amusements like TV—the kit chose to engage in an active, creative, and useful activity. A somewhat eccentric one, but still a good choice on the whole.

I do worry that initiative is being systematically purged from kids today, with all the best intentions. In an effort to keep kids safe and busy, to make sure they're on track with every aspect of their development, and to make life easy, convenient, and pleasant for everyone involved, we are structuring, legislating, and scaring choice and self-determination right out of our kids' lives. I fear we'll pay for it with a generation of kids who are safe and well-prepared to follow directions but who have no sense of self and no ability to make their own decisions.

Last year I spent a series of days visiting a kindergarten class in a high-risk neighborhood. The school and teacher completely wowed me with what a great job they were doing to prepare these kids socially and academically for first grade. The classroom buzzed with activity and contentment and the kids were making remarkable progress in reading, writing, math, and more. But it was only after several visits there that I realized that there was really not ONE minute in the entire day when kids were self-directed—when they decided how to use their time, or what to produce, or how to behave. There wasn't even a choice of food at lunch or unstructured recess— just gym time directed by a teacher. Since then I've talked with pre-school teachers and directors who've commented they no longer have free playtime in their day because they have to make sure that kids are academically prepared to take the state tests administered just after they enter kindergarten. And I've talked with parents who feel pressured by the expectations of their extended families, communities, and their child's future to rush their kids from daycare to soccer to dance class to art enrichment from sunup to bedtime, all the while amusing the little ones with DVDs on the ten-minute drives from school to field to studio. These pressures are real, greater even than when my kids were young, and they do have kernels of justification, but they still pose a danger of their own that you'll have to figure out how to resist.

✳ *Competence*…of a sort anyway. Acquiring a complex skill like making a picture of a heart by hammering lots of nails into a piece of wood tends to be a messy process, but it's a process worth undertaking. Foxy Mama is right that her five-year-old is ready to learn to use a hammer. (Woodworking used to be a formal part of the kindergarten curriculum; when my mother taught it in the 1950s, the state of California issued every kindergartner not only a hammer but an eggbeater drill and a coping saw!) And though some kids need closer supervision than others, the vixen is generally right that the best way to help her kit get better at it is to give him a little time and space to practice and experiment on his own. It's just convenient that doing so also gives her a chance to read her book. And unfortunate that she forgot to mention about not turning the half-nailed wood over.

✳ *Flexibility and creativity.* Okay, the kit didn't quite think through all the consequences, but Foxy Mama can feel proud that when her kit's first attempt to make a heart didn't work out and when he'd seemingly used up an essential supply, he neither gave up nor turned to her to solve the problem but rather worked it out himself. These essential attitudes and skills can't be dictated or learned from a single example or experience. Remember all those challenges I've already covered in this book? While it's probably a relief for you that you likely won't face all of them, it's a good thing for your kid that he'll confront a lot of them—and have you to provide the support, encouragement, and modeling that enables him to see problems as solvable, to try new approaches when one doesn't work, and to summon the energy to persist until things work out.

✳ *Kindness, generosity, gratitude.* Nobody told the kit to make a gift for his mom—to offer a token of his appreciation for all she does for him. The impulse to be altruistic develops gradually over the preschool years, nurtured by discussion, repeated small and casual acts, and opportunities for being the recipient as well as the giver. The completion of this project reflects mutual affection and trust between the kit and his mom, a bond that will serve the kit well throughout his life and prepare him to form other strong relationships.

By the way, keep in mind that the kit is five and at the upper end of the preschooler age group; it takes most kids a long time to work out all the subtle issues involved in prosocial behavior. My friend Julie Stiegemeyer has a great example of an earlier stage in this process. When her son Jacob was about three, he got in the habit of begging for presents on every outing or occasion. Annoyed one day, Julie reminded him, "You know Jacob, it's better to give than to receive."

Jacob mulled this idea over for a few minutes, then replied generously, "Okay, Mommy. I'll let you do the giving and I can just do the receiving."

Good parenting and growing up well are constantly changing processes of facing new challenges and goals, assessing and managing risks and benefits, and making judgment calls. That's what makes them hard. It's the occasional heart that helps you see they're worth the effort.

Moral Number Two: *To err is human, especially if the human is a small child with a hammer or a tired mother with a phone call.*

Everyone makes mistakes. Small children make what seems like more than their fair share of them because their judgment and skills are poor, their patience and experience are limited, and their quirkiness and unpredictability are high—very, very high. The adults in their world have to make up for these shortcomings with lots of instruction, support, reminders, supervision, and (of course) clairvoyance. Even a mere 2.47 seconds is too long to leave most preschoolers unsupervised with a blunt instrument…which means it was mostly Foxy Mama's fault that there are dents in her kitchen table. This does not mean, though, that she has to absolve her kit of all responsibility for the damage; even little guys can be helped to acknowledge their mistakes and make amends. Of course one hopes that they learn from their errors, so that next time they mess up by writing on the table in indelible ink instead of marring it with nail heads again.

Parents misstep for many of the same reasons: inexperience, misjudgment of the situation or the folks involved, fatigue, stress, temptation, etc. The good thing about messing up, though, is that it gives you a chance to model taking responsibility, issuing a sincere apology, and repairing the relationship. It's generally better to do this quickly, but as Foxy Mama has demonstrated, it can happen even after several days.

Moral Number Three: *Things often become clearer if you hold them away and squint.*

I think it's a serious design flaw that we don't develop perspective until an experience is long over, because lots of times situations with our kids look as messy and blobby up close as the kit's heart of nails did, but with a little distance and effort you're able to discern the key features.

So how do you step back while you're stuck in the middle of a rough situation with your kid? There are lots of ways: Seek advice from someone not wallowing in it with you, write it down as if it were happening to someone else and read it over, take the ten-year test (Will this matter ten years from now? How?), or at least lock yourself in the powder room and breathe deeply for a while until some oxygen finds its way to your brain again.

Moral Number Four: *A partner in need is a partner indeed.*

Having someone to get your back when you're losing it is very helpful for everyone involved, and it's equally wonderful to have a caring person share the moments of pride and joy with you. It doesn't have to be a spouse or the child's other parent—a grandparent, godparent, or kindly neighbor (or in a pinch, the dog) will do—but parenting is really a four-hands-and-two-heads job.

Moral Number Five: *Sometimes "sorry" doesn't cut it, but usually it does, especially if it's accompanied by hearts and flowers.*

I don't think this needs any further explanation, except that if the hearts and flowers aren't sufficient, you can always add hugs and kisses, chocolate, a spa certificate, and a little more chocolate. Maybe a bottle of good wine and a reliable babysitter, depending on who is apologizing to whom.

And the Final Moral: *"Valuable heirloom" is in the eye of the beholder.*

Fifteen years later, the Fox family still has the same dented kitchen table, only now those dents are almost the least of its flaws. In many ways, the kit did them a favor, by freeing them to get on with life, meals, and projects without worrying unduly about the table—which the vixen had forgotten in the heat of the moment had been her intent from the beginning. She'd chosen an inexpensive pine table from IKEA over a fancier shinier one from Ethan Allen precisely because her kits were young and she wanted them to feel welcome at the table.

Their kitchen table now has gouges from instruments as varied as ball-point pens, fork tines, X-Acto knives, knitting needles, toy bulldozer blades, staples (don't ask), plastic knives (a word of advice: don't let kids use them to cut Play-Doh pizzas if you have a soft pine table), the dog's nails (she learned how to push out the chairs and use them to leap onto the table so she could get at leftovers when no one was looking) and a whole host of other strange and ordinary implements. The tabletop has blotches of paint, lines from Sharpies, globs of permanent glue, and a glistening patina from a decade and a half of spilled food and beverages being rubbed into the surface.

It's a map of their family life: a reminder of thousands of family meals (both routine and special), celebrations with friends and relatives, and the site of countless hours of homework, craft projects, science experiments, jigsaw puzzles, and artwork for the books Foxy Mama illustrated.

In short, it's a thing of beauty. So even though the Foxes could now afford a newer, nicer table and maybe even convince the kits to be careful with it or at least not pound nails into it, they can't imagine giving it up. And they won't be surprised if the kits fight over it after they're gone.

Besides, there are always tablecloths.

Bibliography

These are the parenting books on my own bookshelves, some aimed specifically at the preschool years, others more general but applicable to this stage of life too. Many of these guided me through my own kids' early years; others are ones I've discovered since and wish I'd had during those years. In no particular order:

✳ THE MOTHER'S ALMANAC, REVISED by Marguerite Kelly and Elia Parsons and THE FATHER'S ALMANAC by S. Adams Sullivan, both time-tested and jam-packed with practical advice from people who actually are parents and seemed to enjoy their kids.

✳ RAISING YOUR SPIRITED CHILD by Mary Sheedy Kurcinka, the perfect guide to living with a child who is "more" everything. (I swear that but for this book I might have yielded to a PMS-fueled temptation to release my oldest child to the wild.)

✳ YOUR CHILD AT PLAY: THREE TO FIVE YEARS by Marilyn Segal, an informative and reassuring guide to how and why kids this age express themselves in play.

✳ HOW TO TALK SO KIDS WILL LISTEN & LISTEN SO KIDS WILL TALK by Adele Faber and Elaine Mazlish, a concise, commonsense how-to guide that really works to improve communication with kids of nearly every age. (I also like Faber's SIBLINGS WITHOUT RIVALRY.)

✳ Martha and William Sears's attachment parenting guides like THE DISCIPLINE BOOK, which help you understand what's going on in kids' heads as well as how to respond. (And I like these books even though I clearly sense that the Searses are way more patient and understanding than I can ever be and thus make me feel slightly guilty.)

✳ The YOUR ___ YEAR OLD series by Louise Bates Ames and Frances L. Ilg, which even though they are somewhat dated and at times oversimplify the characteristics of an age, nonetheless are hard to beat in terms of an easy guide to the normal range of behavior for a child of a particular age.

✻ WHAT KINDERGARTEN TEACHERS KNOW: PRACTICAL AND PLAYFUL WAYS FOR PARENTS TO HELP CHILDREN LISTEN, LEARN, AND COOPERATE AT HOME by Lisa Holewa and Joan Rice, a straightforward, real life cheat-sheet to those "teacher tricks" we all wish we knew.

✻ LAST CHILD IN THE WOODS: SAVING OUR CHILDREN FROM NATURE-DEFICIT DISORDER by Richard Louv, a well-researched and practical book that prescribes one of my favorite ways of spending time with little kids, namely outside getting dirty.

✻ THE BLESSING OF A SKINNED KNEE: USING JEWISH TEACHINGS TO RAISE SELF-RELIANT CHILDREN by Wendy Mogel, a readable discussion of a commonsense, caring philosophy about raising kids that's valuable whatever your religious bent.

✻ Okay, I'll be honest and admit I haven't actually read this book yet, only an excerpt, but I'm going to go out on a limb and recommend it anyhow—FREE RANGE KIDS: GIVING OUR CHILDREN THE FREEDOM WE HAD WITHOUT GOING NUTS WITH WORRY by America's media-designated Worst Mom, Lenore Skenazy, aka the lady who let her nine-year-old son ride the subway by himself. I love her if for no other reason than she debunked the myth about the dangers of eating raw cookie dough.

INDEX